Safety Symbols

These symbols appear in laboratory activities.
They alert you to possible dangers and remind
you to work carefully.

General Safety Awareness Read all directions for an experiment several times. Follow the directions exactly as they are written. If you are in doubt, ask your teacher for assistance.

Physical Safety If the lab includes physical activity, use caution to avoid injuring yourself or others. Tell your teacher if there is a reason that you should not participate.

Safety Goggles Always wear safety goggles to protect your eyes in any activity involving chemicals, heating, or the possibility of broken glassware.

Lab Apron Wear a laboratory apron to protect your skin and clothing from harmful chemicals or hot materials.

Plastic Gloves Wear disposable plastic gloves to protect yourself from contact with chemicals that can be harmful. Keep your hands away from your face. Dispose of gloves according to your teacher's instructions.

Heating Use a clamp or tongs to hold hot objects. Test an object by first holding the back of your hand near it. If you feel heat, the object may be too hot to handle.

Heat-Resistant Gloves Hot plates, hot water, and hot glassware can cause burns. Never touch hot objects with your bare hands. Use an oven mitt or other hand protection.

Flames Tie back long hair and loose clothing, and put on safety goggles before using a burner. Follow instructions from your teacher for lighting and extinguishing burners.

No Flames If flammable materials are present, make sure there are no flames, sparks, or exposed sources of heat.

Electric Shock To avoid an electric shock, never use electrical equipment near water, or when the equipment or your hands are wet. Use only sockets that accept a three-prong plug. Be sure cords are untangled and cannot trip anyone. Disconnect equipment that is not in use.

Fragile Glassware Handle fragile glassware, such as thermometers, test tubes, and beakers, with care. Do not touch broken glass. Notify your teacher if glassware breaks. Never use chipped or cracked glassware.

Corrosive Chemical Avoid getting corrosive chemicals on your skin or clothing, or in your eyes. Do not inhale the vapors. Wash your hands after completing the activity.

Poison Do not let any poisonous chemical get on your skin, and do not inhale its vapor. Wash your hands after completing the activity.

Fumes When working with poisonous or irritating vapors, work in a well-ventilated area. Never test for an odor unless instructed to do so by your teacher. Avoid inhaling a vapor directly. Use a wafting motion to direct vapor toward your nose.

Sharp Object Use sharp instruments only as directed. Scissors, scalpels, pins, and knives are sharp and can cut or puncture your skin. Always direct sharp edges and points away from yourself and others.

Disposal All chemicals and other materials used in the laboratory must be disposed of safely. Follow your teacher's instructions.

Hand Washing Before leaving the lab, wash your hands thoroughly with soap or detergent, and warm water. Lather both sides of your hands and between your fingers. Rinse well.

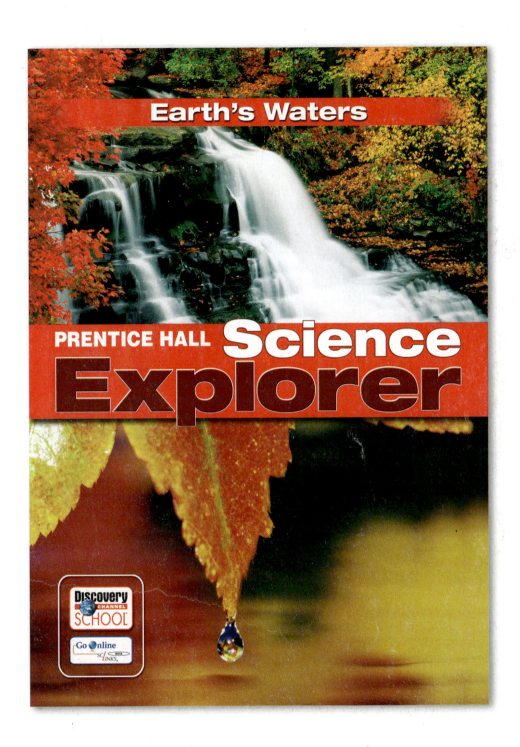

Earth's Waters

PRENTICE HALL Science Explorer

PEARSON

Prentice Hall

Boston, Massachusetts
Upper Saddle River, New Jersey

Earth's Waters

Book-Specific Resources

Student Edition
StudentExpress™ with Interactive Textbook
Teacher's Edition
All-in-One Teaching Resources
Color Transparencies
Guided Reading and Study Workbook
Student Edition on Audio CD
Discovery Channel School® Video
Lab Activity Video
Consumable and Nonconsumable Materials Kits

Program Print Resources

Integrated Science Laboratory Manual
Computer Microscope Lab Manual
Inquiry Skills Activity Books
Progress Monitoring Assessments
Test Preparation Workbook
Test-Taking Tips With Transparencies
Teacher's ELL Handbook
Reading Strategies for Science Content

Differentiated Instruction Resources

Adapted Reading and Study Workbook
Adapted Tests
Differentiated Instruction Guide for Labs and Activities

Program Technology Resources

TeacherExpress™ CD-ROM
Interactive Textbooks Online
PresentationExpress™ CD-ROM
ExamView®, Computer Test Bank CD-ROM
Lab zone™ Easy Planner CD-ROM
Probeware Lab Manual With CD-ROM
Computer Microscope and Lab Manual
Materials Ordering CD-ROM
Discovery Channel School® DVD Library
Lab Activity DVD Library
Web Site at PHSchool.com

Spanish Print Resources

Spanish Student Edition
Spanish Guided Reading and Study Workbook
Spanish Teaching Guide With Tests

Acknowledgments appear on page 214, which constitutes an extension of this copyright page.

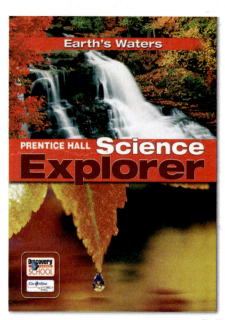

Cover
Brandywine Falls cascades down a rocky slope in Ohio (top). A water droplet falls from a maple leaf (bottom).

PEARSON
Prentice
Hall

ISBN 0-13-201151-4
3 4 5 6 7 8 9 10   10 09 08 07

Program Authors

Michael J. Padilla, Ph.D.
Professor of Science Education
University of Georgia
Athens, Georgia

Michael Padilla is a leader in middle school science education. He has served as an author and elected officer for the National Science Teachers Association and as a writer of the National Science Education Standards. As lead author of Science Explorer, Mike has inspired the team in developing a program that meets the needs of middle grades students, promotes science inquiry, and is aligned with the National Science Education Standards.

Ioannis Miaoulis, Ph.D.
President
Museum of Science
Boston, Massachusetts

Originally trained as a mechanical engineer, Ioannis Miaoulis is in the forefront of the national movement to increase technological literacy. As dean of the Tufts University School of Engineering, Dr. Miaoulis spearheaded the introduction of engineering into the Massachusetts curriculum. Currently he is working with school systems across the country to engage students in engineering activities and to foster discussions on the impact of science and technology on society.

Martha Cyr, Ph.D.
Director of K–12 Outreach
Worcester Polytechnic Institute
Worcester, Massachusetts

Martha Cyr is a noted expert in engineering outreach. She has over nine years of experience with programs and activities that emphasize the use of engineering principles, through hands-on projects, to excite and motivate students and teachers of mathematics and science in grades K–12. Her goal is to stimulate a continued interest in science and mathematics through engineering.

Book Authors

Jan Jenner, Ph.D.
Science Writer
Talladega, Alabama

Thomas R. Wellnitz
Science Instructor
The Paideia School
Atlanta, Georgia

Contributing Writers

Jeffrey C. Callister
Former Earth
   Science Instructor
Newburgh Free Academy
Newburgh, New York

Barbara Brooks Simons
Science Writer
Boston, Massachusetts

Consultants

Reading Consultant

Nancy Romance, Ph.D.
Professor of Science
   Education
Florida Atlantic University
Fort Lauderdale, Florida

Mathematics Consultant

William Tate, Ph.D.
Professor of Education and
   Applied Statistics and
   Computation
Washington University
St. Louis, Missouri

Reviewers

Teacher Reviewers

David R. Blakely
Arlington High School
Arlington, Massachusetts

Jane E. Callery
Two Rivers Magnet Middle
School
East Hartford, Connecticut

Melissa Lynn Cook
Oakland Mills High School
Columbia, Maryland

James Fattic
Southside Middle School
Anderson, Indiana

Dan Gabel
Hoover Middle School
Rockville, Maryland

Wayne Goates
Eisenhower Middle School
Goddard, Kansas

Katherine Bobay Graser
Mint Hill Middle School
Charlotte, North Carolina

Darcy Hampton
Deal Junior High School
Washington, D.C.

Karen Kelly
Pierce Middle School
Waterford, Michigan

David Kelso
Manchester High School Central
Manchester, New Hampshire

Benigno Lopez, Jr.
Sleepy Hill Middle School
Lakeland, Florida

Angie L. Matamoros, Ph.D.
ALM Consulting, Inc.
Weston, Florida

Tim McCollum
Charleston Middle School
Charleston, Illinois

Bruce A. Mellin
Brooks School
North Andover, Massachusetts

Ella Jay Parfitt
Southeast Middle School
Baltimore, Maryland

Evelyn A. Pizzarello
Louis M. Klein Middle School
Harrison, New York

Kathleen M. Poe
Fletcher Middle School
Jacksonville, Florida

Shirley Rose
Lewis and Clark Middle School
Tulsa, Oklahoma

Linda Sandersen
Greenfield Middle School
Greenfield, Wisconsin

Mary E. Solan
Southwest Middle School
Charlotte, North Carolina

Mary Stewart
University of Tulsa
Tulsa, Oklahoma

Paul Swenson
Billings West High School
Billings, Montana

Thomas Vaughn
Arlington High School
Arlington, Massachusetts

Susan C. Zibell
Central Elementary
Simsbury, Connecticut

Safety Reviewers

W. H. Breazeale, Ph.D.
Department of Chemistry
College of Charleston
Charleston, South Carolina

Ruth Hathaway, Ph.D.
Hathaway Consulting
Cape Girardeau, Missouri

Douglas Mandt, M.S.
Science Education Consultant
Edgewood, Washington

Activity Field Testers

Nicki Bibbo
Witchcraft Heights School
Salem, Massachusetts

Rose-Marie Botting
Broward County Schools
Fort Lauderdale, Florida

Colleen Campos
Laredo Middle School
Aurora, Colorado

Elizabeth Chait
W. L. Chenery Middle School
Belmont, Massachusetts

Holly Estes
Hale Middle School
Stow, Massachusetts

Laura Hapgood
Plymouth Community
Intermediate School
Plymouth, Massachusetts

Mary F. Lavin
Plymouth Community
Intermediate School
Plymouth, Massachusetts

James MacNeil, Ph.D.
Cambridge, Massachusetts

Lauren Magruder
St. Michael's Country
Day School
Newport, Rhode Island

Jeanne Maurand
Austin Preparatory School
Reading, Massachusetts

Joanne Jackson-Pelletier
Winman Junior High School
Warwick, Rhode Island

Warren Phillips
Plymouth Public Schools
Plymouth, Massachusetts

Carol Pirtle
Hale Middle School
Stow, Massachusetts

Kathleen M. Poe
Fletcher Middle School
Jacksonville, Florida

Cynthia B. Pope
Norfolk Public Schools
Norfolk, Virginia

Anne Scammell
Geneva Middle School
Geneva, New York

Karen Riley Sievers
Callanan Middle School
Des Moines, Iowa

David M. Smith
Eyer Middle School
Allentown, Pennsylvania

Gene Vitale
Parkland School
McHenry, Illinois

Contents

Earth's Waters

Reference Section

VIDEO

Enhance understanding through dynamic video.

Preview Get motivated with this introduction to the chapter content.

Field Trip Explore a real-world story related to the chapter content.

Assessment Review content and take an assessment.

Get connected to exciting Web resources in every lesson.

$SC_{\color{red}i}$ **LINKS** Find Web links on topics relating to every section.

Active Art Interact with selected visuals from every chapter online.

Planet Diary® Explore news and natural phenomena through weekly reports.

Science News® Keep up to date with the latest science discoveries.

Experience the complete text-book online and on CD-ROM.

Activities Practice skills and learn content.

Videos Explore content and learn important lab skills.

Audio Support Hear key terms spoken and defined.

Self-Assessment Use instant feedback to help you track your progress.

Activities

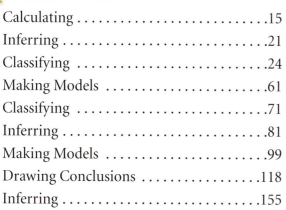

Through the Lens of an Ocean Scientist

Norbert Wu dives for his photographs. (He took all the photographs in this feature.) A trained marine biologist, he roams the underwater world looking for the perfect shot. "Photography has become a way of life for me," Norbert says. "At my best, I am both a scientist and an artist. Photographing new life forms and learning about the connections between different species makes my work a blend of science and art. Taking an in-depth look at the habits and behavior of marine life has become my specialty."

Norbert has followed the trail of manta rays slowly circling the top of an undersea mountain off the Mexican coast. He's photographed octopuses and snails on coral reefs. He's swum with jellyfish in the Antarctic Ocean.

"I went as far south as you can go and still have ocean," Norbert says. "And I fell in love with Antarctica. When you first get there at the beginning of the Antarctic spring, the water is clearer than anywhere in the world. It's really the last untouched place on Earth. That's what draws me back.

In Antarctica, a diver glides toward a jellyfish.

Talking With Norbert Wu

? **What protects divers from the cold?**

Underwater photography in polar seas is a challenge. For one thing, it's very cold. In Antarctica, scientists used to wear wet suits— suits that allow a thin layer of water to touch the skin. Now divers use dry suits, which are waterproof and sealed at the neck and wrists. You can wear long underwear or polyester fleece underneath. Dry suits make polar diving bearable, but it's never very pleasant.

Norbert is shown below with his dogs Ange, a labrador, and Sam, a golden retriever.

Career Path

Norbert Wu attended Stanford University in California, where he received a bachelor's degree and master's degree in electrical and mechanical engineering. He then returned to the subject he loved in high school—marine biology. He attended graduate school at Scripps Institution of Oceanography in San Diego. In 1999, Norbert received a Pew Marine Conservation Fellowship to photograph threatened underwater habitats.

❓ How did you become an underwater photographer?

After college, I decided to pursue a career in marine biology. I got a job with a scientist working off the San Blas Islands near Panama. I counted sea urchins and measured coral growth. Before the trip, I'd never had any interest in photography. But I brought along books on photography, as well as an underwater flash and camera system.

My career didn't happen overnight. I returned to California to continue graduate school in marine biology. I sold some photographs taken at San Blas and gradually my career in photography just took over.

❓ How do you locate ocean organisms?

You learn the places in the world where particular ocean organisms are found. In the waters of Antarctica, you find seals, penguins, and jellyfish. Squid come up in the waters off California at certain times of the year. Local guides can also put you exactly on the right site to locate ocean organisms.

If you dive a reef every day, you get to know the organisms that live there. During the months I spent on the San Blas Islands, I was able to return again and again to photograph an octopus or a flamingo tongue snail. Being able to spend weeks, rather than a few weekends, makes a big difference in the photographs.

Schooling snappers and blue-striped snappers swim around a seamount off the Cocos Island in the Pacific Ocean.

? How is your science background useful?

You need to know how ocean animals behave and how different animals interact with each other. I've taken pictures of manta rays coming to a seamount to be cleaned of parasites by bright orange clarion angelfish. Parasites are small organisms that live on and can harm another organism like a manta ray. As the manta rays swoop past the seamount, the angelfish come out from their shelter, dance about, and flash their bright orange bodies as if signaling their arrival. The manta rays may pause and allow the angelfish to go all about their bodies, picking off parasites.

? Why are you interested in an animal's behavior?

Understanding an ocean animal's behavior and its reactions is essential just to get near enough for a picture. Because of the limited visibility underwater, I am usually close to my subjects—often no more than a meter away. As a diver, the noise of your bubbles tells animals you're there. So an underwater photographer must move slowly and act in ways that won't threaten or frighten animals.

? What do you do on a typical diving trip?

Most of my diving trips last two to three weeks. Once I'm there, almost all my time is on a boat or getting ready to go underwater. My next trip is to Cocos Island, in Costa Rica, where I will photograph seamounts. Seamounts are undersea mountain tops that serve as gathering places for marine life. They attract some of the ocean's largest and most exciting animals.

Seamounts form in areas of volcanic action, where the ocean floor abruptly rises to the surface. These volcanic hot spots can be close to the coast or hundreds of miles offshore. In the Cocos, there are a lot of sharks to photograph—hammerheads and white-tipped reef sharks as well as manta rays and snappers.

Clarion angelfish clean manta rays near a seamount off the coast of Mexico.

❓ What new technology do you use in your work?

Two new technologies have made a big difference—closed-circuit rebreathers and digital cameras. A rebreather recycles your exhaled breath in a closed loop, so you can breathe the unused oxygen you took in during earlier breaths. You can get up to twelve hours on one tank of oxygen. If you can breathe an oxygen-rich mixture in the ocean, you can stay deeper, longer.

With digital cameras, I can also stay down a long time without running out of film. I can put a memory card in the camera and take 300 or 500 exposures. (A large roll of film takes just 36 exposures.)

❓ What would you tell students?

I've talked to young people a good deal. I'm amazed at how much they know about the world and the environment. I'd tell students that any subject you're passionate about is going to lead to good things. I'm very lucky. I've been able to combine a lot of things I love into my career—biology and diving and photography.

◀ Norbert on Antarctic ice

Writing in Science

Career Link For Norbert, one key to taking great scientific photographs is being at the right place at the right time. To do that, he says you need "an understanding of your subject's behavior." Choose an animal you know. In a paragraph, describe the right time and place to take a good photograph of that animal. Explain your choice.

Go Online
PHSchool.com

For: More on this career
Visit: PHSchool.com
Web Code: cfb-3000

Earth: The Water Planet

These waterfalls in the Pacific Northwest ► show the abundance of water on Earth.

Lab zone™ Chapter **Project**

Every Drop Counts

Every living thing depends on water for survival—including you. To learn how water is used in your home and community, design a method for tracking water use over a one-week period.

Your Goal To monitor water use in your home and in another building in your community for one week

To complete the project you will
- track your personal water use at home
- determine the total amount of water that is used in your home
- find out the total amount of water used by a business, school, hospital, or other building in your community
- follow the safety guidelines in Appendix A

Plan It! Begin by brainstorming how you use water at home. Using this list, create a data table to record each time you perform these activities during the week. Preview the chapter to learn how water is used outside the home. Then interview a local building manager to determine how much water is used in a particular building.

The Properties of Water

Reading Preview

Key Concepts
- How does the chemical structure of water molecules cause them to stick together?
- What are some of water's unusual properties?
- What are the three states in which water exists on Earth?

Key Terms
- polar molecule
- capillary action
- surface tension • solution
- solvent • specific heat
- evaporation • condensation

Target Reading Skill
Building Vocabulary A definition states the meaning of a word or phrase by telling about its most important feature or function. After you read this section, reread the paragraphs that contain definitions of Key Terms. Use all the information you have learned to write a definition of each Key Term in your own words.

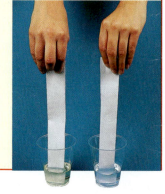

Lab zone Discover Activity

What Are Some Properties of Water?

1. Pour a small amount of water into a plastic cup. Pour an equal amount of vegetable oil into a second cup.
2. Cut two strips of paper towel. Hold the strips so that the bottom of one strip is in the water and the other is in the oil.
3. After one minute, measure how high each substance rose up the paper towel.
4. Using plastic droppers, place equal-sized drops of water and oil next to each other on wax paper.
5. Observe the shape of the two drops from the side.
6. Follow your teacher's instructions for disposing of the oil.

Think It Over
Observing What differences do you notice between the water and the oil in each experiment?

How would you describe water to someone who had never seen it before? You might say that pure water has no color, no taste, and no odor. You might even say that water is a rather plain, ordinary substance. But if you asked a chemist to describe water, the chemist would say that water is very unusual. Its properties differ from those of most other familiar substances.

Hikers awed by waterfalls in ▶ Yosemite National Park

The Structure of Water

Could you and the chemist possibly be talking about the same substance? To understand the chemist's description of water, you need to know something about water's chemical structure.

Like all matter, water is made up of atoms. Just as the 26 letters of the alphabet combine in different ways to form all the words in the English language, about 100 types of atoms combine in different ways to form all types of matter.

Atoms attach together, or bond, to form molecules. Two hydrogen atoms bonded to an oxygen atom form a water molecule. A short way of writing this is to use the chemical formula for water, H_2O.

Figure 1 shows how the hydrogen and oxygen atoms are arranged in a water molecule. Each end of the molecule has a slight electric charge. The oxygen end has a slight negative charge. The hydrogen ends have a slight positive charge. A molecule that has electrically charged areas is a **polar molecule.** Because water consists of polar water molecules, it is called a polar substance.

Have you ever played with bar magnets? If so, then you know that the opposite poles of two magnets attract each other. The same is true with polar molecules, except that an electric force rather than a magnetic force causes the attraction. **The positive hydrogen ends of one water molecule attract the negative oxygen ends of nearby water molecules. As a result, the water molecules tend to stick together.**

 **Reading Checkpoint** Describe the arrangement of the atoms in a water molecule.

Go Online
SciLINKS NSTA

For: Links on water properties
Visit: www.SciLinks.org
Web Code: scn-0811

FIGURE 1

The Structure of Water

Each water molecule has two positive ends and one negative end. The positive ends of one water molecule are attracted to the negative end of another molecule.
Classifying *What makes water a polar substance?*

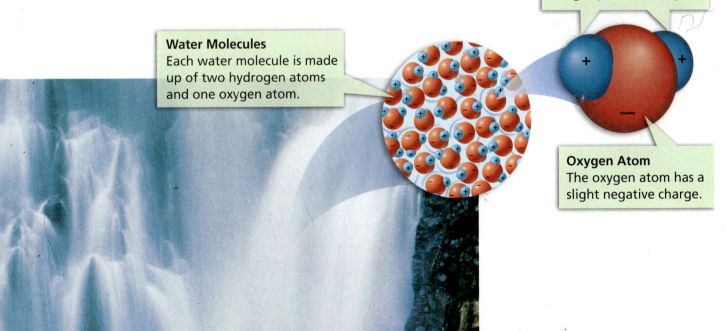

Hydrogen Atoms
Each hydrogen atom has a slight positive charge.

Water Molecules
Each water molecule is made up of two hydrogen atoms and one oxygen atom.

Oxygen Atom
The oxygen atom has a slight negative charge.

FIGURE 2

Three Properties of Water

The attraction among the polar water molecules is responsible for water's unusual properties.

Capillary Action: Water rises in a tube.

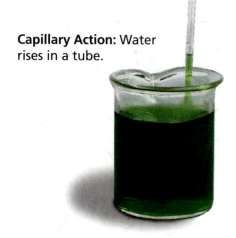

Surface Tension: The tightness of the water's surface keeps a water strider from sinking.

Universal Solvent: Many substances dissolve in water.

Key Properties of Water

Many of water's unusual properties occur because of the attraction among the polar water molecules. **The properties of water include capillary action, surface tension, the ability to dissolve many substances, and high specific heat.**

Capillary Action Just as water molecules stick to one another, they also stick to the sides of a tube, such as a straw. The next time you see a drink with a straw in it, look closely at the level of the liquid outside and inside the straw. You will see that the liquid rises higher inside the straw. As water molecules are attracted to the straw, they pull other water molecules up with them. Similarly, water will climb up into the pores of a brick or a piece of wood.

The combined force of attraction among water molecules and with the molecules of surrounding materials is called **capillary action.** Capillary action allows water to move through materials with pores inside.

Capillary action also causes water molecules to cling to the fibers of materials like paper and cloth. You may have seen outdoor or athletic clothing that claims to "wick moisture away from the skin." Capillary action along the cloth's fibers pulls water away from your skin. By pulling the water away from your skin, the fibers keep you dry.

Surface Tension Have you ever watched water striders skate across the surface of a pond without sinking? They are supported by the surface tension of the water. **Surface tension** is the tightness across the surface of water that is caused by the polar molecules pulling on one another. The molecules at the surface are being pulled by the molecules next to them and below them. The pulling forces the surface of the water into a curved shape. Surface tension also causes raindrops to form round beads when they fall onto a car windshield.

Universal Solvent What happens when you make a fruit drink from a powdered mix? As you stir the powder into the water, the powder seems to disappear. When you make the fruit drink, you are making a solution. A **solution** is a mixture that forms when one substance dissolves another. The substance that does the dissolving is called the **solvent.** In this example, the water is the solvent.

Many substances dissolve in water because water is polar. The charged ends of the water molecule attract the molecules of other polar substances. Water dissolves so many substances that it is called the "universal solvent." It can dissolve solids, such as sugar, and liquids, such as bleach. Water can also dissolve many gases, including oxygen and carbon dioxide. Substances that have molecules with no charged regions are called nonpolar substances. Nonpolar substances do not dissolve well in water.

Specific Heat It is a steamy summer day. The air is hot, the sidewalk is hot, and the sandy beach is hot. But when you jump into the ocean, the water is surprisingly cool! If you go for an evening swim, however, the water is warmer than the cool air.

You feel this difference in temperature because of water's unusually high specific heat. **Specific heat** is the amount of heat needed to increase the temperature of a certain mass of a substance by 1°C. Compared to other substances, water requires a lot of heat to increase its temperature.

Water's high specific heat is due to the strong attraction among water molecules. Other substances, such as air and rocks, have weaker attractions between their molecules. The temperature of each of these substances rises more quickly than that of water that is heated the same amount.

One effect of water's high specific heat is that land areas located near large bodies of water experience less dramatic temperature changes than areas far inland. In summer, the sun's heat warms the land more quickly than the water. The warm land heats the air above it to a higher temperature than the air over the ocean. As a result, the air is warmer inland than on the coast. The opposite effect occurs in winter—land loses heat more quickly than water, so the air above the land is cooler.

 **Reading Checkpoint** Why does water have a high specific heat?

FIGURE 3
Why Water Stays Cool
Although the air is hot, the water offers cool relief. Water's high specific heat keeps it from heating up as quickly as other materials.

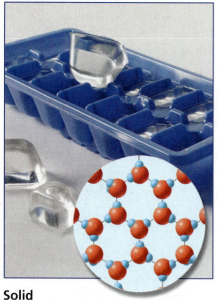

Solid
The molecules in solid ice are close together and form a rigid structure.

Liquid
The molecules move more freely, and the water takes the shape of its container.

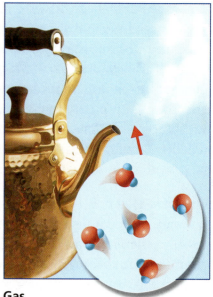

Gas
The molecules in water vapor move very freely and spread out to fill a space.

FIGURE 4
The Three States of Water
Water commonly exists as a solid, a liquid, and a gas.
Comparing and Contrasting
In which state do the molecules move the slowest? The fastest?

Changing State

It's a hot, humid summer day. To cool down, you put some ice cubes in a glass and add cold water. You are interacting with water in three different states, or forms: solid, liquid, and gas. **The ice is solid water, the familiar form of water is a liquid, and the water vapor in the air is a gas.** Water is the only substance on Earth that commonly exists in all of these different states. Figure 4 shows how the arrangement of the water molecules differs in each state.

Boiling and Evaporation If you've ever poured water into a pot, you've seen how the liquid takes the shape of the container. This is true because the molecules in liquid water move freely, bouncing off one another.

What happens if you place the pot of water on a stove and heat it? As more energy is added to the liquid water, the speed of the molecules increases and the temperature rises. At 100°C, the water boils and a change of state occurs. The molecules have enough energy to escape the liquid and become invisible water vapor. The molecules in a gas move even more freely than those in a liquid.

Another way that liquid water can become a gas is through evaporation. **Evaporation** is the process by which molecules at the surface of a liquid absorb enough energy to change to the gaseous state. If you let your hair air-dry after going swimming, you are taking advantage of evaporation.

Condensation As water vapor cools down, it releases some of its energy to the surroundings. The molecules slow down and the temperature decreases. As the temperature of the gas reaches 100°C, the water vapor begins to change back to the liquid state. The process by which a gas changes to a liquid is called **condensation.** When you fog up a window by breathing on it, you are seeing the effects of condensation. The invisible water vapor in your breath is cooled by the window and forms drops of liquid water.

Freezing If those drops of liquid water cooled, the molecules would lose energy. They would start to move more and more slowly. At 0°C, the liquid water freezes, changing into solid ice. If you have ever observed an icicle forming from water dripping off a roof, you have seen this change of state in progress.

Melting Suppose that you put an ice cube in a pot and place it on the stove. As you heated it, the molecules in the ice would start moving faster. The temperature would rise. When the temperature reached 0°C, the solid ice would melt and become liquid water.

 **What is condensation?**

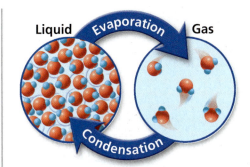

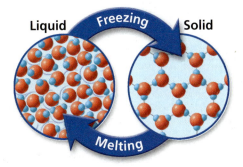

FIGURE 5
Changing State
Water moves between the liquid and gaseous states by evaporation and condensation. Water moves between the liquid and solid states by freezing and melting.

Section 1 Assessment

Target Reading Skill Building Vocabulary Use your definitions to help answer the questions below.

Reviewing Key Concepts

1. a. **Reviewing** What atoms make up a water molecule?
   b. **Describing** Describe the electric charge on each end of a water molecule.
   c. **Relating Cause and Effect** What causes water molecules to be attracted to one another?
2. a. **Listing** Name four unusual properties that water exhibits.
   b. **Explaining** Briefly explain why water exhibits each property.
   c. **Predicting** Oil is a nonpolar molecule. Would it dissolve in water? Why or why not?

3. a. **Identifying** What are the three states in which water exists on Earth?
   b. **Sequencing** Describe how water changes state as a patch of ice is heated by the sun.

Lab zone **At-Home Activity**

Observing Water's Properties Put a penny on a piece of paper. With a plastic dropper or a toothpick, have a family member place a single drop of water on the penny. Ask the person to predict how many more drops he or she can add before the water spills off the penny. Have the person add drops one at a time until the water overflows. How does the result differ from the prediction? Explain what property of water accounts for the results.

Water on Earth

Reading Preview

Key Concepts
- How do people and other living things use water?
- How is Earth's water distributed?
- How does Earth's water move through the water cycle?

Key Terms
- photosynthesis   • habitat
- groundwater   • water cycle
- transpiration   • precipitation

⟳ Target Reading Skill

Identifying Main Ideas As you read the Distribution of Earth's Water section, write the main idea in a graphic organizer like the one below. Then write four supporting details that further explain the main idea.

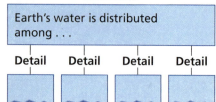

Main Idea

Earth's water is distributed among . . .

Detail	Detail	Detail	Detail

Lab zone Discover **Activity**

Where Does the Water Come From?

1. Fill a glass with ice cubes and water, taking care not to spill any water. Set the glass aside for 5 minutes.
2. Observe the outside of the glass. Pick up the glass and examine the surface it was sitting on.

Think It Over

Inferring Where did the water on the outside of the glass come from? How do you think it got there?

In a galaxy called the Milky Way, nine planets orbit a star known simply as the sun. Some of the planets have spectacular rings. Others have volcanoes that are larger than continents or storms that last for centuries. But only one of the planets, Earth, has a surface covered mainly by water. In fact, oceans cover about 70 percent of our planet's surface. That's why Earth is often called the "blue planet."

Earth differs from the other planets in another important way. It is the only place known thus far where you, your classmates, your pets, your plants, and every other living thing can survive. The wide variety of life on Earth could not exist without water.

▼ All living things need water.

All Living Things Need Water

Here's a riddle for you: What do you and an apple have in common? You both consist mostly of water! Water is a large part of every living thing. Water makes up nearly two thirds of your body's mass. That water is necessary to keep your body functioning. **All living things need water in order to carry out their body processes. In addition, many living things use water for shelter.**

Body Processes All organisms need water to carry out their body processes. Water allows organisms to obtain chemicals from their surroundings, break down food, grow, reproduce, and move substances within their bodies. Humans and other animals drink water or obtain it indirectly by eating foods that contain water. Many animals can live several weeks without food. But they cannot survive more than a few days without water.

Plants and other organisms that make their own food also need water in order to carry out their food-making processes. **Photosynthesis** (foh toh SIN thuh sis) is the process by which plants use water, along with carbon dioxide and energy from the sun, to make their own food. Animals and other organisms depend on the food made by plants during photosynthesis. Animals may eat the plants or eat organisms that eat the plants.

Shelter Bodies of water provide habitats for many living things. An organism's **habitat** is the place where it lives and obtains all the things it needs to survive. You are probably familiar with large water-dwelling organisms such as sharks. But most water-dwelling organisms are microscopic, such as amoebas. In fact, aquatic, or water, habitats contain more organisms than land habitats.

FIGURE 6
Essential for Life
As part of their daily routine, these women in Pakistan must walk to a well to get the water they need.
Interpreting Photographs *What can you infer about the availability of fresh water in the region where these women live?*

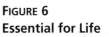 **Reading Checkpoint** What is a habitat?

Distribution of Earth's Water

Look at Figure 8. It shows how water is distributed among saltwater and freshwater sources on Earth. **Most of Earth's water—roughly 97 percent—is salt water found in oceans. Only 3 percent is fresh water.**

Of that 3 percent, about three quarters is frozen in huge masses of ice near the North and South poles. Almost a quarter of the fresh water is underground. A tiny fraction of Earth's fresh water occurs in lakes and rivers. An even tinier fraction is found in the atmosphere, most of it in the form of invisible water vapor, the gaseous form of water.

Oceans To explore Earth's waters, take an imaginary boat trip around the world. Starting in Florida, you head southeast across the Atlantic Ocean toward Africa. Swinging around the continent's southern tip, you enter the smaller but deeper Indian Ocean. Next, you travel east across the Pacific Ocean. This vast ocean covers an area greater than all the land on Earth combined. Pacific, Atlantic, Indian—these are the names used for the different parts of the ocean. But the waters are really all interconnected, making up one big ocean.

✓ **Reading Checkpoint** Where is most fresh water located?

FIGURE 7
Earth's oceans are all connected, enabling a ship to sail all the way around the world. This map also shows some of the world's major rivers and lakes.
Interpreting Maps *Which continents touch the Pacific Ocean? The Atlantic Ocean?*

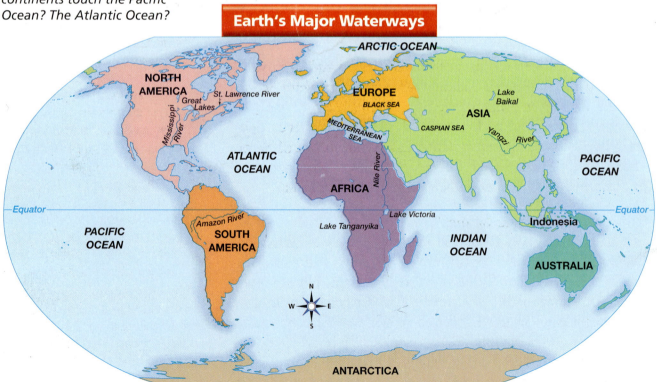

Earth's Major Waterways

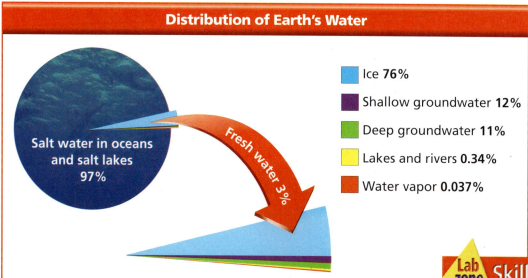

Distribution of Earth's Water

Salt water in oceans and salt lakes 97%

Fresh water 3%

- Ice **76%**
- Shallow groundwater **12%**
- Deep groundwater **11%**
- Lakes and rivers **0.34%**
- Water vapor **0.037%**

FIGURE 8
Only 3 percent of Earth's water is fresh water. Of that fresh water, only a tiny fraction is available for human use. (Percentages in the art have been rounded off.)

Ice How can you get back to Florida? You could sail all the way around South America. But watch out for icebergs! These floating chunks of ice are made of fresh water. Icebergs in the southern Pacific and southern Atlantic oceans have broken off from massive sheets of ice that cover most of Antarctica. If you traveled around the North Pole, you would also find icebergs in the Arctic Ocean and in the North Atlantic.

Rivers and Lakes To see fresh water in rivers and lakes, you'll have to make a side trip inland. Sail north past Nova Scotia, Canada, to the beginning of the St. Lawrence Seaway. Navigate through the series of locks along the St. Lawrence River. Suddenly the river widens and you enter Lake Ontario, one of North America's five Great Lakes. The Great Lakes contain nearly 20 percent of all the water in the world's freshwater lakes.

Groundwater Some of the fresh water on Earth can't be seen from a sailboat. To find it, you would have to go underground. When it rains or snows, some water soaks into the ground. This water trickles down through spaces between particles of soil and rock. Eventually the water reaches a layer of rock that it cannot move through. Water that fills the cracks and spaces in underground soil and rock layers is called **groundwater.** Far more fresh water is located underground than in all of Earth's rivers and lakes. You'll learn more about groundwater in Section 5.

Lab zone Skills Activity

Calculating
This activity shows how Earth's water is distributed.

1. Fill a 1-liter plastic bottle with water to represent the total water on Earth.
2. Measure 97 percent, or 970 milliliters (mL), of the water and pour it into a large bowl to represent salt water on Earth.
3. Label five cups to represent Earth's freshwater sources. Figure 8 shows the percentage of water in each freshwater source. Using this graph, calculate how much of the remaining 30 mL of water should be poured into each cup.
4. Use a graduated cylinder to measure the amount of water for each cup. Use a plastic dropper for amounts that are too small to measure accurately.

Which cups contain water that is easily available to humans? How do these amounts compare to the amount in Step 1?

FIGURE 9
The Water Cycle
Water moves continuously through a cycle, from Earth's surface to the atmosphere and back. The sun's energy drives this process.
Interpreting Diagrams
In which step of the water cycle does water return to Earth's surface?

Condensation

Evaporation

Precipitation

Evaporation from plants

Evaporation from lakes

Evaporation from oceans

Surface runoff

Groundwater

The Water Cycle

Earth's water is naturally recycled through the water cycle. The **water cycle** is the continuous process by which water moves from Earth's surface to the atmosphere and back. **In the water cycle, water moves from bodies of water, land, and living things on Earth's surface to the atmosphere and back to Earth's surface.** As shown in Figure 9, the water cycle has three major steps—evaporation, condensation, and precipitation. The cycle itself has no real beginning or end. But it is driven by an energy source—the sun.

Water Evaporates As you learned earlier, evaporation is the process by which molecules at the surface of a liquid absorb enough energy to change to a gaseous state. Water is constantly evaporating from the surfaces of oceans and large lakes. Smaller amounts evaporate from the soil, puddles, and even from your skin. Plants play a role, too, in this step of the water cycle. Plants draw in water from the soil through their roots. Eventually the water is given off through the leaves as water vapor in a process called **transpiration.**

Condensation Forms Clouds What happens after a water molecule evaporates? Warm air carries the water molecule upward. At higher altitudes, air tends to become much colder. Cold air cannot hold as much water vapor as warm air can. As a result, some of the water vapor cools and condenses into liquid water. Condensed droplets of water clump together around tiny dust particles in the air, forming clouds.

Water Falls As Precipitation As more water vapor condenses, the water droplets in a cloud grow larger and larger. Eventually, they become so heavy that they fall back to Earth. Water that falls to Earth as rain, snow, hail, or sleet is called **precipitation.**

Most precipitation falls directly into the ocean. The precipitation that falls on land may evaporate immediately or run off the surface into rivers and lakes. From there, it may evaporate or flow back into the ocean. In addition, some water may trickle down into the ground. After a long time, this groundwater may reach a river, lake, or ocean and continue the cycle by evaporating again.

Precipitation is the source of all fresh water on and below Earth's surface. The water cycle renews the usable supply of fresh water on Earth. For millions of years, the total amount of water on Earth has remained fairly constant—rates of evaporation and precipitation are balanced.

FIGURE 10
Precipitation
Precipitation is part of the water cycle. But you might not want it falling on your head!

 **Reading Checkpoint** List three sources from which water evaporates.

Section 2 Assessment

Target Reading Skill Identifying Main Ideas Use your graphic organizer to help you answer Question 2 below.

Reviewing Key Concepts

1. a. Describing What are two reasons that living things need water?

b. Applying Concepts Why can't animals survive more than a few days without water?

c. Developing Hypotheses Some desert animals live for many days without drinking water. How do you think these animals survive?

2. a. Listing What are the four main sources of water on Earth?

b. Classifying Which of the four main water sources contain salt water? Which contain fresh water?

c. Making Judgments Which freshwater source is most important to people? Use facts to defend your answer.

3. a. Identifying What three major steps make up the water cycle?

b. Sequencing Starting with a puddle on a sunny day, describe how water might move through the water cycle and eventually fall back as rain.

Writing in Science

Product Label Create a product label for bottled drinking water, explaining to consumers why water is a precious resource.

Water From Trees

Problem

How much water do the leaves on a tree give off in a 24-hour period?

Skills Focus

observing, inferring, calculating

Materials

- 3 plastic sandwich bags • balance
- 3 small pebbles • 3 twist ties

Procedure

1. Copy the data table into your notebook.

2. Place the sandwich bags, twist ties, and pebbles on a balance. Determine their total mass to the nearest tenth of a gram.

3. Select an outdoor tree or shrub with leaves that are within your reach.

4. Put one pebble into a sandwich bag. Place the bag over one of the tree's leaves as shown. Fasten a twist tie around the bag, forming a tight seal around the stem of the leaf.

5. Repeat Step 4 on two more leaves, using the remaining plastic bags. Leave the bags in place for 24 hours.

6. The following day, examine the bags and record your observations in your notebook.

7. Carefully remove the bags from the leaves and refasten each twist tie around its bag so that the bag is closed tightly.

8. Place the three bags, including pebbles and twist ties, on the balance. Determine their total mass to the nearest tenth of a gram.

9. Subtract the original mass of the bags, ties, and pebbles that you found in Step 2 from the mass you found in Step 8.

Analyze and Conclude

1. **Observing** Use the observations you made in Step 6 to account for the difference in mass you found in Step 9.

2. **Inferring** What is the name of the process that caused the results you observed? Explain the role of that process in the water cycle.

3. **Calculating** A single birch tree may give off as much as 260 liters of water in a day. How much water would a grove of 1,000 birch trees return to the atmosphere in a year?

4. **Communicating** Based on what you learned from this lab, write a paragraph explaining why some people are concerned about the destruction of forests around the world.

Design an Experiment

Write a hypothesis about what would happen if you repeated this activity with a different type of tree. Design a plan to test your hypothesis. *Obtain your teacher's permission before carrying out your investigation.*

Data Table	
Starting mass of bags, ties, and pebbles	
Mass of bags, ties, and pebbles after 24 hours	
Difference in mass	

Surface Water

Reading Preview

Key Concepts
- What is a river system?
- How do ponds and lakes form?
- What changes can occur in lakes?

Key Terms
- tributary • watershed
- divide • reservoir • nutrient
- eutrophication

Target Reading Skill
Outlining As you read, make an outline of this section. Use the red headings for the main ideas and the blue headings for the supporting ideas.

Surface Water
I. River systems
A. Tributaries
B.
C.
II. Ponds and lakes
A.

Lab zone Discover Activity

What's in Pond Water?

1. Using a hand lens, observe a sample of pond water.
2. Make a list of everything you see in the water. If you don't know the name of something, write a short description or draw a picture.
3. Your teacher has set up a microscope with a slide of pond water. Observe the slide under the microscope and add any new items to your list. Wash your hands with soap when you are done.

Think It Over

Classifying Use one of these systems to divide the items on your list into two groups: moving/still, living/nonliving, or microscopic/visible without a microscope. What does your classification system tell you about pond water?

Imagine that you are a raindrop falling from the clouds to Earth's surface. Down, down, you go and then, splash! You land in the tumbling waters of a fast-moving stream. You are in one of Earth's freshwater sources. Fresh water on Earth may be moving, as in streams and rivers, or still, as in ponds and lakes. All fresh water, however, comes from precipitation. For example, the Rio Grande—the "Big River"—begins as trickles of melting snow high in the San Juan Mountains in Colorado. But 700 kilometers downstream, the "Big River" lives up to its name as it flows past Albuquerque, New Mexico.

◀ **Kayaker in river rapids**

River Systems

If you were hiking in the mountains of Colorado, you could observe the path of the runoff from melting snow. As you followed one small stream downhill, you would notice that the stream reached another stream and joined it. These streams flow into a small river. Eventually this path would lead you to the Rio Grande itself. Figure 11 shows the parts of a typical river.

Tributaries The streams and smaller rivers that feed into a main river are called **tributaries.** Tributaries flow downward toward the main river, pulled by the force of gravity. **A river and all its tributaries together make up a river system.**

FIGURE 11

Exploring a River

Notice the changes that occur as a river flows from its origin to the ocean.

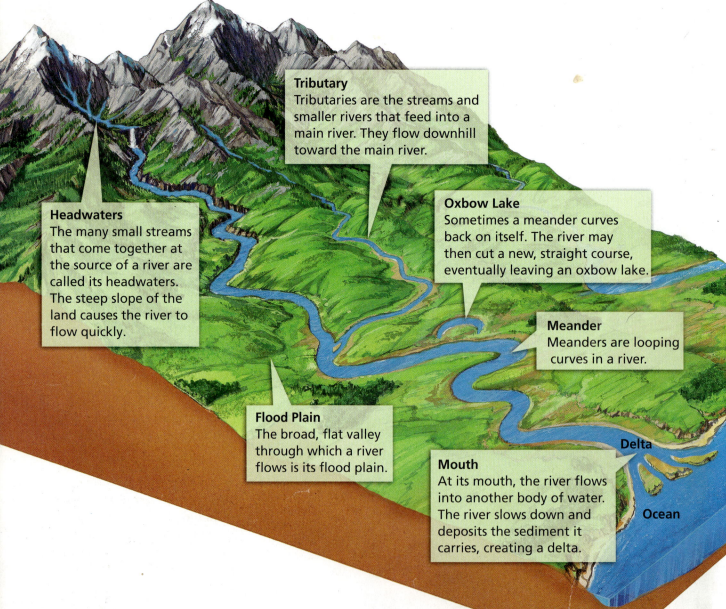

Tributary
Tributaries are the streams and smaller rivers that feed into a main river. They flow downhill toward the main river.

Oxbow Lake
Sometimes a meander curves back on itself. The river may then cut a new, straight course, eventually leaving an oxbow lake.

Headwaters
The many small streams that come together at the source of a river are called its headwaters. The steep slope of the land causes the river to flow quickly.

Meander
Meanders are looping curves in a river.

Flood Plain
The broad, flat valley through which a river flows is its flood plain.

Delta

Mouth
At its mouth, the river flows into another body of water. The river slows down and deposits the sediment it carries, creating a delta.

Ocean

Major Watersheds of the United States

Columbia River Watershed

Missouri River Watershed

Colorado River Watershed

Mississippi River Watershed

Ohio River Watershed

ROCKY MOUNTAINS

SIERRA NEVADA

GREAT BASIN

APPALACHIAN MOUNTAINS

CANADA

Great Lakes

Columbia R.

Snake River

Missouri River

Platte R.

Arkansas River

Mississippi River

Ohio River

Colorado R.

Red River

Rio Grande

PACIFIC OCEAN

ATLANTIC OCEAN

Gulf of Mexico

MEXICO

0 250 500 mi
0 250 500 km

N W E S

Watersheds Just as all the water in a bathtub flows toward the drain, all the water in a river system drains into a main river. The land area that supplies water to a river system is called a **watershed.** Watersheds are sometimes known as drainage basins.

As you can see in Figure 12, the Missouri and Ohio rivers are quite large. Yet they flow into the Mississippi River. So large rivers may be tributaries of still larger rivers. When rivers join another river system, the areas they drain become part of the largest river's watershed. You can identify a river's watershed on a map by drawing an imaginary line around the region drained by all its tributaries. The watershed of the Mississippi River, the largest river in the United States, covers nearly one third of the country!

Divides What keeps watersheds separate? One watershed is separated from another by a ridge of land called a **divide.** Streams on each side of the divide flow in different directions. The Continental Divide, the longest divide in North America, follows the line of the Rocky Mountains. West of the Continental Divide, water either flows toward the Pacific Ocean or into the dry Great Basin. Between the Rocky Mountains and the Appalachian Mountains, water flows toward the Mississippi River or directly into the Gulf of Mexico.

Reading Checkpoint What is a divide?

FIGURE 12
Major Watersheds
This map shows watersheds of several large rivers in the continental United States. Each river's watershed consists of the region drained by the river and all its tributaries. **Interpreting Maps** *What large rivers are tributaries of the Mississippi River?*

Lab zone Skills Activity

Inferring
The Nile River in Africa flows from south to north. What can you infer about the slope of the land through which the Nile River flows? (*Hint:* Think about the factors that determine how a river system forms.)

Go Online
PHSchool.com

For: More on surface water
Visit: PHSchool.com
Web Code: cfd-3013

FIGURE 13
Life in a Pond
From its shallow edges to its muddy bottom, a pond is rich with life.
Inferring *Why can plants grow throughout a pond?*

Ponds and Lakes

Ponds and lakes are bodies of fresh water. Unlike the moving water in streams and rivers, ponds and lakes contain still, or standing, water. How can you tell the difference between ponds and lakes? There is no definite rule. In general, however, ponds are smaller and shallower than lakes. Sunlight usually reaches to the bottom of all parts of a pond. Most lakes have areas where the water is too deep for sunlight to reach the bottom.

Ponds and lakes form when water collects in hollows and low-lying areas of land. Where does the water come from? Some ponds and lakes are supplied by rainfall, melting snow and ice, and runoff. Others are fed by rivers or groundwater. As a pond or lake gains water from these sources, it also loses water to natural processes. For example, water may eventually flow out of a body of fresh water into a river. Water also evaporates from the surface of a pond or lake.

Some of the most important pond dwellers are the smallest. Microscopic algae are the pond's basic food producers.

The roots of water lilies cling to the pond bottom, while their leaves float on the surface. Sponges live under the leaves. Dragonflies pause on top to rest.

A slender-bodied pickerel waits among the duckweed to grab a meal of insects at the water's edge.

Exploring a Pond A pond might seem calm and peaceful at first glance. But look closer—do you notice the silvery minnows gliding beneath the surface? Plop! A frog has jumped into the water. The quiet pond is actually a thriving habitat, supporting a wide diversity of living things, as shown in Figure 13.

If you've ever waded in a pond, you know that the muddy bottom is often covered with weeds. Because the water is shallow enough for sunlight to reach the bottom, plants grow throughout a pond. Plantlike organisms called algae also live in the pond. As the plants and algae use sunlight to make food through photosynthesis, they also produce oxygen. Animals in the pond use the oxygen and food provided by plants and algae.

The shore is edged with grasses and trees that require a lot of water, such as willows and maples. These plants provide shelter and nesting places for red-winged blackbirds and other birds.

Frogs lay eggs in the shallow water near shore. They hatch in the water as tadpoles and move to the land as adults.

Sunfish and perch live in both the weedy shallows and the deeper waters of the pond.

Snails find food on the soft bottom of the pond.

Crayfish lie buried in the mud, waiting for bits of food to drift down.

FIGURE 14

Types of Lakes

A lake can be formed either by a natural process or by human efforts. **Interpreting Photographs** *What are three ways that lakes are formed?*

Volcanic Lake
Volcanic lakes such as this one in Costa Rica form when water fills the craters of old volcanoes.

Classifying

Crumple up a piece of wax paper. Straighten out the paper to model a landscape with hills and valleys. Use a permanent marker to draw lines along the highest divides of the landscape. Then draw circles where lakes and ponds will form on the landscape. Place the wax paper in a sink and sprinkle water over the landscape to simulate rain. Observe where the water collects. Which areas would you classify as ponds? Which would be lakes? Explain your reasoning.

Exploring a Lake Suppose you were shown a picture of a sandy beach. Waves are breaking on the shore. The water stretches as far as the eye can see. Gulls are screeching overhead. Where was the picture taken? Your first guess might be the ocean. But this immense body of water could actually be a lake! You could be viewing a photo of a beach in Indiana, on the shore of Lake Michigan.

Most lakes are not as large as Lake Michigan. But recall that lakes are generally deeper and bigger than ponds. A lake bottom may consist of sand, pebble, or rock, whereas the bottom of a pond is usually covered with mud and algae.

In the shallow water near shore, the wildlife of a lake is similar to that of a pond. Water beetles scurry over the slippery, moss-covered rocks. Loons and kingfishers pluck fishes from the open water. But sunlight does not reach the bottom of a deep lake, as it does in a pond. As a result, only a few organisms can live in lake's chilly, dark depths. There are no plants, but mollusks, such as clams, and worms move along the lake bottom. They feed on food particles that drift down from the surface. Deep lake waters are also home to large, bony fishes such as pike and sturgeon. These fishes eat the tiny bottom-dwellers. They also swim to the surface to feed on other fishes and even small birds.

Glacier-Made Lake
Lake Louise in Alberta, Canada, was formed by the movements of glaciers.

Human-Made Lake
The Lake Mead reservoir is part of the Hoover Dam complex in the southwestern United States.

Lake Formation As you read earlier, lakes and ponds form when water collects in hollows and low-lying areas of land. Let's take a closer look at some natural processes that can result in the formation of a lake. A river channel, for example, can form a lake as it changes over time. It bends and loops as it encounters obstacles in its path. Eventually, a new channel might form, cutting off a loop. The cut-off loop may become an oxbow lake.

Some other natural lakes, such as the Great Lakes, formed in depressions created by ice sheets that melted at the end of the Ice Age. Other lakes were created by movements of Earth's crust. Such movements formed the deep valleys in central Africa that lie below Lake Tanganyika and Lake Victoria. Still other lakes are the result of volcanoes. An erupting volcano can cause a flow of lava or mud that blocks a river and forms a lake. Some lakes form in the empty craters of volcanoes.

People can also create a lake by building a dam across a river. The lake may be used for supplying drinking water, for irrigating fields, and for recreation. A lake that stores water for human use is called a **reservoir.**

 **What is a reservoir?**

How Lakes Can Change

A maple tree in fall looks very different than it does in the summer. The green leaves change to brilliant shades of red, orange, and yellow. Lakes can change with the seasons, too. Lakes change for many reasons. **In addition to seasonal changes, a lake can undergo long-term changes that may eventually lead to its death.**

Seasonal Changes Seasonal changes in lakes are common in cool, northern areas of North America. In summer, the sun warms the upper layer of water in a lake. The warm water floats on top of the cooler, denser, lower layer. But in fall, the top layer cools off, too. As the top layer cools, it becomes denser and sinks. This causes the lake waters to mix. This mixing, also called lake turnover, causes materials to rise from the lake bottom. Lake turnover refreshes the supply of nutrients throughout the lake. **Nutrients** are substances such as nitrogen and phosphorus that enable plants and algae to grow.

Long-Term Changes The second type of change that may occur in a lake happens over a long period of time. The organisms in a lake constantly release waste products into the water. The wastes and the remains of dead organisms contain nutrients such as nitrates and phosphates. Algae feed on these nutrients. Over many years, the nutrients build up in the lake in a process called **eutrophication** (yoo troh fih KAY shun). As eutrophication causes more algae to grow, a thick, green scum forms on the surface of the water. Recall that algae are present in ponds as well as lakes. So eutrophication can also occur in ponds.

FIGURE 15
Long-Term Changes in a Lake
Lakes and ponds change gradually over time. **Relating Cause and Effect** *What effect does an increase in nutrient levels have on a lake?*

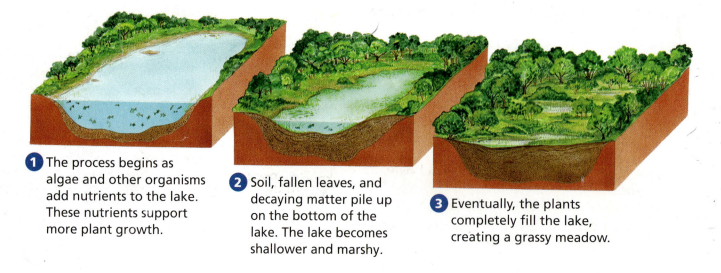

1. The process begins as algae and other organisms add nutrients to the lake. These nutrients support more plant growth.

2. Soil, fallen leaves, and decaying matter pile up on the bottom of the lake. The lake becomes shallower and marshy.

3. Eventually, the plants completely fill the lake, creating a grassy meadow.

Death of a Body of Fresh Water When the algae layer becomes so thick that it blocks out the sunlight, plants in the lake or pond can no longer carry out photosynthesis. They stop producing food and oxygen, and they die. As dead organisms in the water decay, the amount of oxygen in the water decreases. Many of the fishes and other water animals no longer have enough oxygen to live. Material from decaying plants and animals piles up on the bottom, and the lake or pond becomes shallower. The sun warms the water to a higher temperature and more plants take root in the rich bottom mud. Eventually, the body of fresh water becomes completely filled with plants. The remaining water evaporates, and a grassy meadow takes the place of the former lake or pond.

Eutrophication is not the only change that can lead to the death of a lake or pond. Sometimes, water may leave a pond more rapidly than it enters it. This can happen when the source of water for a pond—a stream, for example—dries up or is cut off from the pond by natural processes such as erosion. In addition, streams and rivers carry sediments into ponds or lakes. Over a long period of time, these sediments can fill in the body of water.

FIGURE 16
Slowing Eutrophication
In some locations, a community will periodically pull plants out of a pond or lake in order to prolong its life.

 **Reading Checkpoint** What kinds of materials can build up over time at the bottom of a lake?

Section 3 Assessment

🎯 **Target Reading Skill Outlining** Use the information in your outline to help you answer the questions below.

Reviewing Key Concepts

1. a. **Identifying** What bodies of water make up a river system?
   b. **Summarizing** How is a watershed related to a river system?
   c. **Applying Concepts** How could you determine the boundaries of a river system by studying a map of the United States?
2. a. **Reviewing** How are lakes different from ponds?
   b. **Explaining** Explain how ponds and lakes form.
   c. **Comparing and Contrasting** What is the major difference between a reservoir and most other types of lakes?

3. a. **Explaining** What causes lake turnover?
   b. **Sequencing** Describe the changes that take place at each stage of eutrophication.

Lab zone **At-Home Activity**

The Knuckle Divide Have a family member make a fist and put it on a paper towel, knuckles facing up. Dribble water from a spoon so that it falls onto the person's knuckles. As you both observe how the water flows over the hand, explain how the knuckles model a mountain range. Which parts of the hand represent a watershed?

Wetland Environments

Reading Preview

Key Concepts
- What are the common types of freshwater wetlands?
- Which human activities threaten the Florida Everglades?
- What important functions do wetlands serve?

Key Term
- wetland

Target Reading Skill
Asking Questions Before you read, preview the red headings. In a graphic organizer like the one below, ask a *what* or a *how* question for each heading. As you read, write the answers to your questions.

Wetland Environments

Question	Answer
What are the types of wetlands?	Three types of wetlands are . . .

Wet or Dry?

1. Hold a kitchen sponge under water until it is soaked. Then squeeze out the water until the sponge is just damp.
2. Place the damp sponge next to a dry sponge in a pan.
3. Pour water into two paper cups until each is half full.
4. Hold a cup in each hand, about 10 centimeters above the pan. Pour the water onto both sponges at the same time.

Think It Over

Observing Which of the sponges absorbs water faster? How are your observations related to what might happen in areas of wet and dry land?

Imagine coming home from a long trip, only to find that your house is gone and has been replaced by a parking lot! Millions of migrating birds have had a similar experience. But people are beginning to understand the importance of wetlands, both to wildlife and to people. A **wetland** is a land area that is covered with a shallow layer of water during some or all of the year. These soggy regions, as you'll learn, are important in many ways.

FIGURE 17
Freshwater Wetlands
Freshwater wetlands can differ in many ways. **Predicting** *Which types of wetlands are you more likely to find in northern areas?*

Marsh Marshes, such as this one in Washington State, are grassy areas covered with shallow water.

Types of Wetlands

Wetlands help control floods and provide habitats for many species. They form in places where water is trapped in low areas or where groundwater seeps to the surface. Wetlands may be as small as a roadside ditch or cover as much area as a city. Some wetlands fill up during spring rains, only to dry up during long, hot summers. Others are covered with water year-round.

The three common types of freshwater wetlands are marshes, swamps, and bogs. As shown in Figure 17, these wetlands are quite diverse. Marshes are usually grassy areas covered by shallow water or a stream. They teem with cattails and other tall, grasslike plants. Swamps look more like flooded forests, with trees and shrubs sprouting from the water. Many swamps are located in warm, humid climates, where trees grow quickly. Bogs are more common in cooler northern areas. They often form in depressions left by melting ice sheets thousands of years ago. The water in bogs tends to be acidic, and mosses thrive in these conditions.

Wetlands along coasts usually contain both fresh and salt water. Coastal wetlands include salt marshes and mangrove forests. Salt marshes are found along both coasts of the United States. Tall, strong grasses grow in the rich, muddy bottoms of salt marshes. Mangrove forests are found along the southeastern coast of the United States. In these forests, the mangrove trees are short and have thick, tangled roots.

 **Reading Checkpoint** Name three types of fresh-water wetlands.

Go Online
SciLINKS NSTA

For: Links on wetlands
Visit: www.SciLinks.org
Web Code: scn-0814

Swamp Swamps look like flooded forests. Curtains of Spanish moss hang from cypress trees in this Louisiana swamp.

Bog Mosses thrive in the acidic water in bogs. Colorful flowers dot a bed of velvety moss in this bog in Montana.

FIGURE 18
Florida Everglades

A rich variety of living things make their homes in the Everglades. **Observing** *Why is the Everglades sometimes called a "river of grass"?*

Mangrove forests
Everglades National Park
Rivers and canals

The Everglades: A Wetland

If you were to walk down a path in Florida's Everglades National Park, you would feel the ground squish under your feet. Water is the key to the Everglades, a unique region of wetlands. A shallow stream of water moves slowly over the gently sloping land from Lake Okeechobee south to Florida Bay. Tall, sharp-edged blades of sawgrass grow in the water. The thick growth of sawgrass gave this region its Native American name, *Pa-hay-okee*, which means "river of grass." Low-lying islands are scattered throughout the sawgrass marsh.

Everglades Wildlife In the Everglades, fishes and snakes gobble up tiny organisms in the warm, muddy water. Wading birds in bright colors—pink flamingos, white egrets, and purple gallinules—stand on skinny legs in the water. A raccoon digs for alligator eggs, unaware of the alligator lying low in the water nearby.

The Everglades provide habitats for many rare or endangered species. The endangered Florida panther lives in the wildest parts of the Everglades. Many species of birds, such as the wood stork and the roseate spoonbill, depend on the Everglades as a nesting area. The manatee, or sea cow, lives in the mangrove forests along the coast. Because manatees swim slowly, they are easily injured by the propellers of powerboats. They have become an endangered species as a result of increased boating.

Everglades palm

White-tailed deer

Flamingos

Raccoon

American alligator

Purple gallinule

Threats to the Everglades The Everglades are a fragile environment. Nearby farming has introduced new chemicals into the slow-moving waters of the marsh, upsetting the balance of nutrients. Outside the protected limits of the national park, developers have filled in areas of wetland to build homes and roads. New organisms brought into the area accidentally or for pest control compete with other organisms for space and food. **Agriculture, development, and the introduction of new species are some human activities that threaten the Florida Everglades.**

Water that once flowed into the Everglades from Lake Okeechobee has been diverted for farming and household use. New canals and levees built to provide drinking water and to control flooding have changed the flow of water into and out of the Everglades. Some areas are drying up, while others are flooded.

Preserving the Everglades Scientists, concerned citizens, and government officials have been trying for many years to develop a plan to preserve the Everglades and save its endangered wildlife. One plan involves building an elaborate system of pipes and canals to refill some drained areas with fresh water. The National Park Service, the state of Florida, and the U.S. Army Corps of Engineers are working together to manage the supply of water to areas around and within the Everglades.

Reading Checkpoint What is one way that farming has affected the Everglades?

Roseate spoonbill

Great egret

Snowy egret

Sawgrass

Little blue heron

Anhinga

Florida panther

Lab zone Try This **Activity**

A Natural Filter

1. Cover your work surface with newspaper. In one end of a loaf pan, build a sloping hill of damp soil.
2. Add water to the other end of the pan to form a lake.
3. Use a watering can to sprinkle rain onto the hill. Observe what happens to the hill and the lake.
4. Empty the water out of the pan and rebuild the hill.

5. Now push a sponge into the soil across the bottom of the hill to model a wetland.
6. Repeat Steps 2 and 3.

Observing Based on your observations, describe how wetlands filter water.

Importance of Wetlands

If you've ever enjoyed tart cranberry sauce or tasty wild rice, you've eaten plants that grow in wetlands. The layer of water covering a wetland can range from several centimeters to a few meters deep. Dead leaves and other plant and animal materials serve as natural fertilizers. They add nitrogen, phosphates, and other nutrients to the water and soil.

Importance to Wildlife **Because of their sheltered waters and rich supply of nutrients, wetlands provide habitats for many living things.** Recall the many plants and animals that live in or near a pond—reeds, frogs, snails, dragonflies, turtles. Some of these same organisms live in freshwater wetlands year-round. Insects dart about, finding food and shelter among wetland plants. Birds nest in and around the wetlands, feeding on the plants and darting insects. In addition, some larger animals, such as manatees, live in the wetlands year-round.

Other animals spend only part of their lives in the wetlands. Have you ever seen or heard a flock of geese flying overhead? The geese may be flying south to make a temporary home in a wetland. As winter approaches, geese, ducks, and other waterfowl travel from Alaska and Canada to warmer climates. They pass millions of small, shallow marshes along their routes. The birds stop at these marshes to rest and feed. The birds then make their way to the large southern marshes where they spend the winter.

FIGURE 19
Wetlands Wildlife
Manatees depend on rich wetland habitats for food and breeding sites.

Importance to People Many people, including farmers and builders, once thought wetlands were worthless. They assumed that wetland areas could not be used unless they were drained and filled in. Thousands of square kilometers of wetlands were developed for farms, homes, and businesses. Beginning in the 1970s, however, the government passed laws to protect wetland habitats.

What prompted these laws? Scientific studies showed that wetlands serve important functions for people as well as for wildlife. For example, as water moves slowly through a wetland, some waste materials settle out. Other wastes may be absorbed by plants, such as those shown in Figure 20. The thick network of plant roots also traps silt and mud. **In this way, wetlands act as natural water filters. They also help control floods by absorbing extra runoff from heavy rains.** Wetlands are like giant sponges, storing water until it gradually drains or evaporates. When wetlands are destroyed, the floodwaters are not absorbed. Instead, the water runs off the land quickly, worsening flood problems.

FIGURE 20
Natural Filters
Some wetland plants, such as the pickerel weed shown here, filter pollutants from water. **Inferring** *How are wetland plants like pickerel weed important to people?*

 **Reading Checkpoint** What prompted wetlands protection laws?

Section 4 Assessment

Target Reading Skill **Asking Questions** Use the answers to the questions you wrote about the headings to help you answer the questions below.

Reviewing Key Concepts

1. a. **Defining** What is a wetland?
   b. **Classifying** What are the three major types of freshwater wetlands?
   c. **Comparing and Contrasting** How are the three major types of freshwater wetlands similar? How are they different?
2. a. **Listing** List three activities that threaten the Florida Everglades.
   b. **Summarizing** What is being done to preserve the Everglades?
   c. **Making Judgments** Some of the plans to restore the Everglades will require millions of dollars and would negatively affect local farmers. What information would you consider in deciding what should be done?

3. a. **Describing** Name one way that wetlands benefit wildlife and one way that wetlands benefit people.
   b. **Explaining** How do wetlands help reduce water pollution?
   c. **Developing Hypotheses** Without plants, could a wetland still filter water? Explain.

Lab zone **At-Home Activity**

Runoff Take a family member outside to observe how water runs off different materials. Pour some water in the grass and watch what happens. Then pour some water on the sidewalk or driveway. What happened to the water in each case? How does this relate to the role of wetlands in controlling floods? Why would floods be more frequent if wetlands were paved over?

Water Underground

Reading Preview

Key Concepts
- How does water move through underground layers of soil and rock?
- How do people obtain water from an aquifer?

Key Terms
- permeable • impermeable
- saturated zone • water table
- unsaturated zone • aquifer
- artesian well

🔄 Target Reading Skill

Previewing Visuals Before you read, preview Figure 22. Then write one question that you have about the diagram in a graphic organizer like the one below. As you read, answer your question.

Springs and Wells

Q.	What is an artesian well?
A.	
Q.	

Discover **Activity**

Where Does the Water Go?

1. Add pebbles to a jar to form a layer about 5 centimeters deep. Cover the pebbles with a layer of dry sand about 3 centimeters thick. Pour the sand in slowly to avoid moving the pebbles. These materials represent underground soil layers.
2. Sprinkle water onto the sand to simulate rainfall.
3. Looking through the side of the jar, observe the path of the water as it soaks through the layers. Wash your hands when you are finished with this activity.

Think It Over

Observing Describe what happened when the water reached the bottom of the jar.

When you were a little child, did you ever dig a hole in the ground hoping to find a buried treasure? You probably never found a trunk full of gold. But there was a certain kind of treasure hidden underground. If you had dug past the tangled grass roots and small stones, the bottom of your hole would have filled with water. You would have "struck groundwater"! In the days before public water systems, water underground was truly a hidden treasure. Today, many people still rely on the water underground to meet their water needs.

How Water Moves Underground

Where does this underground water come from? Like the water in rivers, lakes, and glaciers, it comes from precipitation. Recall that precipitation can evaporate, run off the surface, or soak into the ground. If water soaks into the ground, it trickles downward, following the pull of gravity.

If you pour water into a glass full of pebbles, the water trickles down around the pebbles until it reaches the bottom of the glass. Then the water begins to fill up the spaces between the pebbles. **In the same way, water underground trickles down between particles of soil and through cracks and spaces in layers of rock.**

Effects of Different Materials Different types of rock and soil have different-sized spaces, or pores, between their particles, as shown in Figure 21. The size of the pores determines how easily water moves through rock and soil. If the pores are connected, this too affects water movement. Because they have large and connected pores, materials such as sand and gravel allow water to pass through, or permeate. They are thus known as **permeable** (PUR mee uh bul) materials.

As water soaks down through permeable rock and soil, it eventually reaches layers of material that it cannot pass through. These materials have few or no pores or cracks. Two examples are clay and granite. Clay and granite are **impermeable,** meaning that water cannot pass through easily.

Water Zones Once water reaches an impermeable layer, it is trapped. It can't soak any deeper. Instead, the water begins to fill up the spaces above the impermeable material. The area of permeable rock or soil that is totally filled, or saturated, with water is called the **saturated zone.** The top of the saturated zone is the **water table.** If you know the depth of the water table in your area, you can tell how deep you must dig to reach groundwater.

Soil and rock layers above the water table contain some moisture, too. But here the pores contain air as well as water. They are not saturated. Therefore, the layer of rocks and soil above the water table is called the **unsaturated zone.**

 **Reading Checkpoint** **Give an example of a permeable material.**

Go Online
SciLINKS NSTA

For: Links on water underground
Visit: www.SciLinks.org
Web Code: scn-0815

FIGURE 21
Groundwater Formation
Differences in the materials that form layers underground determine where groundwater forms. Water can move through certain layers but not others.
Interpreting Diagrams *What is the saturated zone? Where is it located?*

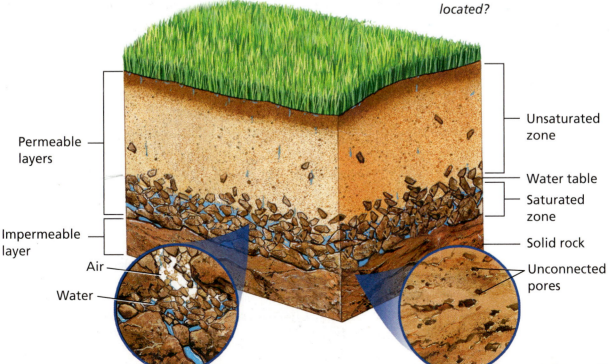

Permeable layers

Impermeable layer

Air

Water

Unsaturated zone

Water table

Saturated zone

Solid rock

Unconnected pores

Bringing Up Groundwater

Suppose you live far from a city, town, or body of fresh water. How could you reach groundwater to use it for your daily needs? You may be in luck: the water table in your area might be only a few meters underground. In fact, in some places the water table actually meets the surface. Springs can form as groundwater bubbles or flows out of cracks in the rock. A short distance away, the water table may be deep underground.

Aquifers Any underground layer of permeable rock or sediment that holds water is called an **aquifer.** Aquifers can range in size from a small underground patch of permeable material to an area the size of several states. The huge High Plains aquifer lies beneath the plains of the Midwest, from South Dakota to Texas. Millions of people obtain drinking water from this underground storehouse. The aquifer also provides water for crops and livestock.

Do you picture groundwater as a large, still pool beneath Earth's surface? In fact, the water is moving, seeping through layers of rock. The rate of movement depends largely on the slope of the aquifer and the permeability of the rocks. Groundwater in some aquifers moves only a few centimeters a day. At that rate, the water moves about 10 meters a year. Groundwater may travel hundreds of kilometers and stay in an aquifer for thousands of years before coming to the surface again.

Math ▶ Analyzing Data

Uses of Water

The graph shows water use in the United States. Each category of water use is represented by a different color. Use the graph to answer the questions below.

1. **Reading Graphs** How many categories of water use are shown on the graph?

2. **Interpreting Data** The two largest categories of water use combine to make up about what percentage of the total water used in the United States?

3. **Interpreting Data** Which of the categories of water use shown in the graph represents the largest use of water in the United States? Which represents the smallest?

4. **Predicting** How would an increase in the number of farms affect this graph?

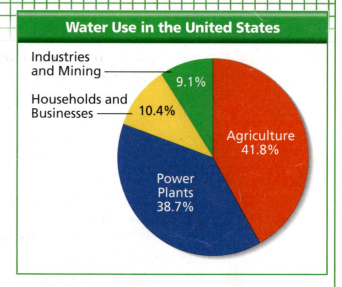

Water Use in the United States

Industries and Mining — 9.1%
Households and Businesses — 10.4%
Agriculture 41.8%
Power Plants 38.7%

5. **Calculating** If the total daily usage of water in the United States is 1,280 billion liters, about how many liters are used each day by power plants?

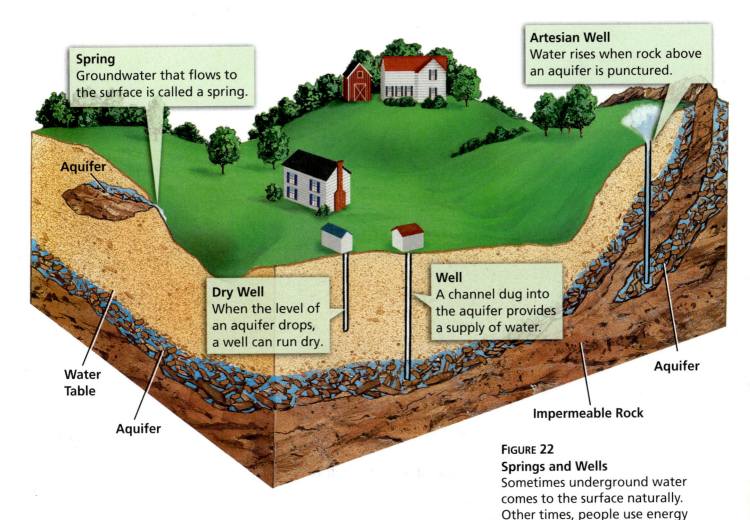

Spring
Groundwater that flows to the surface is called a spring.

Artesian Well
Water rises when rock above an aquifer is punctured.

Aquifer

Dry Well
When the level of an aquifer drops, a well can run dry.

Well
A channel dug into the aquifer provides a supply of water.

Water Table

Aquifer

Aquifer

Impermeable Rock

FIGURE 22
Springs and Wells
Sometimes underground water comes to the surface naturally. Other times, people use energy to obtain groundwater.
Comparing and Contrasting *How do the ordinary well, artesian well, and dry well differ?*

Wells The depth of a water table can vary greatly over a small area. Its level may vary as well. Generally, the level of a water table follows the shape of underground rock layers, as shown in Figure 22. But it can rise during heavy rains or snow melts, and then fall in times of dry weather. So what do you do if the depth and level of the water table in your area is far underground? How can you bring the water to the surface?

Since ancient times, people have brought groundwater to the surface for drinking and other everyday uses. **People can obtain groundwater from an aquifer by drilling a well below the water table.** Locate the well near the center of Figure 22. Because the bottom of the well is in a saturated zone, the well contains water. Notice the level of the bottom of the dry well in the diagram. Because this well does not reach below the water table, water cannot be obtained from it.

 **Reading Checkpoint** Why might a water table rise? Why might a water table fall?

Lab zone Try This Activity

An Artesian Well

For this activity, cover your desk with newspaper.

1. Cover the bottom of a loaf pan with clay. Pile the clay higher at one end. Cover the clay with about 4 cm of moist sand.

2. Cover the sand with a thin sheet of clay. Seal the edges of the clay tightly against the pan.

3. Push a funnel into the high end so the bottom of the funnel is in the sand.

4. Insert a short piece of plastic straw through the clay and into the sand layer at the low end. Remove the straw, discard it, and then insert a new piece of straw into the same hole.

5. Slowly pour water into the funnel. Do not let the water overflow.

6. Observe the level of water in the straw.

Making Models How is your model like a real artesian well? How is it different?

Using Pumps Long ago, people dug wells by hand. They lined the sides of the well with brick and stone to keep the walls from collapsing. To bring up the water, they lowered and raised a bucket. People may also have used simple pumps, like the one shown in Figure 23. Today, however, most wells are dug with well-drilling equipment. Mechanical pumps bring up the groundwater.

Pumping water out of an aquifer lowers the water level near the well. If too much water is pumped out too fast, a well may run dry. The owners of the well will have to dig deeper to reach the lowered water table, or wait for rainfall to refill the aquifer. New water that enters the aquifer from the surface is called recharge.

Relying on Pressure Now you know how to bring groundwater to the surface. But what if that didn't work? You might not be out of luck. You might be able to drill an artesian well. In an **artesian well** (ahr TEEZH un), water rises because of pressure within an aquifer.

Look back at Figure 22 and locate the artesian well. In some aquifers, groundwater becomes trapped between two layers of impermeable rock or sediment. This water is under great pressure from the weight of the rock above. If the top layer of rock is punctured, the pressure sends water spurting up through the hole. No pump is necessary—in an artesian well, pressure does the job.

FIGURE 23
Working for Water Here a resident of Bangladesh uses a hand pump to bring groundwater to the surface.
Interpreting Photographs *What is one disadvantage of a hand pump?*

Springs and Geysers Sometimes, groundwater comes to the surface through natural processes. You read that places where groundwater bubbles or flows out of cracks in the rock are called springs. Most springs contain water at normal temperatures. Others, like those in Figure 24, contain water that is warmed by the hot rocks deep below the surface. The heated water bubbles to the surface in hot springs.

In some areas, you might see a fountain of boiling hot water and white steam burst into the air. This is a geyser, a type of hot spring from which the water periodically erupts. The word *geyser* comes from an Icelandic word, *geysir*, which means "gusher."

A geyser forms when very hot water that has been circulating deep underground begins to rise through narrow passages in the rock. Heated gases and bubbles of steam are forced up these passages by the pressure of the hot water boiling below. Just as pressure builds up in a partly blocked water pipe, the pressure within these narrow openings in the rock increases. Finally, the gases, steam, and hot water erupt high into the air.

FIGURE 24
A Hot Spring
A Japanese macaque takes advantage of the warm water that rises to the surface of a hot spring in Nagano, Japan.

 Reading Checkpoint How do geysers form?

Section 5 Assessment

 Target Reading Skill **Previewing Visuals** Refer to your questions and answers about Figure 22 to help you answer Question 2 below.

Reviewing Key Concepts

1. a. **Reviewing** What happens to water in the ground when it reaches impermeable materials?
   b. **Explaining** What two factors determine how easily water can move through underground materials?
   c. **Inferring** Would an impermeable material have large or small pores? Would the pores be connected or unconnected? Explain.
2. a. **Describing** How can people obtain water from an aquifer?
   b. **Interpreting Diagrams** Using Figure 22 as a guide, explain why is it important to know the depth of an aquifer before drilling a well.

c. **Problem Solving** During the winter, you draw your water from a well on your property. Every summer, the well dries up. What might be the reason for the change?

Writing in Science

Formal Letter Water usage in your town has risen in recent years due to population growth. Your town obtains its water from a nearby aquifer. You are concerned that the water level of the aquifer may be going down. Write a letter to local government officials explaining your concerns. Describe the effect of heavy water usage on the aquifer and suggest measures that can be taken to avoid a water shortage.

Soil Testing

Problem

How fast does water move through sand, clay, and pebbles?

Skills Focus

observing, developing hypotheses, designing experiments

Suggested Materials

- hand lens
- 100 mL of sand
- stopwatch
- 3 rubber bands
- 3 100-mL beakers
- 300 mL of water
- 100 mL of pebbles
- 100 mL of powdered potter's clay
- 3 squares of cheesecloth
- 3 large funnels or cut-off plastic bottle tops

Procedure

PART 1 Observing the Flow of Water Through Sand

1. Copy the data table in your notebook.

2. Use a hand lens to observe the sand sample closely. Record your observations in your data table.

3. Place a piece of cheesecloth over the bottom of one funnel or bottle top and secure it with a rubber band.

4. Place the sand in the funnel. Be sure that there is about 5 cm of space above the sand in the funnel.

5. Place the funnel on top of a beaker.

Data Table		
Material	Observations	Time for Water to Stop Dripping
Sand		
Clay		
Pebbles		

6. Slowly pour 100 mL of water into the funnel. Do not let the water overflow the funnel.

7. Start the stopwatch when the water begins to flow or drip out of the funnel.

8. Stop the stopwatch when the water stops dripping out of the funnel or after 5 minutes. Record the time to the nearest second in your data table.

PART 2 Comparing the Flow of Water Through Different Soil Samples

9. Use a hand lens to observe each of the two other material samples closely. Record your observations in the data table.

10. Using the procedures you followed in Part 1, design an experiment to compare the flow of water through sand, clay, and pebbles. Be sure to write a hypothesis and to control all necessary variables.

11. Submit your experimental plan to your teacher. After making any necessary changes, carry out your experiment. Record your observations in your data table.

12. When you are finished with this activity, dispose of the materials according to your teacher's instructions. Wash your hands thoroughly with soap.

Analyze and Conclude

1. **Observing** In Part 1, how did the sand look under the hand lens? How long did it take the water to flow through the sand?

2. **Developing Hypotheses** What hypothesis did you test in Part 2? On what did you base your hypothesis?

3. **Designing Experiments** What was the manipulated variable in Part 2? What was the responding variable?

4. **Drawing Conclusions** Through which material did water move the fastest? The slowest? What can you conclude about the permeability of the three materials?

5. **Predicting** Based on the results of this lab, would you expect to get more water from a well dug in sand, pebbles, or clay? Explain.

6. **Communicating** You and your neighbor are discussing your gardens. You're explaining that it's important for a gardener to know the permeability of different soils. Write your conversation in dialogue form. Use quotation marks for each speaker.

More to Explore

Of the soil samples you tested, which do you think most resembles the soil on the grounds at your school? Explain your reasoning. How might you test your hypothesis?

1 The Properties of Water

Key Concepts

- The positive hydrogen ends of one water molecule attract the negative oxygen ends of nearby water molecules. As a result, the water molecules tend to stick together.

- The properties of water include capillary action, surface tension, the ability to dissolve many substances, and high specific heat.

- Ice is solid water, the familiar form of water is a liquid, and water vapor is a gas.

Key Terms

polar molecule	solvent
capillary action	specific heat
surface tension	evaporation
solution	condensation

2 Water on Earth

Key Concepts

- All living things need water in order to carry out their body processes. In addition, many living things use water for shelter.

- Most of Earth's water—roughly 97 percent—is salt water found in oceans. Only 3 percent is fresh water.

- In the water cycle, water moves from bodies of water, land, and living things on Earth's surface to the atmosphere and back to Earth's surface.

Key Terms

photosynthesis	water cycle
habitat	transpiration
groundwater	precipitation

3 Surface Water

Key Concepts

- A river and all its tributaries together make up a river system.

- Ponds and lakes form when water collects in hollows and low-lying areas of land.

- In addition to seasonal changes, a lake can undergo long-term changes that may eventually lead to its death.

Key Terms

tributary	reservoir
watershed	nutrient
divide	eutrophication

4 Wetland Environments

Key Concepts

- The three common types of freshwater wetlands are marshes, swamps, and bogs.

- Agriculture, development, and the introduction of new species are some human activities that threaten the Florida Everglades.

- Wetlands provide habitats for many living things. Wetlands help people by acting as natural water filters and by helping to control floods.

Key Term

wetland

5 Water Underground

Key Concepts

- Water underground trickles down between particles of soil and through cracks and spaces in layers of rock.

- People can obtain groundwater from an aquifer by drilling a well below the water table.

Key Terms

permeable	unsaturated zone
impermeable	aquifer
saturated zone	artesian well
water table	

Review and Assessment

Organizing Information

Sequencing Copy and complete the cycle diagram to show how water moves throughout the water cycle. (For more on Sequencing, see the Skills Handbook.)

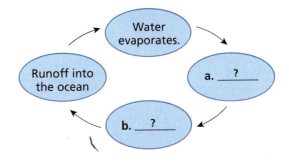

Reviewing Key Terms

Choose the letter of the best answer.

1. A molecule with electrically charged parts is a
   a. nonpolar molecule.
   b. solution.
   c. polar molecule.
   d. gas.

2. More than 97 percent of Earth's total water supply is found in
   a. ice sheets.
   b. the atmosphere.
   c. the oceans.
   d. groundwater.

3. The land area that supplies water to a river system is called a
   a. divide.
   b. watershed.
   c. wetland.
   d. tributary.

4. Wetlands help control floods by absorbing
   a. silt and mud.
   b. extra runoff.
   c. nutrients.
   d. waste materials.

5. The water table is the top of the
   a. saturated zone.
   b. unsaturated zone.
   c. aquifer.
   d. artesian well.

If the statement is true, write *true*. **If it is false, change the underlined word or words to make the statement true.**

6. The property of specific heat allows some insects to walk on water.

7. In the process of condensation, water vapor is given off through the leaves of a plant.

8. One watershed is separated from another by a divide.

9. An aquifer is an area of land covered with a shallow layer of water during some or all of the year.

10. Water moves easily through permeable materials.

Writing in Science

Brochure Write a brochure describing the Florida Everglades. Be sure to include information about why so many organisms live here and why people need to protect the Everglades.

Earth: The Water Planet
Video Preview
Video Field Trip
▶ Video Assessment

Review and Assessment

Checking Concepts

11. Draw a diagram of a water molecule that shows how it is polar. Be sure to label your diagram.

12. Give examples of two properties of water that are caused by the attractions between water molecules.

13. Explain why Earth is called the "blue planet."

14. Why is so little of Earth's water available for human use?

15. When can a large river be considered a tributary?

16. What is lake turnover and how does it relate to changing seasons?

17. Why doesn't an artesian well require a pump?

Thinking Critically

18. **Comparing and Contrasting** Compare the three states of water in terms of the speed and arrangement of their molecules.

19. **Relating Cause and Effect** A molecule of water is likely to evaporate more quickly from the Caribbean Sea near the equator than from the Arctic Ocean. Explain why this statement is true.

20. **Predicting** The city of Charleston, South Carolina, is located on the Atlantic coast. The city of Macon, Georgia, is located about 340 kilometers inland to the west. Predict which city is likely to be cooler in the summer. Explain your answer in terms of specific heat.

Macon, Ga.

Charleston, S.C.

340 km

Atlantic Ocean

21. **Comparing and Contrasting** How would the variety of organisms in the center of a pond be different from those you would find in deep water at the center of a lake?

22. **Applying Concepts** Explain why some rivers experience severe springtime flooding as snow and ice melt along small mountain streams.

23. **Classifying** On a walk in a northern state, you come upon an area of spongy soil. It is carpeted with mosses along with some low-growing, flowering plants. What type of wetland is this likely to be? Explain.

Applying Skills

Use the diagram of underground layers to answer Questions 24–27.

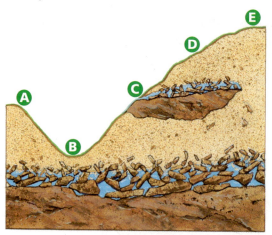

24. **Drawing Conclusions** Would point D or point E be a better location to dig a well? Explain your reasoning.

25. **Inferring** At which location could you obtain groundwater without having to use a pump? What is this location called?

26. **Interpreting Data** At which point is the water table closest to the surface?

27. **Predicting** Draw a simple diagram showing how this area might look during a very rainy season.

Lab zone Chapter Project

Performance Assessment Make graphs of your household and community water-use data. Then share your graphs with your classmates. As a class, discuss any surprising results. How do your findings compare to those of your classmates?

Standardized Test Prep

Choose the letter of the best answer.

1. What characteristic of water explains why it has many unusual properties?
   A Water is a nonpolar molecule.
   B Water is a polar molecule.
   C Water molecules do not have electrically charged areas.
   D Water is not a molecule.

2. Why don't plants normally grow on the bottoms of deep lakes?
   F The water is too salty.
   G The water is too cold.
   H Photosynthesis does not occur in water.
   J There is not enough sunlight for photosynthesis to occur.

3. For a science project you must build a model of an aquifer. What material would be the best to use for the layer that will hold water?
   A an impermeable material, such as clay
   B an impermeable material, such as granite
   C a permeable material, such as gravel
   D a material that does not have pores

Use the diagram below and your knowledge of science to answer Questions 4–5.

4. Which of the following is a process that occurs in the water cycle?
   F evaporation
   G precipitation
   H condensation
   J all of the above

5. What is the energy source that drives the continuous process shown in the diagram?
   A the sun
   B the ocean
   C gravity
   D the tides

Constructed Response

6. Explain what a wetland is and why wetlands are important. Describe one threat to wetlands and the actions being taken to protect wetlands from this threat.

Chapter 2

Freshwater Resources

Chapter Preview

This family is enjoying a ▶
freshwater resource—fish.

Lab zone™ Chapter **Project**

A Precious Resource

You need water to cook, to clean, to shower—and, most importantly, to survive. Water is a precious resource. But when people use water, it can become polluted. In this chapter project, you'll explore how to clean up water pollution.

Your Goal To design and build a water treatment system to clean one liter of dirty water

Your treatment system should

● consist of at least two treatment steps
● be made from materials that have been approved by your teacher
● recover as much clean water as possible
● be assembled following the safety guidelines in Appendix A

Plan It! Your teacher will give you a sample of dirty water. Carefully observe your sample and record your observations. Preview the chapter to learn about water pollution and water treatment systems. Then choose materials for your model. After your teacher approves your design, build your model and conduct several trials to see how well it works. **CAUTION:** *Do not taste or drink the water samples before or after treatment.*

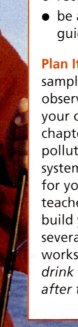

Water Supply and Demand

Reading Preview

Key Concepts
- How do people use water?
- What are some ways to conserve available fresh water?
- What are some possible sources of water for the future?

Key Terms
- irrigation
- conservation
- desalination

⊙ Target Reading Skill

Using Prior Knowledge Your prior knowledge is what you already know before you read about a topic. Before you read, write what you know about water conservation in a graphic organizer like the one below. As you read, continue to write in what you learn.

What You Know
1. I can conserve water by taking shorter showers.
2.

What You Learned
1.
2.

Discover **Activity**

Can You Find a Balance?

1. Fill a large measuring cup with water to represent a reservoir. Record the level of the water. One partner, the water supplier, should have a plastic dropper and a small bowl of water. The other partner, the water user, should have a spoon and an empty bowl.
2. Start a stopwatch. For two minutes, the water supplier should add water to the measuring cup one dropperful at a time. Each time the water supplier adds a dropperful of water, the water user should remove one spoonful of water from the reservoir.
3. At the end of two minutes, record the level of water in the cup.
4. Now increase the rate of water use by removing two spoonfuls of water for every dropperful added.
5. After another two minutes, record the level of water in the cup again.

Think It Over
Predicting What changes will you need to make so that the water level in the reservoir stays constant?

Imagine this: you're eating dinner with your family and you ask someone to pass the rolls. As the basket makes its way around the table, each person takes a roll. By the time it gets to you, there's nothing left in the basket but crumbs!

This scenario is an example of a limited resource—the rolls—being used by many people. A similar thing can happen to a river.

For example, the Colorado River holds a resource that is precious to the Southwest—water. In this desert region, there is too little precipitation to meet people's water needs. As the river flows through five states and into Mexico, it is tapped again and again to provide water for drinking, irrigation, and other uses. Each time the river is tapped, the flow decreases. As a result, the river's mouth at the Gulf of California is often only a dry riverbed. The Colorado River often dries up before it reaches the ocean.

How People Use Water

The deserts of Nevada and Arizona, two states along the Colorado River, are home to some of the fastest-growing cities in the country. As more people move to Las Vegas, Phoenix, and Tucson, the demand for water—already scarce in this dry region—increases.

People use water for household purposes, industry, transportation, agriculture, and recreation. As cities grow, so too does the water needed for household uses. Industries, such as mining companies, need water to cool machinery and flush out mines. Meanwhile, farmers need a large amount to water their fields. Cities, industries, and farms compete for water rights—the legal right to take water from a particular source.

The Southwest is just one of many places where water is scarce. As you know, water is constantly recycled in the water cycle. However, sometimes water is used faster than it can be replaced by precipitation. A water shortage occurs when there is too little water or too great a demand in an area—or both. A water shortage may occur because of natural processes or it can occur because of rapidly growing human water needs.

FIGURE 1
The Colorado River
The Colorado River flows through five states. The river is used by cities, mines, and farms for drinking, irrigation, and other uses.

Huge dams have been constructed along the Colorado River to store water and generate electric power.

At the beginning of the river, water is plentiful.

At the end of the river, little water is flowing.

Nevada

Utah

Colorado River

Colorado

Lake Powell

Las Vegas

Hoover Dam

Glen Canyon Dam

Lake Mead

Grand Canyon

Colorado River

Arizona

Phoenix

Tucson

In the Home Take a minute to list all of the ways you used water this morning. You probably washed your face, brushed your teeth, and flushed the toilet. Perhaps you drank a glass of water or used water to make oatmeal. These are some common uses of water in the home.

Industry and Transportation Think about the objects in your backpack—books, pens, folders. Even though water is not part of these things, it plays a role in making them. Industries use water in other ways, too. For example, power plants and steel mills both need huge volumes of water to cool hot machinery. Water that is used for cooling can often be recycled.

Since ancient times, water has been used to transport people and goods. If you look at a map of the United States, you will notice that many large cities are located on the coasts. Ocean travel led to the growth of these port cities. In early America, rivers also served as natural highways.

• Tech & Design in History •

Water and Agriculture
Plants require a steady supply of water to grow. How have farmers throughout history provided their crops with water? This timeline shows some methods developed in different parts of the world.

3000 B.C. Irrigation
One of the oldest known methods of irrigation was developed for growing rice. Farmers built paddies, or artificial ponds with raised edges. The farmers flooded the paddies with water from a nearby stream. This ancient technique is still widely used throughout Southeast Asia.

2000 B.C. Shadufs
Egyptian farmers invented a device to raise water from the Nile River. The shaduf acted as a lever to make lifting a bucket of water easier. The farmers then emptied the water into a network of canals to irrigate their fields. The shaduf is still in use in Egypt, India, and other countries.

700 B.C. Canals and Aqueducts
Sennacherib, king of the ancient nation Assyria, surrounded the capital city of Nineveh with fruit trees and exotic plants. To help irrigate the gardens, he built a canal and an aqueduct to transport water from the nearby hills.

3000 B.C.   **2000 B.C.**   **1000 B.C.**

Agriculture Has your family ever had a garden? If so, you know that growing fruits and vegetables requires water. On a large farm, a constant supply of fresh water is essential. However, some areas don't receive enough regular rainfall for agriculture. In such places, farmland must be irrigated. **Irrigation** is the process of supplying water to areas of land to make them suitable for growing crops. In the United States, more water is used for irrigation than for any other single purpose.

Recreation Do you like to swim in a neighborhood pool? Catch fish from a rowboat in the middle of a lake? Walk along a beach collecting seashells? Or maybe just sit on the edge of a dock and dangle your feet in the water? Then you know some ways that water is used for recreation. And if you brave the winter cold to ski or skate, you are enjoying water in its frozen form.

 **Reading Checkpoint** List a household use, an industrial use, and an agricultural use of water.

Writing in Science

Research and Write Find out more about one of these agricultural techniques. Imagine that you are a farmer seeing the method in action for the first time. Write a letter to a friend describing the new technique. What problem will it solve? How will it improve your farming?

A.D. 1200 *Chinampas*
To grow crops in swampy areas, the Aztecs built raised plots of farmland called *chinampas*. A grid of canals kept the crops wet and allowed the farmers to navigate boats between the *chinampas*.

A.D. 1870 Wind-Powered Pumps
When homesteaders arrived on the dry Great Plains of the central United States, they had to rely on groundwater for irrigation. Windmills provided the energy to pump the groundwater to the surface. The farmers dug ditches to transport the water to their fields.

Today Drip Irrigation
Irrigation is the key to survival in desert regions. Today, methods such as drip irrigation ensure that very little water is wasted when crops are watered. Holes in the pipe allow water to drip directly onto the soil around the roots of each plant.

A.D. 1   A.D. 1000   A.D. 2000

Take shorter showers. If you take baths, fill the tub only halfway.

If you have a lawn, water it early in the morning or late in the afternoon so the sun won't evaporate the water.

Scrub vegetables in a basin of water, not under running water.

Keep drinking water in the refrigerator instead of running the water until it gets cold.

Turn off the faucet instead of letting the water run while you brush your teeth.

Only run the washing machine when you have a full load.

FIGURE 2
Conserving Water at Home
There are many simple ways to conserve water at home.
Developing Hypotheses *Which of these ideas do you think would save the most water per day in your home? How could you test your hypothesis?*

Conserving Water

During a water shortage, people often try to avoid wasting water. **Conservation** is the practice of using less of a resource so that it will not be used up. **Reducing water use, recycling water, and reusing water are three ways to conserve water.**

In the Home Most people in the United States have access to as much clean, safe water as they want. As a result, we often use more water than we need without thinking much about it. But as Figure 2 shows, there are some simple things you can do to help conserve water around your home.

Can these suggestions really help? Figure it out. For every minute you shower, you use about 18 liters of water. If you shower for 10 minutes, that's about 180 liters. But if you showered for 5 minutes, you would use only 90 liters. And if each student in a class of 25 showered for 5 minutes instead of 10, they would save a total of 2,250 liters of water!

In Industry Many industries have made changes in their manufacturing processes to use less water. For example, in the 1950s it took about 227,000 liters of water to make 1,000 kilograms of writing paper. By the 1980s, paper mills needed only half that much water to make the same amount of paper.

New water-saving techniques help industries save money in water costs and meet the requirements of environmental laws. These techniques conserve water while also reducing the amount of wastewater that plants release. For example, some factories that use water to cool machinery now build cooling pools on their property. The heated water cools off in the pools and then can be used again.

In Agriculture Agriculture accounts for the highest consumption of water in the United States. In the last few decades, farmers have found new ways to use less water. When water flows into fields in open ditches, much of it is lost through evaporation. Using pipes to carry water reduces the water loss.

Sprinkler irrigation and drip irrigation both use pipes to conserve water. Sprinkler irrigation sprays water onto crops from overhead pipes. Drip irrigation distributes water through pipes with tiny holes that lie close to the ground. Water drips onto the soil near the plants' roots so that very little is wasted.

 **Reading Checkpoint** **How do sprinkler irrigation and drip irrigation differ?**

Go Online
PHSchool.com

For: More on water conservation
Visit: PHSchool.com
Web Code: cfd-3021

FIGURE 3
Conserving Water on Farms
One way that farmers can conserve water is to use sprinkler irrigation systems to water their crops.
Relating Cause and Effect *How does sprinkler irrigation conserve water?*

Household Water Use

A family conducted a survey of their current water use. Their average daily use is shown in the bar graph. Study the graph and answer the following questions.

1. **Reading Graphs** What variable is shown on the horizontal axis? What variable is shown on the vertical axis?

2. **Interpreting Data** Where does this family use the greatest amount of water?

3. **Calculating** The family found that they used an average of about 800 liters of water per day. About what percentage of the water is used for laundry?

4. **Inferring** Do you think the family's water use would vary at different times of the year? Explain.

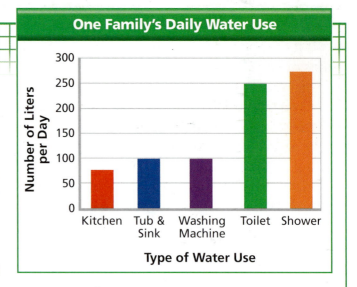

One Family's Daily Water Use

5. **Predicting** Suggest three ways that this family might be able to save a significant amount of water each day.

Fresh Water for the Future

As the use of water in the world increases, so does the need for water. Where can people find new sources of water for the future? One obvious place would seem to be the oceans. **Two possible methods of obtaining fresh water for the future are desalination and melting icebergs.**

Desalination For thousands of years, people have tried to make salty ocean water drinkable. One possible method of obtaining fresh water from salt water is called **desalination.**

There are several ways to desalinate water. A technique called distillation involves boiling water so that it evaporates, leaving the salt behind. The water vapor is then condensed to produce liquid fresh water. Another desalination method involves freezing the water, which also leaves the salt behind. Still another method is to pump water at high pressure through a very fine filter. The filter separates out pure water and returns salty water to the ocean.

Desalination is very expensive because of the energy and equipment it requires. In spite of the cost, however, many nations in dry Southwest Asia depend on this technology. A few cities in the United States, such as Santa Barbara, California, have also built desalination plants.

Icebergs Another possible source of fresh water is icebergs. Tugboats could tow a wrapped iceberg from Antarctica to a coastal area of Africa or South America. As the iceberg melted, it would provide millions of liters of pure water that could be piped to shore.

Such plans raise environmental questions, however. How would a huge mass of ice offshore affect the local weather? What would happen to living things in the ocean as the ice cooled the water around it? These questions must be answered before icebergs could be used to meet future water needs.

 **What is desalination?**

FIGURE 4
A Future Source of Drinking Water?
Icebergs are one possible source of drinking water for the future. **Applying Concepts** *How can water from icebergs reach people on shore?*

Section 1 Assessment

Target Reading Skill **Using Prior Knowledge** Revise your graphic organizer based on what you learned.

Reviewing Key Concepts

1. a. **Listing** Name five ways that people use water.
   b. **Explaining** Why are towns and cities often located near bodies of water?
   c. **Calculating** Growing wheat for one loaf of bread takes about 435 liters of water. If your family eats three loaves a week, about how much water would be used each year to make bread for your family?

2. a. **Identifying** What are three ways to conserve water?
   b. **Describing** Describe the techniques that industries can use to conserve water.
   c. **Making Judgments** To conserve water, should communities limit how often people can water their lawns or wash their cars? Why or why not?

3. a. **Reviewing** What are two possible ways to meet people's future water needs?
   b. **Inferring** What is one disadvantage of each method?

Lab zone **At-Home Activity**

Monitoring Water Use Place a stopper over the drain in a sink. Ask a family member to brush his or her teeth over the sink, allowing the water to run until he or she is done. Mark the level of the water in the sink with a small piece of tape. Remove the stopper and let the water drain. Replace the stopper and have the person repeat the brushing, this time turning the water on only when needed. Mark the water level with another piece of tape. Point out the difference in the amount of water used in each case.

Getting the Salt Out

Problem

How can distillation be used to obtain fresh water from salt water?

Skills Focus

observing, making models

Materials

- hot plate • aluminum foil • 250-mL beaker
- plastic spoon • water, 100 mL
- shallow pan • ice • plastic tube
- 500-mL flask • stirring rod • rubber stopper
- salt • rubber tubing, 50 cm

Procedure

1. Pour 100 mL of water into the flask.

2. Add one spoonful of salt to the water in the flask and stir until it is dissolved. The solution should not be cloudy.

3. Gently insert the plastic tube through the hole of the rubber stopper. Do not force the tube into the hole; ask your teacher for help if you are having difficulty.

4. Insert one end of the plastic tube into the rubber tubing.

5. Put the rubber stopper in the flask. The bottom of the plastic tube should be above the surface of the solution.

6. Cover the beaker with aluminum foil. Press the edges of the foil against the beaker.

7. Push the free end of the rubber tubing through the center of the aluminum foil covering the top of the beaker.

8. Place the beaker into the pan, surrounded by ice.

9. Put the flask on the hot plate, keeping it away from the pan of ice. Turn the hot plate on. Bring the solution to a boil. **CAUTION:** *Do not touch the hot plate or flask. Do not allow the solution to boil completely away.*

10. Observe what happens in the flask and in the beaker. Continue heating the solution until a liquid has accumulated in the beaker.

11. Turn off the hot plate and allow the flask and the beaker to cool. What is left behind in the flask? Record your observations.

Analyze and Conclude

1. **Observing** What happened to the water in the flask during the boiling process? What happened to the salt?

2. **Making Models** What did the water in the flask represent? What did the water in the beaker represent?

3. **Drawing Conclusions** Based on your results, is distillation a useful method for obtaining fresh water from salt water? Why or why not?

4. **Communicating** Imagine building a desalination plant that uses distillation to obtain water for a city. Write a paragraph describing any difficulties you might encounter using this process on such a large scale.

Design an Experiment

How could you change the setup and procedure to recover fresh water from salt water without using the hot plate? *Obtain your teacher's permission before carrying out your investigation.*

Water to Drink

Reading Preview

Key Concepts
- What factors affect water quality?
- Why is drinking water often treated before people drink it?
- What happens to wastewater in most communities?

Key Terms
- water quality • concentration
- pH • hardness • filtration
- coagulation • sewage

Target Reading Skill

Sequencing As you read, make a flowchart that shows the steps of drinking-water treatment. Put the steps of the process in separate boxes in the flowchart in the order in which they occur.

Drinking-Water Treatment

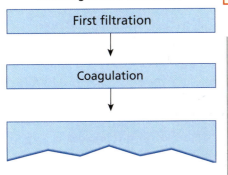

First filtration

↓

Coagulation

↓

Discover Activity

How Hard Is It to Move Water?

1. Line two large trash barrels with heavy plastic bags. Fill one barrel with 100 liters of water. This is about how much water a person uses during a five-minute shower.
2. With your classmates, form a line between the barrels. Your goal is to transfer all the water from one barrel to the other.
3. The first person in line should fill a large plastic pitcher with water, put the cover on, and hand it to the next person. **CAUTION:** *Avoid spilling the water. Be careful of slippery floors if you are indoors.*
4. Pass the pitcher to the end of the line, where the last person should empty it into the second barrel. Hand the empty pitcher back down the line to the first person.
5. Repeat Steps 3 and 4 until all the water is in the second barrel. How many times did you pass the pitcher down the line?

Think It Over

Calculating Suppose a person uses an average of 250 liters of water a day. How many times would you have to pass the pitcher to move that amount of water?

Where does the water in your kitchen faucet come from? Its source may be a lake or reservoir, or it may come from water in underground rock layers. Most people in the United States get their drinking water from one of these sources.

Your drinking water comes from either a public or private water supply. Most large communities maintain public water supplies. These communities collect, treat, and distribute water to residents. In less-populated areas, people often rely on private wells that supply water for individual families.

Calculating a Concentration

Concentrations are often measured in parts per million (ppm). What does this unit mean? If you own one compact disc by your favorite band, and the disc sells one million copies, your disc is one of the one million sold, or one part per million. When a concentration is written in this form, you can rewrite it as a fraction. To do this, put the number of parts on top, and the "whole" on the bottom.

$$1 \text{ part per million} = \frac{1}{1,000,000}$$

Practice Problem The concentration of iron in a water sample is 500 parts per million. Write this concentration as a fraction.

Water Quality

Now you know where your water comes from. Before you raise a glass to your lips, however, you'll want to be sure the water is safe to drink. Would you be willing to take a sip if the water were rust-colored or had a funny smell? Color and odor are two factors that affect water quality.

Standards of Quality **Water quality** is a measurement of the substances in water besides water molecules. **Certain substances, such as iron, can affect the taste or color of water but are harmless unless present at very high levels. Other substances, such as certain chemicals and microorganisms, can be harmful to your health.**

In the United States, the Environmental Protection Agency (EPA) is responsible for developing water-quality standards. These standards set concentration limits for certain substances. A **concentration** is the amount of one substance in a certain volume of another substance. Figure 5 shows some water-quality standards for different substances.

Acidity The pH level of water also affects its quality. The **pH** of water is a measurement of how acidic or basic the water is, on a scale of 0 to 14. Pure water has a pH of 7—it is neutral, meaning it is neither an acid nor a base. The higher the pH, the more basic the water. The lower the pH, the more acidic the water. Acidic water can cause problems by dissolving lead or other metals from the pipes it passes through.

FIGURE 5
The EPA has set water-quality standards for drinking water.
Interpreting Data *Based on this table, is a concentration of 0.09 ppm of arsenic in drinking water acceptable? Is a concentration of 0.05 ppm of cyanide acceptable?*

Selected Water-Quality Standards	
Substance	**Limit**
Arsenic	0.01 parts per million (ppm)
Carbon tetrachloride	0.005 ppm
Copper	1.3 ppm
Cyanide	0.2 ppm
Lead	0.015 ppm
Coliform count	No more than 5% of samples taken in a month can be positive.
pH	6.5 – 8.5

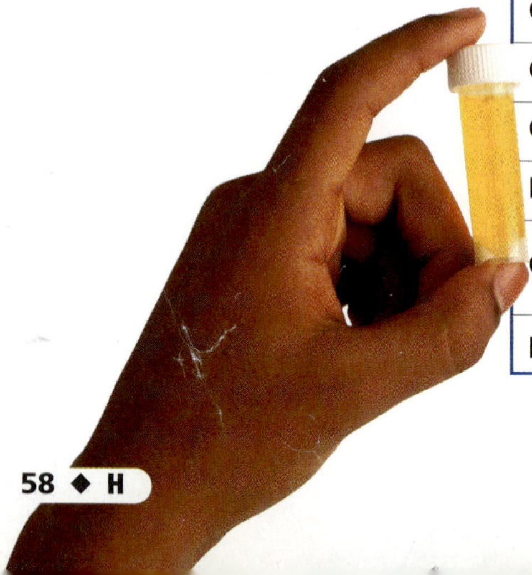

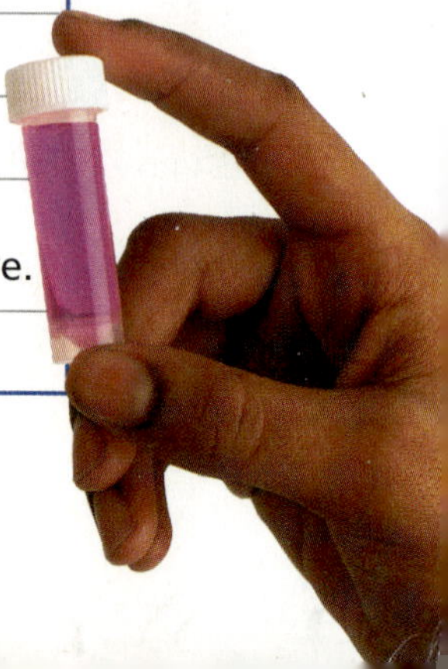

Hardness The combined level of two minerals—calcium and magnesium—in a sample of water is referred to as the **hardness** of that sample. Hard water contains high levels of calcium and magnesium. The minerals come from rocks, such as limestone, that water flows through underground.

For most people, the main drawback of hard water is that it does not form suds well when mixed with soap or detergent. Suds are very important to the cleaning process. So it takes more soap or detergent to get laundry clean in hard water.

The minerals in hard water can also form deposits that can clog pipes and machinery. Soft water, on the other hand, contains lower levels of calcium and magnesium. Soft water leaves fewer deposits and forms better soapsuds than hard water.

Disease-Causing Organisms The presence of disease-causing organisms affects water quality. Such organisms can be detected in water by conducting a coliform count, which measures the number of *Escherichia coli* bacteria. These bacteria are found in human and animal wastes. Thus, their presence in water shows that it contains waste material. A high coliform count is an indicator, or sign, that the water may also contain other disease-causing organisms.

FIGURE 6
Hardness of Water
Hard water does not form suds easily. The water being used to wash this car is probably soft water.

 **What two minerals affect a water sample's hardness?**

FIGURE 7
Drinking-Water Treatment

A typical drinking-water treatment process includes several steps that remove unwanted substances from water.
Interpreting Diagrams *What occurs during aeration?*

Treating Drinking Water

Picture a huge, smooth-surfaced lake under a sky dotted with puffy, white clouds. Leaves drift upon the water's sparkling surface. Fish swim along the muddy bottom. That lake may be your source of drinking water.

How can you be sure that the quality of the water is good? **Water from both public and private supplies often needs some treatment to ensure that it is clean and safe to drink.** Treatment may be simple, such as a filter on a household well. Water treatment may also be complex, such as the many processes water undergoes at public treatment plants. Follow the water in Figure 7 to see what happens in a typical water treatment plant.

Filtration and Coagulation The first step in treating water from a lake or river is usually filtration. **Filtration** is the process of passing water through a series of screens that allows the water through, but not larger solid particles. During this step, trash, leaves, branches, and other large objects are removed from the water.

In the second step, a chemical is added to cause sticky globs, called flocs, to form. Other particles stick to the flocs, a process known as **coagulation.** The heavy clumps then sink into the settling basins. The water is then filtered again.

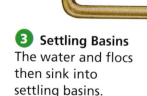

1 First Filtration
Water is filtered through screens that remove fish, leaves, and trash.

2 Coagulation
Alum is added to form sticky flocs. Mud, bacteria, and other particles stick to the flocs.

3 Settling Basins
The water and flocs then sink into settling basins.

Chlorination The next step is to chlorinate the water. If you have ever been to a public swimming pool, you have probably smelled chlorine. Chlorine is added to drinking water for the same reason it is added to swimming pools: to kill disease-causing microorganisms. At this point, the water is usually ready to be distributed to homes.

Water from an aquifer may require less treatment than water from a lake. Flowing through rocks or sand naturally filters and purifies the water. However, most public water supplies that use a groundwater source still add chlorine to kill disease-causing organisms.

Aeration and Additional Treatment Air is then forced through the purified water. This process reduces unpleasant odors and tastes. Minerals may then be added to soften the water or for other purposes.

Testing Samples Public health officials regularly test samples from water treatment plants to assess water quality. They test for the substances covered by the drinking-water standards, including chemicals, dissolved solids, pH, hardness, and disease-causing organisms. Private well owners should also test their water regularly to make sure no treatment is needed.

 **Reading Checkpoint** What is the goal of drinking-water treatment?

Lab zone Skills **Activity**

Making Models
Cover an empty jar with a paper towel; tuck the paper towel slightly into the mouth of the jar. Fill a second jar with water. Add a handful of materials to the water, such as sand, soil, and leaves. While holding the paper towel in place, slowly pour the water onto the paper towel so that it enters the empty jar. Observe what happens to the materials in the water. How does this activity relate to the process of treating drinking water?

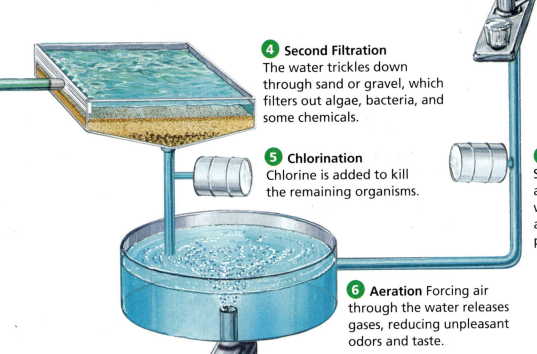

4 Second Filtration
The water trickles down through sand or gravel, which filters out algae, bacteria, and some chemicals.

5 Chlorination
Chlorine is added to kill the remaining organisms.

6 Aeration Forcing air through the water releases gases, reducing unpleasant odors and taste.

7 Additional Treatment
Sodium or lime may be added to soften hard water. Some communities add fluoride to help prevent tooth decay.

Moving Water Uphill

1. Pile a stack of books on a table. Place one bowl on top of the books and another bowl on the table. Pour water into the higher bowl until it is about half full.

2. Submerge a piece of plastic tubing in the water in the upper bowl. When the tubing is full of water, put a finger over each end.

3. Keeping one end of the tubing underwater, place the other end in the lower, empty bowl. Release both fingers and watch what happens.

Observing In what direction does the water first have to travel to get out of the higher bowl? Can you explain this movement?

Water Distribution Once it has been treated, water is ready to be distributed to homes and businesses. From a treatment plant, water goes to a central pumping station. There the water is pumped into an underground network of pipes called water mains. The water mains branch off to smaller pipes. These pipes feed into even smaller pipes that carry water into buildings.

Water pressure causes the water to move through this system of pipes. Whenever water is in an enclosed space, it exerts pressure in all directions. Pumping stations are designed to keep water pressure steady throughout the system.

Rather than use a central pumping station, some communities store their water in a water tower or tank on top of a hill. Treated water is pumped up into the water tower. When the water is needed, it is released. Then the water rushes downward, into the town's water mains and pipes.

Treating Wastewater

Finally, after a long journey, the water reaches your house. You take a shower, flush the toilet, or wash a load of laundry. What happens to the used water that goes down the drain? The wastewater and the different kinds of wastes in it are called **sewage. Two ways that communities deal with sewage are wastewater treatment plants and septic systems.**

Wastewater Treatment Plants Most communities treat their wastewater to make it safe to return to the environment. In many communities, household wastewater flows into a network of pipes called sanitary sewers. Sanitary sewers carry sewage away to wastewater treatment plants. You'll learn more about public wastewater-treatment systems in the Technology and Society feature later in this chapter.

Septic Systems Some people dispose of their sewage and treat their wastewater using a septic system. A septic system centers around a septic tank, which is an underground tank containing bacteria that treat wastewater as it passes through. Sludge and scum are materials that bacteria cannot break down or that break down very slowly. These materials must be pumped out regularly so they don't fill the tank.

The remaining water in the septic tank filters out through holes. The area around the septic tank that the water filters through is called a leach field. Over time, wastes remaining in the water break down naturally in the soil of the leach field.

 **Reading Checkpoint** What is a leach field?

FIGURE 8
A Septic System

Sewage flows into a septic tank, where bacteria break down the waste material into simpler chemicals. Cleaner water leaves the tank and flows into a leach field.
Observing *What is the purpose of the outlet pipe?*

Scum
Less-dense wastes that break down slowly float to the top of the tank and build up there. Scum must be pumped out regularly.

Inlet Pipe From House
Sewage enters the system through the inlet pipe. Bacteria begin to break down most of the wastes.

Sludge
Denser wastes that break down slowly sink to the bottom of the tank. Sludge must be pumped out.

Outlet Pipe to Leach Field
Water and wastes that have broken down filter into the leach field through the outlet pipe.

Section 2 Assessment

 **Target Reading Skill** **Sequencing** Refer to your flowchart about drinking-water treatment as you answer Question 2 below.

Reviewing Key Concepts

1. a. Listing Name the factors that affect water quality.
   b. Comparing and Contrasting How does hard water differ from soft water?
   c. Inferring Dissolved lead has been found in your drinking supply. What can you infer about the acidity of your water? Explain.
2. a. Reviewing Explain why drinking water is treated.
   b. Sequencing Create a flowchart showing how drinking water is delivered to homes and businesses in a community that has a central pumping station.

3. a. Defining What is sewage?
   b. Sequencing List in order the steps involved in the treatment of sewage in a septic system.
   c. Applying Concepts Why it is important to know the depth and location of drinking-water wells before deciding where to build a septic system?

Math Practice

4. Calculating a Concentration Review the EPA selected water-quality standards in Figure 5. Note that the concentrations of the first five substances are limited to certain amounts, given in parts per million (ppm). Write the concentration of each substance as a fraction.

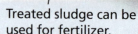

Treated sludge can be used for fertilizer.

Treating Wastewater

In the morning, you roll out of bed and head for the bathroom. You take a shower, flush the toilet, brush your teeth. What happens to the water that goes down the drain? You might be surprised to learn that someday, this water might be part of your drinking supply. Don't panic—the wastewater goes through many changes to make this possible.

Wastewater Treatment Plant
Wastewater treatment at a plant includes several steps that remove unwanted substances from water. Water flows through the plant, becoming cleaner after each stage.

1 Preliminary Treatment
First, wastewater flows through screens to catch large particles such as food and bits of trash.

2 Primary Treatment
The flow of the water slows as it enters settling tanks. Gravity causes particles to settle to the bottom of the tanks, forming sludge.

3 Secondary Treatment
Next, the wastewater is filtered through a bed of gravel. The gravel is covered with colonies of bacteria. These bacteria break down the wastes left in the sewage.

Public Treatment Systems

Most communities rely on public treatment systems to clean their wastewater. Different communities often use slightly different processes. A typical wastewater treatment process, like the one shown here, involves several steps. Once treatment is complete, the water is returned to the environment. The clean water may be released back into lakes, rivers, or oceans, or pumped back into the ground. There the water rejoins the water cycle.

How Clean Is Clean?

Until recently, wastewater was often dumped into open gutters and allowed to run directly into rivers and oceans. This practice spread disease. Cleaning wastewater before it is returned to the environment is healthier for everyone. However, treating wastewater does have some tradeoffs. By law, costly chemical tests are performed regularly to verify the water's cleanliness. Updating old systems or increasing system capacities for growing populations is expensive also. Small amounts of unwanted substances may remain in the water after treatment. The long-term effects of these substances are not known.

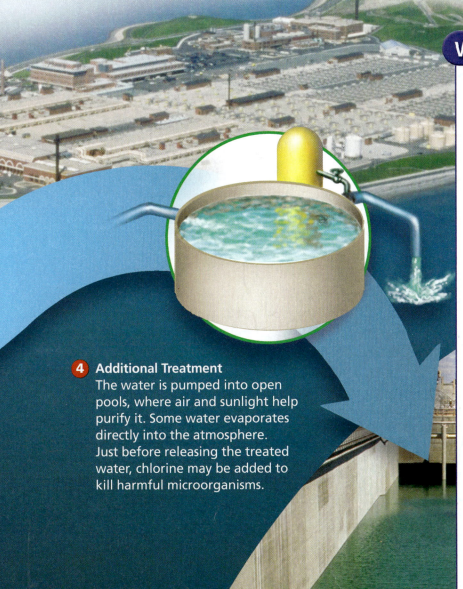

4 **Additional Treatment**
The water is pumped into open pools, where air and sunlight help purify it. Some water evaporates directly into the atmosphere. Just before releasing the treated water, chlorine may be added to kill harmful microorganisms.

Weigh the Impact

1. Identify the Need
Why is wastewater treated?

2. Research
Use the Internet to research wastewater treatment. What new technologies are being developed? Choose one of these technologies and make a list of its advantages and disadvantages.

3. Write
Your community is considering upgrading its wastewater treatment plant. Some residents believe the plan can reduce water pollution. Others are concerned about the cost. State your views in a letter to the newspaper. Back up your opinions with facts from your research.

For: More on wastewater treatment
Visit: PHSchool.com
Web Code: cfh-3020

Testing Water

Problem

How do distilled water, spring water, and mineral water differ from tap water?

Skills Focus

observing, inferring, drawing conclusions

Materials

- hot plate
- liquid soap
- ruler
- wax pencil
- tap water, 200 mL
- distilled water, 200 mL
- spring water, 200 mL
- mineral water, 200 mL
- 4 250-mL beakers
- 4 test tubes and stoppers
- 4 pieces of pH paper
- test tube rack
- 25-mL graduated cylinder
- pH indicator chart
- 4 paper cups per person

Procedure

1. Copy the data table into your notebook.

2. Label the beakers A, B, C, and D. Pour 100 mL of tap water into beaker A. Pour 100 mL of the other water samples into the correct beaker (refer to the data table).

3. Heat each water sample on a hot plate until about 20 mL remains. Do not allow the water to boil completely away. **CAUTION:** *Do not touch the hot plate or beakers with your bare hands.*

4. After the water samples have cooled, look for solids that make the water cloudy. Rank the samples from 1 to 4, where 1 has the fewest visible solids and 4 has the most visible solids. Record your rankings in the data table.

5. Label the test tubes A, B, C, and D. Pour 10 mL of each water sample from the source bottle into the correct test tube.

6. Dip a piece of pH paper into test tube A to measure its acidity. Match the color of the pH paper to a number on the pH indicator chart. Record the pH (0–14) in your data table.

7. Repeat Step 6 for the other samples.

8. Add two drops of liquid soap to test tube A. Put a stopper in the test tube and shake it 30 times. With the ruler, measure the height of the soapsuds in the test tube. Record the measurement in your data table.

9. Repeat Step 8 for the other samples.

10. Label the four cups A, B, C, and D. Write your name on each cup.

11. Pour a little tap water into cup A directly from the original source bottle. Taste the tap water. In your data table, describe the taste using one or more of these words: *salty, flat, bitter, metallic, refreshing, tasteless.* **CAUTION:** *Do not conduct the taste test in a lab room. Use a clean cup for each sample and discard it after use.*

12. Repeat Step 11 with the other samples.

Data Table				
Water Sample	Visible Solids (1–4)	pH (0–14)	Soapsud Height (cm)	Taste
A – Tap Water				
B – Distilled Water				
C – Spring Water				
D – Mineral Water				

Analyze and Conclude

1. **Observing** Review your data table. Compare each of the bottled water samples to the tap water sample. What similarities and differences did you detect?

2. **Inferring** Rank the samples from the one with the fewest soapsuds to the one with the most. Compare this ranking to the one for visible solids. What pattern do you see? What do both of these tests have to do with the hardness of water?

3. **Posing Questions** What other information about the water samples might you need before deciding which one to drink regularly? Explain.

4. **Drawing Conclusions** Based on your results, which sample would you most want to use for (a) drinking, (b) boiling in a teakettle, and (c) washing laundry? Which sample would you least want to use for each purpose? Explain.

5. **Communicating** Create a brochure to educate consumers about water quality. Include information about acidity, hardness, and other factors that can affect the appearance, taste, and safety of drinking water.

More to Explore

Conduct a survey to find out what percentage of people buy bottled mineral water, distilled water, and spring water. Why do they buy each type of water, and how do they use it in their homes?

Freshwater Pollution

Reading Preview

Key Concepts
- What is one way that sources of pollution are classified?
- What are three sources of water pollution?
- What are the two parts of the solution to water pollution?

Key Terms
- water pollution
- pollutant
- point source
- nonpoint source
- pesticide
- acid rain

Target Reading Skill

Outlining As you read, make an outline about freshwater pollution that you can use for review. Use the red headings for the main ideas and the blue headings for the supporting ideas.

Freshwater Pollution
I. What is pollution?
A. Point and nonpoint sources
B.
II. Human wastes
A.

Lab zone Discover **Activity**

Will the Pollution Reach Your Wells?

1. With a permanent marker, draw three rings on a coffee filter as shown in the photo. Draw three dots and label them A, B, and C. These dots represent the locations of wells that supply drinking water.
2. Place the coffee filter on a paper plate. Moisten the coffee filter with a wet sponge. The damp coffee filter represents an aquifer.
3. Squirt five drops of food coloring onto the center of the damp coffee filter. Observe how the "pollution" travels.

Think It Over

Observing Which wells were affected by the pollution? Describe the pattern the pollution forms.

Only 50 years ago, the French Broad River in North Carolina was a river to avoid. Its color changed daily, depending on the dyes used at a nearby blanket factory. Towns dumped raw sewage into the water. Sediment and fertilizers from farms washed into the river with every rainfall. The few fish that lived in the river were unhealthy and covered with sores. Mostly, the river was home to wastes and bacteria—certainly not a place for people to play. Today, however, the river is a popular white-water rafting spot. Fish thrive in the clear water. Factories have stopped releasing wastes into the river. The towns have sewage treatment plants. And ponds catch the runoff from farm fields before it reaches the river.

FIGURE 9
The French Broad River
Canoers can once again safely enjoy the French Broad River in North Carolina.

Freshwater Pollutants		
Kind of Pollutant	**Examples**	**Sources**
Disease-causing organisms	*Giardia*, *Cryptosporidium*, bacteria	Human wastes, runoff from livestock pens
Pesticides and fertilizers	DDT, nitrates, phosphates	Runoff from farm fields, golf courses
Industrial chemicals	PCBs, carbon tetrachloride, dioxin	Factories, industrial waste disposal sites
Metals	Lead, mercury, copper	Factories, waste disposal sites
Radioactive wastes	Uranium, carbon-14	Medical and scientific disposal sites, nuclear power plants
Petroleum products	Oil, gasoline	Road runoff, leaking underground storage tanks

FIGURE 10
This table lists examples of different types of freshwater pollutants.
Relating Cause and Effect *Why might it be helpful to know the source of a particular pollutant detected in a body of water?*

What Is Pollution?

People near the French Broad River still carry out the same activities—farming, building houses, and making blankets. But by changing how they do these things, they have reduced water pollution in the river. **Water pollution** is the addition of any substance that has a negative effect on water or the living things that depend on the water. The substances that cause water pollution are called **pollutants**. Figure 10 shows different types of pollutants.

Point and Nonpoint Sources Sources of pollution are classified, in part, by how they enter a body of water. For example, suppose you notice a pipe gushing brightly colored water into a river. The pipe is a **point source,** a specific source of pollution that can be identified. More often, though, the source of pollution is less obvious. Pollutants may be carried along in runoff from a farm field, a street, or a construction site. The pollutants eventually flow into a lake or river or seep into groundwater and may be carried far away. It's hard to trace the exact source of this pollution. A widely spread source of pollution that can't be tied to a specific point of origin is called a **nonpoint source.**

FIGURE 11
Point Source Pollution
The pipe gushing polluted water into a river is an example of a point source of pollution.

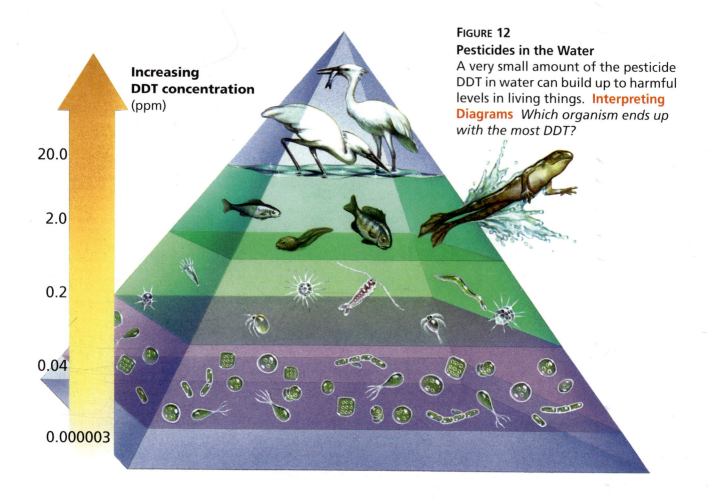

Increasing
DDT concentration
(ppm)

20.0

2.0

0.2

0.04

0.000003

FIGURE 12
Pesticides in the Water
A very small amount of the pesticide DDT in water can build up to harmful levels in living things. **Interpreting Diagrams** *Which organism ends up with the most DDT?*

Effects of Pollutants Some pollutants, such as pesticides, can build up in the bodies of living things. **Pesticides** are chemicals intended to kill insects and other organisms that damage crops. Trace the path of one such pesticide, DDT, in Figure 12. DDT dissolves in water and is absorbed by microscopic algae. The algae, which contain only low levels of DDT, are eaten by small water animals. When frogs or fish eat these smaller animals, they also consume the chemicals from the algae these animals have eaten. The frogs and fish are in turn eaten by birds or other animals. Each larger organism consumes a greater number of the smaller organisms, and therefore more of the DDT.

When humans regularly eat contaminated fish, the toxic chemicals also build up in their bodies. Over a long time, certain pollutants can build up to levels that can cause birth defects or illnesses such as cancer. Contaminated fish and impure drinking water are not the only means by which water pollutants can affect human health. Bathing or swimming in polluted water can irritate the skin or cause more serious problems.

Reading Checkpoint What is a pesticide?

Human Wastes

One way or another, human activities cause most water pollution. **The three major sources of water pollution are human wastes, industrial wastes, and chemical runoff.** Today it seems obvious that dumping human wastes into drinking water can spread disease. But scientists have understood this connection for only the last 150 years. For example, cholera is a disease caused by bacteria that live in human wastes. It can be fatal. In 1854, an English doctor named John Snow discovered the cause of a cholera outbreak in London. In the poorer sections of the city, people carried water home in buckets from public wells. After 500 people in one neighborhood died in just ten days, Dr. Snow traced the cholera to a well near a pipe carrying sewage. He ended the epidemic by removing the pump handle so no one could get water from that source. Dr. Snow's work showed the danger of releasing untreated sewage into bodies of water that might be used for drinking.

Sewage in Cities Today, wastewater is usually treated before being released to the environment. However, while water treatment kills most bacteria, some viruses and parasites are able to resist chlorine and other water-treatment processes. Most of these organisms come from human or animal wastes that get into the water supply.

During heavy rains and floods, sanitary sewers sometimes overflow and run into storm sewers. Because the storm sewers generally lead directly into surface water, the sewage from the sanitary sewers can pollute the water. For this reason, people are often told to boil water for drinking and cooking after a flood. The boiling kills many disease-causing organisms.

Sewage in Rural Areas Disposing of human waste is not just a problem in big cities. In rural areas, people must be careful where they locate septic tanks. If a tank is too near a stream or on a hill, wastewater can leak into the stream or flow downhill into the area of a well.

Wastes from cattle, pigs, and chickens can also be a problem in rural areas. Animal wastes can run off from pastures and barnyards and pass disease-causing bacteria and other kinds of pollution into bodies of water.

 **Reading Checkpoint** Why should drinking water and sewage be kept separate?

FIGURE 13
Cholera Epidemic
This engraving from the late 1800s shows people in Hamburg, Germany, getting water from a tank during a cholera epidemic. The city wells were closed, and water was brought in from the countryside.

Lab zone Skills Activity

Classifying
Classify the following as point sources or nonpoint sources of water pollution.

- a sanitary sewer pipe with a leak
- salt used on icy roads
- an open drain in a sink at a paint factory
- fertilizer sprayed onto an orchard

Explain why you classified each source as you did.

FIGURE 14
Industrial Pollutants
Water pollution caused by industrial wastes is a serious pollution problem.

Industrial Wastes

In many cities and towns in the United States, water pollution from factories and mines is a more serious problem than pollution from sewage. This is because most areas have wastewater treatment systems that handle sewage effectively. Chemicals, smoke, and heated water are three types of pollutants produced by factories, mines, and other industries.

Chemicals Many factory processes involve toxic chemicals and strong acids. Other toxic wastes are produced as a result of manufacturing and mining processes. Although laws control many point sources of chemical pollution, some factories still release toxic chemicals directly into nearby rivers and lakes.

Another problem is pollution caused by nonpoint sources. In the past, many industries stored toxic wastes in barrels or other containers buried underground. Over the years, however, many of these containers rusted or broke. The chemicals leaked out, polluting both the soil and the groundwater.

Smoke and Exhaust Many power plants and factories burn coal or oil to fuel their processes. The engines of millions of cars, trucks, and buses burn gasoline. Smoke and exhaust from these sources pour into the air, especially around large cities.

Chemical Waste — Point Source
Some factories release chemical

Chemical Waste — Nonpoint Source
Chemical wastes can leak out of storage containers and pollute

When coal, oil, and gasoline are burned, the gases sulfur dioxide and nitrogen oxide are released into the atmosphere. There the sulfur and nitrogen react with water, forming sulfuric and nitric acids. The result is **acid rain,** which is rain or another form of precipitation that is more acidic than normal. When acid rain falls on lakes and ponds, the water can become so acidic that fish and other wildlife cannot survive. Acid rain also harms trees and eats away the stone of buildings and statues.

Heat Pollution Think about how hot a metal playground slide gets on a sunny day. Imagine taking water from a swimming pool to cool the slide, and then returning the water to the pool. How would this change the temperature of the pool water? Would you still want to jump in to cool off?

Much of the water in factories is used to cool machinery or metal objects. Even if it contains no chemicals, the warm water alone can act as a pollutant. Many water organisms can live in only a narrow range of temperatures. Warm water released by a factory into a nearby river or pond raises the temperature of the water, sometimes enough to harm the living things there.

 **Reading Checkpoint** What are three types of industrial pollutants?

Smoke and Exhaust
Pollutants released from smokestacks can cause acid rain.

Heat Pollution
Heated water released by factories can

FIGURE 15
Runoff From Roads
Chemical runoff from roads can enter rivers and lakes or seep underground to pollute groundwater. **Inferring** *How might cars add to chemical runoff?*

Lab zone
Try This Activity

How Do Algae Grow?

1. Label two jars A and B. Pour tap water into each jar until it is half full.
2. Add water from a pond or aquarium to each jar until it is three-quarters full.

3. Add 5 mL of liquid fertilizer to jar A only.
4. Cover both jars tightly and place them on a windowsill in the sunlight. Wash your hands with soap.
5. Observe the jars every day for a week.

Drawing Conclusions How did the fertilizer affect the growth of the algae in jar A? What was the purpose of jar B in this experiment?

Chemical Runoff

Have you ever "fed" a houseplant with fertilizer to make it grow? On a larger scale, farmers spread or spray fertilizing chemicals on their fields to produce better crops. When rain falls on the fields, it washes some of the chemicals away as runoff. Water used for irrigation also creates runoff. The fertilizers in the runoff are a nonpoint source of pollution.

Runoff From Farms As you know, ponds and lakes naturally change over time during eutrophication. With the addition of fertilizers, this natural process speeds up. A thick, soupy scum of algae forms on top of the water. The scum blocks sunlight and chokes the flow of water, changing the living conditions for other organisms. The rich supply of nutrients from fertilizers encourages the growth of plants and algae in and around nearby bodies of water.

Runoff and irrigation water also carry away other pollutants from farm fields. Pesticides may be sprayed on crops and then carried by runoff into streams and ponds. Sometimes they are sprayed directly on ponds to kill mosquitoes. But these chemicals can also harm insects that are not pests, as well as insect-eating animals.

Runoff From Roads Have you ever noticed an oily sheen on a puddle in a parking lot after it rains? The sheen was probably caused by gasoline and motor oil that leaked from cars. When it rains, runoff carries these oily substances into rivers and lakes, or underground and into the groundwater. During winter, runoff also picks up salt that is spread on roads and sidewalks to melt ice. Gasoline, oil, and salt are nonpoint sources that pollute rivers and lakes. They can also seep underground and pollute wells and aquifers.

Reading Checkpoint How can pesticides pollute water?

Water Pollution Solutions

In the late 1960s, as people became more aware of the problems of pollution, they urged governments to create laws to clean up and reduce pollution. The goals of those laws include the cleanup of polluted lakes and rivers, better waste-water treatment, and limits on the amounts of pollutants released. Governments also monitor the health of bodies of water and enforce water-quality standards and the cleanup of waste disposal sites.

Despite some success cleaning up some water pollution, most pollutants are very difficult to remove. It is often easier to avoid causing the pollution in the first place than to clean it up. **Solving pollution problems involves cleaning up existing problems as well as preventing new ones.**

Cleanup Many pollutants are removed from fresh water through natural cleanup processes. Living things in lakes, streams, and wetlands help reduce pollution by filtering out and breaking down waste materials. For example, plant roots filter larger particles from the water. Some plants can absorb metals and chemicals. And just as certain bacteria are used in purifying wastewater, some are also useful in cleaning up toxic chemicals. Bacteria that consume oil have been used to help clean up oil spills. Waste-eating bacteria may also prove to be useful in breaking down toxic chemicals in rivers and lakes.

Pollution cleanup programs can be based on such natural treatment processes. For example, both natural and artificial wetlands can be used to clean up water pollution. Wetlands have been built near coal mines to treat acidic mining runoff before it returns to the environment.

FIGURE 16
Testing Water for Pollutants
Many lakes and rivers have been polluted by wastes from nearby industries. These environmental scientists are collecting water samples from a pond for testing.

FIGURE 17
Pollution Solutions

People can prevent or clean up pollution in many ways. **Interpreting Diagrams** *How can people prevent their septic systems from polluting the environment?*

Roads
Using sand instead of salt on roadways reduces the amount of pollution in the winter.

Factories
Factories cool water and reuse it instead of dumping hot water into a river.

Farms
Farmers collect runoff from pastures and barnyards to use for irrigation. They also plant coarse grasses to filter pollutants before they reach rivers and ponds.

Hazardous waste collection site

Runoff

Irrigated Fields

Homes
In rural areas, people place septic tanks away from freshwater sources and maintain their tanks to avoid leaking pollutants.

Cities
In the city, sewage treatment plants clean wastewater. Hazardous waste collection days discourage people from dumping pollutants such as motor oil down their drains.

Wetlands
Natural and artificial wetlands filter out pollutants from the runoff produced by mines.

Prevention Many industries have found that recycling techniques that conserve water also reduce pollution. For example, factories cool the water used to cool machinery and reuse it instead of releasing it into a river. This reduces heat pollution. Industries also look for ways to use fewer toxic materials. Printing inks, for instance, can be made with water instead of chemical solvents.

Farmers are trying to reduce the pollution problem caused by the runoff of animal wastes from pastures. Some collect and reuse this water for irrigation. Other farmers plant fields of grasses that filter out pollutants before the water reaches a river or pond. These and other techniques to reduce water pollution are shown in Figure 17.

You can also help keep pollutants from entering the environment. Dispose of toxic substances properly. For example, chemicals like paint and motor oil should never be poured down the drain, but instead should be taken to sites that collect hazardous waste. Remember, water pollution can be difficult to clean up. So the most important place to stop pollution is at its source.

 **Reading Checkpoint** What can governments do to clean up water pollution?

FIGURE 18
Preventing Water Pollution
One way you can help prevent water pollution is to educate others about its causes. This student has stenciled a storm drain to remind people of its connection to a nearby river.

Section 3 Assessment

Target Reading Skill Outlining Use the information in your outline about freshwater pollution to help you answer the questions below.

Reviewing Key Concepts

1. a. **Defining** What is a point source of pollution? What is a nonpoint source?
   b. **Comparing and Contrasting** Compare and contrast point and nonpoint sources of water pollution.
   c. **Classifying** A substance added to gasoline is found in the wells of people who live miles from a gas station. Is this an example of a point source of pollution or a nonpoint source? Explain.

2. a. **Listing** List three sources of water pollution.
   b. **Developing Hypotheses** The trees in a wooded area near a factory look like burnt toothpicks. What might be causing the problem?

c. **Making Judgments** To prevent water pollution, a factory proposes pumping its wastes into the ground instead of into a river. Would you support this change? Why or why not?

3. a. **Reviewing** What are two ways to solve a water pollution problem?
   b. **Making Generalizations** Which is easier: preventing pollution or cleaning up pollution? Give an example to support your answer.

Writing in Science

Product Label Write a "warning label" that can be pasted on a gasoline pump. In your label, include a paragraph describing how burning gasoline can cause acid rain. Be sure to explain the reaction that takes place when certain chemicals are released into the atmosphere and react with water. Also describe the effects of acid rain.

Droughts and Floods

Reading Preview

Key Concepts
- What is a drought?
- What is a flood, and how can the dangers of floods be reduced?

Key Terms
- drought
- flash flood
- levee

Target Reading Skill
Comparing and Contrasting As you read, compare and contrast droughts and floods by completing a table like the one below.

Droughts and Floods

Feature	Droughts	Floods
Cause	Scarce rainfall	
Possible to predict?		
Preparation		
Major effects		

How Does Dryness Affect Soil?
1. Spread a layer of soil about 3 centimeters thick in a rectangular pan.
2. Add water to the soil and stir so that it forms a thick mud.
3. Place the pan under a lamp for several hours. At the end of the day, check the soil.

Think It Over
Observing What does the soil look like? How does it feel? If the soil in your area looked similar to this soil sample, do you think it could support plants? Explain your answer.

Imagine trying to drink from a tall glass of milk through a straw no longer than a toothpick. When the level of the milk falls below the bottom of the straw, you can no longer reach the milk. In the same way, when the water table falls below the bottom of a well, the well runs dry. A water shortage may occur.

As you read in Chapter 1, water shortages can be triggered by human activities, such as overuse of an aquifer. However, natural processes also can cause areas to receive too little water—or, conversely, too much water. In this section, you'll learn what causes these conditions and how they impact people.

Droughts

A certain area might receive, on average, enough rainfall to meet its water needs. But if the area experiences a long period of scarce rainfall, a condition known as a **drought** (drowt) might occur. A drought reduces the supplies of groundwater and surface water. Without precipitation to recharge the aquifer, the amount of groundwater in the aquifer decreases. A decrease in the amount of water in the aquifer can result in a shortage of water for homes and businesses.

Causes and Effects of Droughts Droughts are weather-related events. **They are usually caused by dry weather systems that remain in one place for weeks or months at a time.**

Long-term droughts can devastate a region. Droughts can cause crop failure or even widespread famine. Streams and ponds dry up, and both people and animals suffer. During the drought that struck Florida in 1998, plants withered and died. The dry conditions set the stage for drought-related fires—more than 475,000 acres burned, causing an estimated $500 million in damage.

Predicting and Preparing for Droughts Droughts are difficult to predict. However, since the 1980s, federal and state governments have begun monitoring soil and water conditions, as well as precipitation levels. This information allows scientists to pinpoint areas that may, in the near future, experience droughts. As soon as the level of rainfall drops below normal, state agricultural officials may contact farmers to warn them of a possible drought.

Little can be done to actually control a drought. However, people can prepare for droughts in several ways. When dry conditions first occur, people can begin conserving water. Washing cars and watering lawns, for example, are two activities that can be curtailed. Farmers can grow drought-resistant plants that have been especially bred to withstand dry conditions. In general, practicing water conservation and soil conservation ensures that when droughts do occur, the effects will be as mild as possible.

 **What is a drought?**

Go Online
PLANET DIARY

For: More on droughts
Visit: PHSchool.com
Web Code: cfd-3024

FIGURE 19

A Drought

Europe experienced a severe drought in the summer of 2003, causing the Rhine River to dry up. The smaller photo shows Düsseldorf, Germany, during a normal summer.

FIGURE 20

Floods

Severe flooding can leave many homes and farms under water. **Inferring** *What characteristic of the land along this river allowed floodwaters to spread out over a large area?*

Floods

The floods caused by Hurricane Katrina in 2005 were devastating. The huge, powerful hurricane hit the United States coast of the Gulf of Mexico in late August. Katrina brought 20-foot waves from the gulf and more than 10 inches of rain to the hardest hit areas, which were in Louisiana and Mississippi. Lakes overflowed and rivers flooded. Two weeks after the hurricane, parts of New Orleans were still under 10 feet of water and mud. More than 100,000 homes and businesses were destroyed, along with many bridges and highways. More than 1,000 people died.

Causes and Effects of Floods Not all floods are as devastating as those caused by Hurricane Katrina. Some cause relatively little damage. **Small or large, however, all floods occur when the volume of water in a river increases so much that the river overflows its channel.** As rain and melting snow add more and more water, a river gains in speed and strength. When the speed of a river increases, the amount of energy it has increases, too. A flooding river can uproot trees and pluck boulders from the ground. As it overflows its banks, the powerful water can even wash away bridges and buildings.

 **Reading Checkpoint** What happens to a river's speed and strength during a flood?

Flash Floods Floods are the most dangerous weather-related events in the United States. Unexpected floods, called flash floods, are the most dangerous of all because the water rises very rapidly—"in a flash"—and people have little time to reach safe ground. A **flash flood** is a sudden, violent flood that occurs within a few hours, or even minutes, of a storm. Figure 21 shows one way in which a flash flood can occur.

Most flash floods are due to large amounts of rain. For example, a line of thunderstorms may remain over an area, dropping heavy rain for several hours or days. Hurricanes or tropical storms bring downpours that quickly fill stream channels. A flash flood can also be caused by a dam breaking, releasing millions of liters of water all at once. Similarly, if ice that has jammed a river breaks free, the sudden rush of water can cause a flash flood.

Some of the most dangerous flash floods occur in the deserts of the southwestern United States. For example, in 1997, a serious flash flood struck Antelope Canyon in the northern Arizona desert. On August 12, a group of 12 hikers entered the dry, narrow canyon. That afternoon, a severe thunderstorm dropped several inches of rain on the Kaibeto Plateau, 24 kilometers away. Dry stream channels that drain into Antelope Canyon quickly filled with rainwater. The water rushed into the canyon, creating a wall of water over 3 meters high. Only one hiker survived.

FIGURE 21
Flash Floods
Flash floods (left) occur when large amounts of rain are funneled into a narrow valley. This process flooded Antelope Canyon in Arizona (right) in 1997.

Heavy rain falls on the plateau.

Instead of soaking into the hard soil, the water runs into the canyon.

The rainwater is funneled into the narrow canyon and floods it.

Flood Precautions

Despite efforts to control flooding, floods have killed millions of people around the world in the last century. In the United States alone, 20 million people live in places where flooding is likely. What can people do to protect themselves and their homes?

Predicting Floods Using different types of technology, scientists can often issue flood warnings. **Advance warnings help reduce flood damage and loss of life.** Weather satellites supply information about snow cover so that scientists can estimate how much water will run into rivers when the snow melts. Radar can track and measure the size of an approaching rainstorm. Scientists check river gauges that measure water levels. With this information, forecasters can predict flood heights at different points along a river. Their goal is to issue warnings in time for people to prepare and evacuate if necessary.

Controlling Floods For as long as people have lived near rivers, they have tried to control floods. **Building dams is one method of flood control.** A dam is a barrier across a river that may redirect the flow of a river to other channels. It can also be used to store water in an artificial lake. Engineers can open the dam's floodgates to release water in dry seasons. Dams work fairly well to control small floods. During severe floods, however, powerful flood waters can wash over the top of a dam or break through it.

FIGURE 22
Trying to Control a Flood
These people are working together to protect their community during a flood.

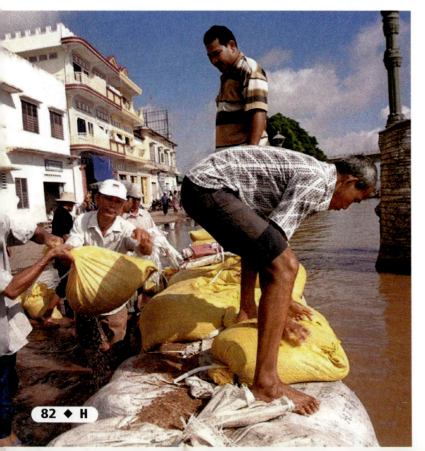

There is also a natural defense against floods—sediments. Sediments are particles of rock and soil that are picked up and carried along by forces such as flowing water. As a river overflows, it slows down, depositing its heavier sediments alongside the river channel.

Over time, these deposits build up into long ridges called **levees.** Levees that form naturally help keep the river inside its banks. People sometimes strengthen natural levees with sandbags or stone and concrete to provide further protection against floods.

 **Reading Checkpoint** How do sediments help protect against a flood?

1 The car stalls. Moving water pushes against the car.

2 As the water rises, the car begins to float.

3 Sixty centimeters of water can wash a car away.

Flood Safety What should you do in the event of a flood? When the danger becomes too great or the water rises too high, people are usually evacuated. The first rule of flood safety is: Move to higher ground and stay away from flood waters. If your family is in a car, the driver shouldn't try to drive on a flooded road. Sometimes less than 60 centimeters of fast-moving water can sweep a car away.

High water is not the only hazard in a flood. Floods can knock down electrical poles and wires. Downed electrical poles can leave dangerous live wires hanging loose and cause power outages. Flood waters can also saturate soil, causing landslides or mudslides. If roads have been flooded or washed away, emergency vehicles such as fire trucks and ambulances may not be able to get through.

Flood waters can wash into wells and water treatment plants, polluting the water. Therefore, be careful with food and water that flood waters have touched. Boil drinking water after a flood if you are instructed to do so.

FIGURE 23
Dangers of a Flood
Flood waters can wash away cars. It is extremely dangerous to remain in a car during a flood.
Applying Concepts *Why is it dangerous to stay in a car that is caught in a flood?*

Section **4** Assessment

Target Reading Skill Comparing and Contrasting Use your table to quiz a partner about droughts and floods.

Reviewing Key Concepts

1. a. Reviewing What causes droughts?
  b. Summarizing What are some effects of droughts?
  c. Problem Solving What are two ways to reduce the effects of droughts?
2. a. Describing When do floods occur?
  b. Explaining What are two ways to help reduce the dangers of floods?
  c. Making Judgments Your community is considering building a dam and on a nearby river to reduce flooding. Would you support this proposal? Explain.

Writing in Science

Radio Announcement Write a script for a 30-second public service radio announcement in which you tell about the dangers of floods. Include safety steps to follow in case of a flood.

Water Power

Reading Preview

Key Concepts
- How can the energy of moving water be used to produce electricity?
- What are some advantages and disadvantages of hydroelectric power plants?

Key Terms
- kinetic energy
- potential energy
- hydroelectric power

Target Reading Skill

Asking Questions Before you read, preview the red headings. In a graphic organizer like the one below, ask a *how* or *what* question for each heading. As you read, write the answers to your questions.

Water Power

Question	Answer
How are energy and moving water related?	Hydroelectric power . . .

A raging river that overflows its banks can wash away homes and uproot trees. The river has power. Imagine if we could harness this power as an energy resource. Guess what? We can. Since ancient times, people have used the energy of moving water to grind corn and transport goods. Today, that energy is also used to produce electricity. One of the world's largest dams, the Itaipu, produces more electricity than 13 nuclear power plants. Straddling the border between Brazil and Paraguay, the dam took 18 years to build and contains enough iron and steel to make 380 Eiffel Towers! More than 75 percent of Paraguay's electrical needs are supplied by the dam. Paraguay is just one of many countries that rely on the energy of moving water as a source of electrical power.

▼ Itaipu Dam

FIGURE 24
A Water Wheel
The potential energy of water is changed to kinetic energy when it hits a water wheel.

Energy and Moving Water

Have you ever seen a fast-moving river propel a kayaker along? If so, you know how much energy moving water can have. It can move boats, carve out canyons, and sweep away cars in a flood.

Kinetic and Potential Energy The energy that sends the kayak through the rapids is kinetic energy. **Kinetic energy** is the form of energy that an object has when it is moving.

Energy can change from one form to another. If the water's movement is stopped, all of its energy becomes potential energy. **Potential energy** is energy that is stored and waiting to be used. To understand how energy changes form, imagine that you're holding a baseball bat at the top of your swing. The bat at that point has potential energy. As you swing at a ball, the bat's energy becomes kinetic energy. If you hit the ball, the energy is transferred again, becoming the kinetic energy of the ball.

Energy From Moving Water Electricity produced by the kinetic energy of water moving over a waterfall or through a dam is called **hydroelectric power.** To generate hydroelectric power (or "hydropower"), engineers build a dam across a river. Water backs up behind the dam, floods the valley, and creates a reservoir. The water stored behind the dam has potential energy, which is changed to kinetic energy when the water is released. **Hydroelectric power plants capture the kinetic energy of moving water and change it into electrical energy.**

 **Reading Checkpoint** What is potential energy?

Chapter 2 H ◆ 85

FIGURE 25
Hydroelectric Power

Hydroelectric power is generated by changing energy from one form to another. **Interpreting Diagrams** *At what point in the process is the kinetic energy of moving water converted to mechanical energy?*

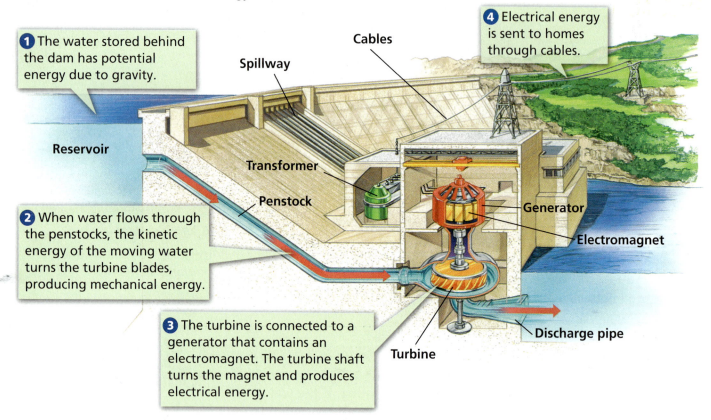

1 The water stored behind the dam has potential energy due to gravity.

2 When water flows through the penstocks, the kinetic energy of the moving water turns the turbine blades, producing mechanical energy.

3 The turbine is connected to a generator that contains an electromagnet. The turbine shaft turns the magnet and produces electrical energy.

4 Electrical energy is sent to homes through cables.

Cables

Spillway

Reservoir

Transformer

Penstock

Generator

Electromagnet

Turbine

Discharge pipe

Go **O**nline
active art

For: Hydroelectric Power activity
Visit: PHSchool.com
Web Code: cfp-3025

Hydroelectric Power Plants

Figure 25 shows a hydroelectric power plant. In this diagram, you can see how the kinetic energy of moving water is changed into the electrical energy that lights homes and runs computers.

Advantages In some ways, hydroelectric power seems like an ideal way to produce electricity. **Hydroelectric power is clean, safe, and efficient. Building a dam is expensive, but the water is free and is naturally renewed by the water cycle.** Unlike power plants that burn coal or oil, hydroelectric plants do not contribute to air pollution.

In the United States, hydroelectric power accounts for about 9 percent of the electricity produced, while worldwide it generates about 20 percent. Some countries, such as Norway and Brazil, produce almost all of their electrical energy through hydropower.

Disadvantages Hydroelectric plants do have limitations, however. Only certain locations are suitable for building a dam. A fast-moving river is necessary, as is an area that can be flooded to create a reservoir.

Dams affect all living things in the area around them. What was once a fast-moving river becomes the still, deep waters of a reservoir. Some organisms cannot survive the change. **Flooding the land behind a dam can destroy wildlife habitats as well as farms and towns. In addition, the dam forms a barrier across the river.** It may prevent fish from traveling to the parts of the river where they usually lay their eggs and hatch their young.

In some places, people have suggested building small dams to supply power to a local area. Smaller dams uproot fewer people and do less harm to the environment, while still providing energy for a region. However, since dams are expensive to build, small dams may not produce enough power to be worthwhile. Large dams, on the other hand, produce great amounts of power, but they also have a major effect on the land around them.

FIGURE 26
The Three Gorges Dam
The Three Gorges Dam in China has displaced more than 500,000 people. Eventually, it may displace more than 1 million. Also, historical artifacts such as the one shown here have had to be relocated.

 **Reading Checkpoint** **What is the main disadvantage of small dams?**

Section 5 Assessment

Target Reading Skill **Asking Questions** Use your graphic organizer about the section headings to help you answer the questions below.

Reviewing Key Concepts

1. a. **Reviewing** What type of energy does moving water have?
   b. **Comparing and Contrasting** Compare and contrast the energy of moving water and the energy of water that is stored.
   c. **Sequencing** Make a flowchart that shows how the energy of moving water is used to produce electricity.
2. a. **Defining** What is a hydroelectric power plant?
   b. **Listing** Give two advantages and two disadvantages of hydroelectric power.
   c. **Problem Solving** Suppose you were hired to build a dam. What features would you look for in a site? Be sure to consider the impact on living things as well as the physical characteristics of the site.

Lab zone **At-Home Activity**

Modeling a Dam With the help of a family member, construct a model dam in your bathtub. Use a sturdy piece of plastic foam as wide as the tub and about 12 cm high. Cut a 3-cm square in the center of the foam, then cover the hole with tape. Place the plastic foam upright in the tub. If necessary, trim the foam so that it fits snugly against the side of the tub. Turn the water on to create a reservoir. Then carefully peel the tape off the hole and observe what happens to the water. What energy change took place?

① Water Supply and Demand

Key Concepts

- People use water for household purposes, industry, transportation, agriculture, and recreation.
- Reducing water use, recycling water, and reusing water are three ways to conserve water.
- Two possible methods of obtaining fresh water are desalination and melting icebergs.

Key Terms

irrigation   conservation   desalination

② Water to Drink

Key Concepts

- Certain substances can affect the taste or color of water but are usually harmless. Other substances, such as certain chemicals and microorganisms, can be harmful to your health.
- Water often needs some treatment to ensure that it is clean and safe to drink.
- Two ways that communities deal with sewage are wastewater treatment plants and septic systems.

Key Terms

water quality   filtration
concentration   coagulation
pH   sewage
hardness

③ Freshwater Pollution

Key Concepts

- Sources of pollution are classified, in part, by how they enter a body of water.
- The three major sources of water pollution are human wastes, industrial wastes, and chemical runoff.
- Solving pollution problems involves cleaning up existing problems and preventing new ones.

Key Terms

water pollution   nonpoint source
pollutant   pesticide
point source   acid rain

④ Droughts and Floods

Key Concepts

- Droughts are usually caused by weather systems that remain in one place for weeks or months at a time.
- Floods occur when the volume of water in a river increases so much that the river overflows its channel.
- Advance warnings help reduce flood damage and loss of life. Building dams is one method of flood control.

Key Terms

drought   levee
flash flood

⑤ Water Power

Key Concepts

- Hydroelectric power plants capture the kinetic energy of moving water and change it into electrical energy.
- Hydroelectric power is clean, safe, and efficient. Building a dam is expensive, but the water is free and is naturally renewed by the water cycle.
- Flooding the land behind a dam can destroy wildlife habitats as well as farms and towns. In addition, the dam is a barrier across the river.

Key Terms

kinetic energy
potential energy
hydroelectric power

Review and Assessment

Go Online
PHSchool.com

For: Self-Assessment
Visit: PHSchool.com
Web Code: cfa-3020

Organizing Information

Concept Mapping Copy the concept map about freshwater pollution onto a separate sheet of paper. Then complete it and add a title. (For more on Concept Mapping, see the Skills Handbook.)

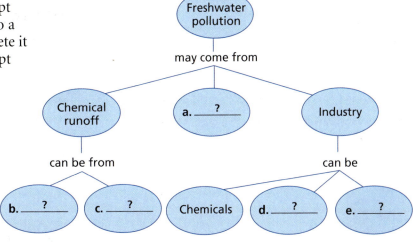

Reviewing Key Terms

Choose the letter of the best answer.

1. One process used to obtain fresh water from salt water is
   a. coagulation.
   b. filtration.
   c. recharge.
   d. desalination.

2. Chlorine is added during water treatment in order to
   a. make particles form flocs.
   b. kill disease-causing organisms.
   c. improve the taste of the water.
   d. remove objects such as fish and trash.

3. Acid rain results from
   a. burning of coal, oil, and gasoline.
   b. pesticides sprayed in the air.
   c. runoff from farm fields.
   d. toxic chemicals buried underground.

4. A prolonged period of scarce rainfall is a(n)
   a. levee.
   b. reservoir.
   c. drought.
   d. aquifer.

5. Water flowing swiftly possesses
   a. mechanical energy.
   b. electrical energy.
   c. potential energy.
   d. kinetic energy.

If the statement is true, write *true*. If it is false, change the underlined word or words to make the statement true.

6. <u>Conservation</u> is the practice of using less of a resource so that it will not be used up.

7. The <u>pH</u> of water is a measurement of the amount of calcium and magnesium it contains.

8. People sometimes strengthen natural <u>levees</u> with sandbags to protect against floods.

Writing in Science

Cause and Effect Description Suppose that you were a news reporter assigned to write about a new hydroelectric power plant. Explain how the water will be harnessed to generate electricity.

DISCOVERY CHANNEL SCHOOL™

Freshwater Resources
Video Preview
Video Field Trip
▶ Video Assessment

Review and Assessment

Checking Concepts

9. Why are water rights an important issue in dry areas?

10. Describe one way that farmers can reduce the amount of water lost during irrigation.

11. Why isn't most of the water on Earth's surface available for people to use?

12. Describe one possible path of drinking water from its source to a home.

13. How does acid rain form?

14. How might building a dam affect people living nearby?

Thinking Critically

15. **Comparing and Contrasting** How is the process of distillation similar to the water cycle? How is it different?

16. **Relating Cause and Effect** Why does the concentration of pollutants build up as shown in the diagram?

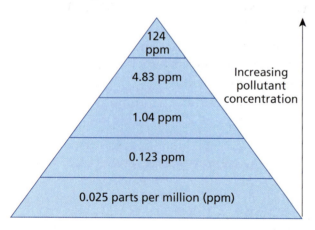

Increasing pollutant concentration

124 ppm

4.83 ppm

1.04 ppm

0.123 ppm

0.025 parts per million (ppm)

17. **Applying Concepts** What type of energy does a diver have while standing at the edge of a diving board?

18. **Making Judgments** Do you think that the benefits of hydroelectric power outweigh the disadvantages? Give reasons to support your answer.

Math Practice

19. **Calculating a Concentration** Look at the concentrations of lead and copper shown in the data table on this page. Write the concentrations in fraction form.

Applying Skills

Use the data in the table to answer Questions 20–22.

A family tested their drinking-water well to check the water quality. The test results are shown in the table below.

Drinking Water Sample Test Results

Lead	0.2 parts per million
Copper	0.006 parts per million
pH	5.0
Coliform count	5 out of 5 samples positive

20. **Inferring** The family suspects that their septic tank is polluting the well. What evidence exists to support this conclusion?

21. **Designing Experiments** What might be the source of the lead in the water? How could you test your answer?

22. **Developing Hypotheses** How might the low pH of the water be related to the lead contamination?

Lab zone — Chapter **Project**

Performance Assessment It's time to put your treatment system to the test! Use your system to clean up the dirty water sample. Measure the volume of water recovered by your system. Share your results with your classmates. How do your results compare with theirs?

Standardized Test Prep

Choose the letter of the best answer.

1. In which step of the drinking-water treatment process are disease-causing microorganisms killed?
   A chlorination
   B filtration
   C coagulation
   D desalination

2. Which of the following is an example of a point source of water pollution?
   F runoff of pesticides from wheat fields
   G salt spread on roads and parking lots to melt ice
   H chemicals flowing from a factory into a stream
   J fertilizer from corn fields that runs off into streams

3. Two students are measuring the volume of water they use while brushing their teeth. Which of the following pieces of equipment should they use for their measurement?
   A a metric ruler   **B** a balance
   C a graduated cylinder   **D** a test tube

Use the data table below and your knowledge of science to answer Questions 4–5.

Hydroelectric Power in the United States	
Region	**Annual Power Generation (megawatt-hours)**
Great Lakes	24,987,042
Upper Mississippi	3,543,100
Lower Mississippi	1,192,680
Rio Grande	441,821
Pacific Northwest	146,085,711
Lower Colorado	6,916,259
Upper Colorado	6,339,303

4. According to the data table, which region produces the most hydroelectric power?
   F Upper Colorado   **G** Great Lakes
   H Pacific Northwest   **J** Rio Grande

5. The Rio Grande region produces the least hydroelectric power. Why might this be?
   A Dams cannot be built on the rivers in the region.
   B It is a dry area, and most of the water in the rivers is used for other purposes.
   C There is no need for hydroelectric power in the region.
   D all of the above

Constructed Response

6. You are on a committee that is planning whether or not to build a dam on a nearby river to produce hydroelectric power. Describe some of the advantages and disadvantages you should consider before deciding to build the dam.

Chapter Preview

Powerful waves have created odd-looking ▶
landforms at Cape Kiwanda in Oregon.

Lab zone™ Chapter **Project**

Design and Build an Erosion-Proof Beach

Waves, tides, and currents move Earth's waters in different ways. These movements change the land. In this project, you will build a model of a shoreline with a lighthouse and use the model to demonstrate how some ocean motions can affect the land along the coast.

Your Goal To design and build a model ocean beach and test methods for preventing shoreline erosion

To complete this project, you must

- build a model beach and use it to demonstrate the effects of wave erosion
- test methods of protecting the lighthouse from damage
- follow the safety guidelines outlined in Appendix A

Plan It! Begin now by previewing the chapter. Find out how engineers protect structures from beach erosion. Begin to design your model ocean beach. Consider what materials you will use for your shoreline and lighthouse. Then develop a plan for protecting your lighthouse.

Wave Action

Reading Preview

Key Concepts
- How does a wave form?
- How do waves change near the shore?
- How do waves affect shorelines and beaches?

Key Terms
- wave • wavelength
- frequency • wave height
- tsunami • longshore drift
- rip current • groin

🔄 Target Reading Skill

Using Prior Knowledge Before you read, look at the section headings and visuals to see what this section is about. Then write what you know about waves in a graphic organizer like the one below. As you read, continue to write in what you learn.

What You Know
1. There are waves in the ocean.
2.

What You Learned
1.
2.

Lab zone Discover **Activity**

How Do Waves Change a Beach?

1. In one end of an aluminum pan, build a "beach" of sand and pebbles. Put a book under that end of the pan to raise it about 5 centimeters.
2. Pour water slowly into the other end of the pan until it covers the edge of the sand, just as water touches the edge of a beach.
3. Place a wooden tongue depressor in the water. Move it back and forth gently in a regular rhythm to make waves in the pan. Continue for about 2 minutes.
4. Once the water has stopped moving, observe what has happened to the beach. Wash your hands after completing this activity.

Think It Over

Observing How has the motion of the water changed the edge of the beach?

Hundreds of years ago, kings and queens ruled the islands of Hawaii. If you could travel back in time, you could watch the royal family engaging in the islands' favorite sport. It wasn't baseball or tennis or polo. Instead, the ancient rulers paddled into the ocean on heavy wooden boards to catch the perfect wave. They were "wave-sliding," a sport we know today as surfing.

If you've ever seen a surfer like the one in Figure 1, you know that they make this difficult sport look almost easy. But even experienced surfers can seldom predict when the next good wave will roll into shore. As you will read in this section, many different forces influence the size, shape, and timing of waves.

What Is a Wave?

When you watch a surfer's wave crash onto a beach, you are seeing the last step in the development of a wave. A **wave** is the movement of energy through a body of water. Wave development usually begins with wind. Without the energy of wind, the surface of the ocean would be as smooth as a mirror. **Most waves form when winds blowing across the water's surface transmit their energy to the water.**

Wave Size Waves start in the open ocean. The size of a wave depends on the strength of the wind and on the length of time it blows. A gentle breeze creates small ripples on the surface of the water. Stronger winds create larger waves.

The size of a wave also depends on the distance over which the wind blows. Winds blowing across longer distances build up bigger waves. Winds blowing across the Pacific Ocean can create bigger waves than winds blowing across the narrower Atlantic Ocean.

Wave Energy Although waves may appear to carry water toward shore, the water does not actually move forward in deep water. If it did, ocean water would eventually pile up on the coasts of every continent! The energy of the wave moves toward shore, but the water itself remains in place. You can test this by floating a cork in a bowl of water. Use a spoon to make a wave in the bowl. As the wave passes, the cork lurches forward a little; then it bobs backward. It ends up in almost the same spot where it started.

Figure 1
Wave Energy
A surfer cruises along a cresting wave. The wave's energy moves, but the water mostly stays in one place. **Applying Concepts** *In which direction is the energy of this wave moving?*

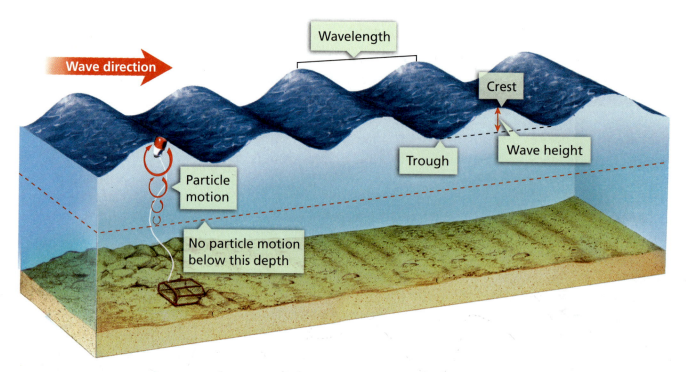

Wave direction

Wavelength

Crest

Particle motion

Trough

Wave height

No particle motion below this depth

FIGURE 2
Water Motion
As a wave passes, water particles move in a circular motion. The buoy on the surface swings down into the trough of one wave, then back up to the crest of the next. Below the surface, water particles move in smaller circles. At a depth equal to about one half the wavelength, water particles are not affected by the surface wave.

Go Online
active art

For: Water Motion activity
Visit: PHSchool.com
Web Code: cfp-3031

Water Motion Figure 2 shows what happens to the water as a wave travels along. As the wave passes, water particles move in a circular path. They swing forward and down with the energy of the wave, then back up to their original position.

Notice that the deeper water particles move in smaller circles than those near the surface. The wind affects the water at the surface more than it affects the deep water. Below a certain depth, the water does not move at all as the wave passes. If you were inside a submarine in deep water, you would not be able to tell whether the water above you was rough or calm.

Other Wave Characteristics Scientists have a vocabulary of terms to describe the characteristics of waves. The name for the highest part of a wave is the crest. The horizontal distance between crests is the **wavelength.** Long, rolling waves with lots of space between crests have long wavelengths. Short, choppy waves have shorter wavelengths. Waves are also measured by their **frequency,** the number of waves that pass a point in a certain amount of time.

The lowest part of a wave is the trough. The vertical distance from the crest to the trough is the **wave height.** The energy and strength of a wave depend mainly on its wave height. In the open ocean, most waves are between 2 and 5 meters high. During storms, waves can grow much higher and more powerful.

Reading Checkpoint Which have longer wavelengths—waves that are close together or waves that are far apart?

How Waves Change Near Shore

Have you ever seen an area of ocean water swell, resulting in a wave? Waves begin this way out in the ocean, but as they approach the shore, they change.

Breakers The white-capped waves that crash onto shore are often called "breakers." In deep water, these waves usually travel as long, low waves called swells. As the waves approach the shore, the water becomes shallower. Follow the waves in Figure 3 as they enter the shallow water. The bottoms of the waves begin to touch the sloping ocean floor. Friction between the ocean floor and the water causes the waves to slow down. As the speed of the waves decreases, their shapes change. **Near shore, wave height increases and wavelength decreases.** When the wave reaches a certain height, the crest of the wave topples. The wave breaks onto the shore, forming surf.

As the wave breaks, it continues to move forward. At first the breaker surges up the beach. But gravity soon slows it down, eventually stopping it. The water that had rushed up the beach then flows back out to sea. Have you ever stood at the water's edge and felt the pull of the water rushing back out to the ocean? This pull, often called an undertow, carries shells, seaweed, and sand away from the beach. A strong undertow can be dangerous to swimmers.

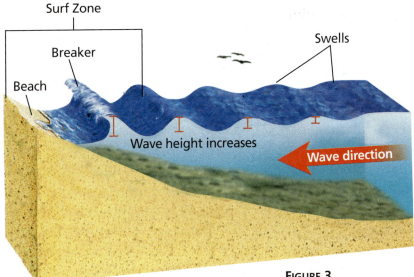

Surf Zone
Breaker
Beach
Swells
Wave height increases
Wave direction

FIGURE 3
How Breakers Change Near Shore
Friction with the ocean floor causes waves to slow down in the shallow water near shore. The wave height increases until the waves break, forming surf.
Comparing and Contrasting *How do swells and breakers differ?*

Lab zone Try This Activity

Wave Motion

This activity shows how waves that form at the surface affect deeper water.

1. Fill an aquarium about three-quarters full of water.
2. Tie enough metal washers to a cork so that the cork floats about 3 cm from the bottom of the tank.

3. Repeat Step 2 with more corks so that they float 9 cm from the bottom, 15 cm from the bottom, and so on, until the last cork floats on the surface.
4. Make small, steady waves in the tank by moving your hand up and down in the water. Note what happens to each cork.
5. Repeat Step 4, increasing the height of the waves by moving your hand faster.

Observing How does increasing the wave height affect the motion of each cork?

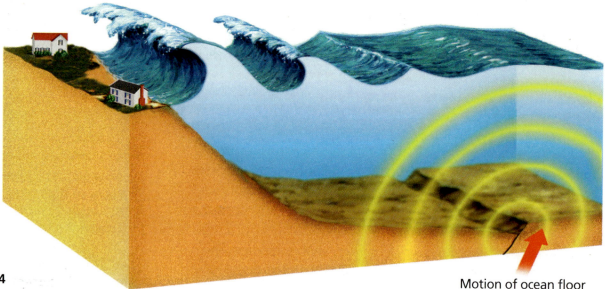

Motion of ocean floor

FIGURE 4
Tsunamis
At sea, a tsunami travels as a long, low wave. Near shore, the wave height increases suddenly. The wall of water smashes onto land, tossing ships onto the shore and destroying buildings.

Ocean Motions

Video Preview
▶ Video Field Trip
Video Assessment

Tsunamis So far you have been reading about waves that are caused by the wind. Another kind of wave, shown in Figure 4, forms far below the ocean surface. This type of wave, called a **tsunami,** is usually caused by an earthquake beneath the ocean floor. The abrupt movement of the ocean floor sends pulses of energy through the water above it. When tsunamis reach the coast, they can be as devastating as an earthquake on land, smashing buildings and bridges.

Despite the tremendous amount of energy a tsunami carries, people on a ship at sea may not even realize a tsunami is passing. How is this possible? A tsunami in deep water may have a wavelength of 200 kilometers or more, but a wave height of less than a meter. When the tsunami reaches shallow water near the coast, friction with the ocean floor causes the long wavelength to decrease suddenly. The wave height increases as the water "piles up." The tsunami becomes a towering wall of water. Some tsunamis have reached heights of 20 meters or more—taller than a five-story building!

Tsunamis are most common in the Pacific Ocean, often striking Alaska, Hawaii, and Japan. In response, nations in the Pacific have developed a warning system, which can alert them to an approaching tsunami.

But not all tsunamis occur in the Pacific Ocean. On December 26, 2004, a major earthquake in the Indian Ocean caused tremendous tsunamis that hit 11 nations. Tragically, these tsunamis took the lives of more than 230,000 people. Several nations are now developing a tsunami warning system for the Indian Ocean.

How Waves Affect the Shore

What happens on shore as waves pound the beach? Figure 5 shows some of their effects. Because wave direction at sea is determined by the wind, waves usually roll toward shore at an angle. But as they touch bottom, the shallower water slows the shoreward side of the wave first. The rows of waves gradually turn and become more nearly parallel to the shore.

Longshore Drift **As waves come into shore, water washes up the beach at an angle, carrying sand grains. The water and sand then run straight back down the beach.** This movement of sand along the beach is called **longshore drift.** As the waves slow down, they deposit the sand they are carrying on the shallow, underwater slope in a long ridge called a sandbar.

Rip Currents As a sandbar grows, it can trap the water flowing along the shore. In some places, water breaks through the sandbar and begins to flow back down the sloping ocean bottom. This process creates a **rip current,** a rush of water that flows rapidly back to sea through a narrow opening. Rip currents can carry a swimmer out into deep water. Because rip currents are narrow, a strong swimmer can usually escape by swimming across the current, parallel to the beach.

 **Reading Checkpoint** In what direction does a rip current pull a swimmer?

Making Models

Half fill an aluminum pan with water. The pan represents the ocean floor. Make the "ocean floor" slope by placing a book or other object under one long end of the pan. Add enough sand in the middle of the pan to create a sandbar. Then pour water from a beaker onto the sand to model a rip current. Use the model to explain why rip currents can be dangerous to swimmers.

FIGURE 5
Longshore Drift
Waves approach the shore at an angle. This results in a gradual movement of sand along the beach. **Interpreting Diagrams** *In which direction is longshore drift moving the sand along this beach?*

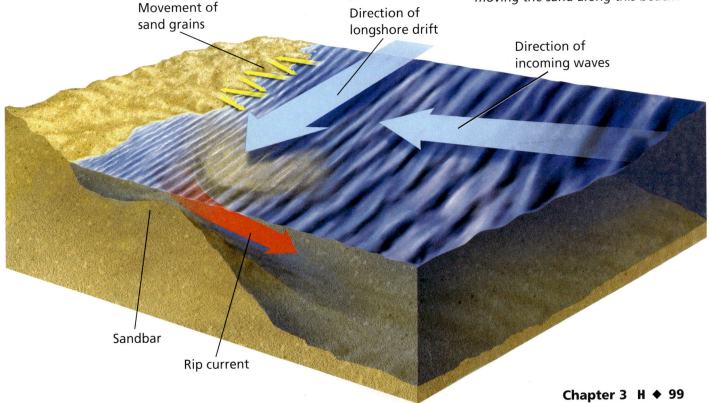

Movement of sand grains

Direction of longshore drift

Direction of incoming waves

Sandbar

Rip current

FIGURE 6
A Barrier Beach
Barrier beaches are sand deposits that form parallel to a shore. Sand dunes are hills of wind-blown sand that help protect the beach.
Interpreting Photographs *How does a barrier beach protect the mainland from erosion by waves?*

Waves and Beach Erosion

The boundary between land and ocean is always changing shape. If you walk on the same beach every day, you might not notice that it is changing. From day to day, waves remove sand and bring new sand at about the same rate. But if you visit a beach just once each year, you might be startled by what you see. **Waves shape a beach by eroding the shore in some places and building it up in others.**

At first, waves striking a rocky shoreline carve the rocks into tall cliffs and arches. Over many thousands of years, waves break the rocks into pebbles and grains of sand. A wide, sandy beach forms. Then the waves begin to eat away at the exposed beach. The shoreline slowly moves farther inland. Longshore drift carries the sand along the coast and deposits it elsewhere. This process of breaking up rock and carrying it away is known as erosion.

Barrier Beaches A natural landform that protects shorelines from wave action occurs along low-lying beaches. Long sand deposits called barrier beaches form parallel to the shore. Such beaches are separated from the mainland by a shallow lagoon. Waves break against the barrier beach instead of against the land inside. For this reason, people are working to preserve natural barrier beaches like those off Cape Cod, the New Jersey shore, and the Georgia and Carolina coasts.

Sand Dunes Other natural landforms also help protect beaches and reduce erosion, although they can't completely stop the movement of sand. Sand dunes, which are hills of windblown sand, can make a beach more stable and protect the shore from erosion. The strong roots of dune plants, such as beach grass and sea oats, hold the sand in place. These plants help to slow erosion caused by wind and water. But the dunes and plants can be destroyed by cars, bicycles, or even by many people walking over them. Without plants to hold the sand in place, dunes can be easily washed away by wave action.

Groins Many people like to live near the ocean. But over time, erosion can wear away the beach. This threatens the homes and other buildings near the beach. To avoid losing their property, people look for ways to reduce the effect of erosion.

One method of reducing erosion along a stretch of beach is to build a wall of rocks or concrete, called a **groin,** outward from the beach. Sand carried by the water piles up against the groins instead of moving along the shore. Figure 7 shows how groins interrupt the movement of water. However, groins increase the amount of erosion farther down the beach.

Groin

FIGURE 7
Groins
Sand piles up against a series of groins people have built along the New Jersey coast. Building groins to stop longshore drift is one way to reduce beach erosion.

 **Reading Checkpoint** Name two natural landforms that help reduce beach erosion.

Section 1 Assessment

⊙ Target Reading Skill Using Prior Knowledge
Review your graphic organizer and revise it based on what you just learned in the section.

Reviewing Key Concepts

1. a. **Reviewing** How do waves form?
   b. **Explaining** Explain how both a wave's energy and the water in a wave move.
   c. **Applying Concepts** Why does an ocean buoy bob up and down as a wave passes by?
2. a. **Defining** What is the wavelength of a wave? What is wave height?
   b. **Describing** How do wavelength and wave height change as a wave enters shallow water?
   c. **Developing Hypotheses** Using what you know about the wavelength and wave height of tsunamis, propose an explanation of why tsunamis can cause so much damage when they reach the shore.

3. a. **Explaining** What is longshore drift, and how does it affect a shoreline?
   b. **Relating Cause and Effect** Explain how building a groin affects longshore drift. What happens to the beach on each side of the groin?

Lab zone **At-Home Activity**

Wave Model With a family member, make a construction paper model of a wave. Your model should show the wave from the time it develops in the ocean to the time it breaks on the shore. Be sure to label the features of the wave, including crests, troughs, wavelengths, wave heights, swells, and breakers.

Tides

Reading Preview

Key Concepts
- What causes tides?
- What affects the heights of tides?
- How are tides a source of energy?

Key Terms
- tides • spring tide • neap tide

🎯 Target Reading Skill
Previewing Visuals Before you read, preview Figure 11. Then write two questions that you have about the diagram in a graphic organizer like the one below. As you read, answer your questions.

Spring and Neap Tides

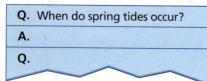

Q.	When do spring tides occur?
A.	
Q.	

🔺 Lab zone Discover **Activity**

When Is High Tide?

Twice a day, the ocean rises and falls on Earth's coasts. These changes in water level are called tides. The map shows the times of the two high tides in two cities on a specific day.

1. Calculate the length of time between the two high tides for each city. Remember to consider both hours and minutes.
2. Compare the times of the high tides in Bar Harbor and in Portsmouth. Do you see a pattern?

Think It Over

Predicting Based on the times of the high tides in Bar Harbor and Portsmouth, predict when the high tides will occur in Portland.

You're standing on a riverbank in the town of Saint John, New Brunswick, in Canada. In the distance there's a roaring sound. Suddenly a wall of water twice your height thunders past. The surge of water rushes up the river channel so fast that it almost looks as if the river is flowing backward!

This thundering wall of water is an everyday event at Saint John. The town is located where the Saint John River enters the Bay of Fundy, an arm of the Atlantic Ocean. The Bay of Fundy is famous for its dramatic daily tides. When the tide comes in, fishing boats float on the water near the piers. But once the tide goes out, the boats are stranded on the muddy harbor bottom!

FIGURE 8
Differences in Tides
The Bay of Fundy in Canada is noted for the great differences between its high and low tides. Near the mouth of the bay, boats float at high tide (left). At low tide, the boats are grounded (right).

High Tide

What Causes Tides?

The daily rise and fall of Earth's waters on its coastlines are called **tides.** As the tide comes in, the level of the water on the beach rises gradually. When the water reaches its highest point, it is high tide. Then the tide goes out, flowing back toward the sea. When the water reaches its lowest point, it is low tide. Unlike the surface waves you read about earlier, tides happen regularly no matter how the wind blows. Tides occur in all bodies of water, but they are most noticeable in the ocean and large lakes.

Gravity and Tides Tides are caused by the interaction of Earth, the moon, and the sun. How can distant objects like the moon and sun influence water on Earth? The answer is gravity. Gravity is the force exerted by an object that pulls other objects toward it. Gravity keeps you and everything around you on Earth's surface. As the distance between objects increases, however, gravity's pull grows weaker.

Figure 9 shows the effect of the moon's gravity on the water on Earth's surface. The moon pulls on the water on the side of Earth closest to it more strongly than it pulls on the center of the Earth. This pull creates a bulge of water, called a tidal bulge, on the side of Earth facing the moon. The water farthest from the moon is pulled toward the moon less strongly than are other parts of Earth. The water farthest from the moon is "left behind," forming a second bulge.

In the places where there are tidal bulges, high tide is occurring along the coastlines. In the places between the bulges, low tide is occurring. Earth's rotation through the tidal bulges causes most coastlines to experience two high tides and two low tides every 25 hours.

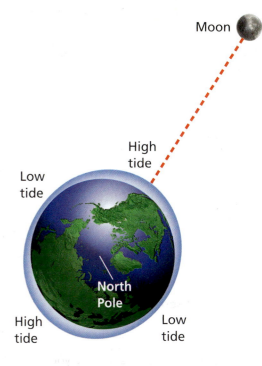

FIGURE 9
How the Moon Causes Tides
The pull of the moon's gravity on Earth's water causes tidal bulges to form on the side closest to the moon and the side farthest from the moon. **Inferring** *Why is the water level high on the side of Earth farthest from the moon?*

 **Reading Checkpoint** What force causes tides to occur on Earth's surface?

Low Tide

FIGURE 10
Sea Turtles and Spring Tides
Some animals are very dependent on tide cycles. Sea turtles can only come to shore to lay their eggs during certain spring tides.

The Daily Tide Cycle As Earth turns completely around once each day, people on or near the shore observe the rise of tides as they reach the area of a tidal bulge. High tides occur about 12 hours and 25 minutes apart in any location. As Earth rotates, easternmost points pass through the area of the tidal bulge before points farther to the west. Therefore, high tide occurs later the farther west you travel along the coast.

In some places, the two high tides and two low tides are easy to observe each day. But in other places, the difference between high tide and low tide is less dramatic. One set of tides may even be so minimal that there appears to be only one high tide and one low tide per day.

Several factors affect the height of a tide in any particular location. For example, certain landforms can interrupt the water's movements. A basin at the mouth of a river can also increase the difference between high and low tide. The speed and depth of moving water increases as it flows into a narrower channel. That is what causes the dramatic tides in the mouth of the Saint John River you read about earlier.

The Monthly Tide Cycle Even though the sun is about 150 million kilometers from Earth, it is so massive that its gravity affects the tides. The sun pulls the water on Earth's surface toward it. In Figure 11, you can follow the positions of Earth, the moon, and the sun at different times during a month. **Changes in the positions of Earth, the moon, and the sun affect the heights of the tides during a month.**

Twice a month, at the new moon and the full moon, the sun and moon are lined up. Their combined gravitational pull produces the greatest difference between the heights of high and low tide, called a **spring tide.** These tides get their name from an Old English word, *springen*, which means "to jump."

At the first and third quarters of the moon, the sun and moon pull at right angles to each other. This arrangement produces a **neap tide,** a tide with the least difference between low and high tide. During a neap tide, the sun's gravity pulls some of the water away from the tidal bulge facing the moon. This acts to "even out" the water level over Earth's surface, decreasing the difference between high and low tides.

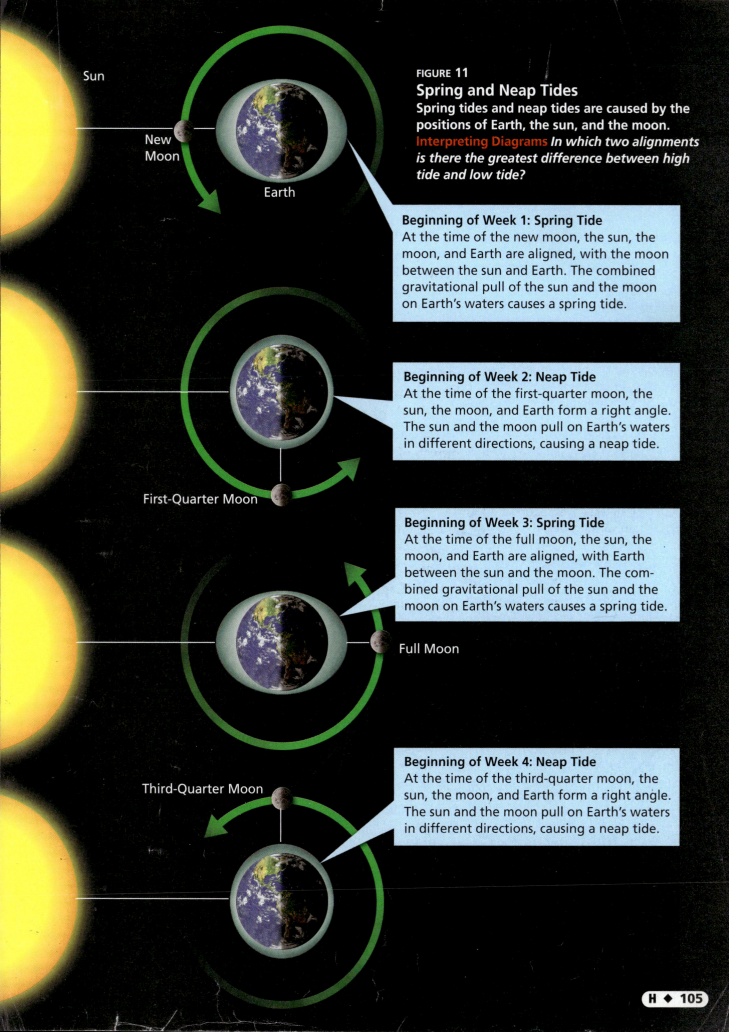

Sun

New
Moon

Earth

First-Quarter Moon

Third-Quarter Moon

Full Moon

FIGURE 11
Spring and Neap Tides
Spring tides and neap tides are caused by the positions of Earth, the sun, and the moon. **Interpreting Diagrams** *In which two alignments is there the greatest difference between high tide and low tide?*

Beginning of Week 1: Spring Tide
At the time of the new moon, the sun, the moon, and Earth are aligned, with the moon between the sun and Earth. The combined gravitational pull of the sun and the moon on Earth's waters causes a spring tide.

Beginning of Week 2: Neap Tide
At the time of the first-quarter moon, the sun, the moon, and Earth form a right angle. The sun and the moon pull on Earth's waters in different directions, causing a neap tide.

Beginning of Week 3: Spring Tide
At the time of the full moon, the sun, the moon, and Earth are aligned, with Earth between the sun and the moon. The combined gravitational pull of the sun and the moon on Earth's waters causes a spring tide.

Beginning of Week 4: Neap Tide
At the time of the third-quarter moon, the sun, the moon, and Earth form a right angle. The sun and the moon pull on Earth's waters in different directions, causing a neap tide.

Plotting Tides

This table lists the highest high tides and the lowest low tides for one week at the mouth of the Savannah River, where it meets the Atlantic Ocean in Georgia.

1. **Graphing** Use the data in the table to make a graph. On the horizontal axis, mark the days. On the vertical axis, mark tide heights ranging from 3.0 to –1.0 meters. (*Hint:* Mark the negative numbers below the horizontal axis.)

2. **Graphing** Plot the tide heights for each day on the graph. Connect the high tide points with one line and the low tide points with another line.

Tide Table		
Day	**Highest High Tide (m)**	**Lowest Low Tide (m)**
1	1.9	0.2
2	2.1	0.1
3	2.3	0.0
4	2.4	–0.2
5	2.5	–0.2
6	2.6	–0.3
7	1.9	0.3

3. **Interpreting Data** How do the high and low tides change during the week?

4. **Inferring** What type of tide might be occurring on Day 6? Explain.

Tide Tables Despite the complex factors affecting tides, scientists can predict tides quite accurately for many locations. They combine knowledge of the movements of the moon and Earth with information about the shape of the coastline and other local conditions. If you live near the coast, your local newspaper probably publishes a tide table. Knowing the times and heights of tides is important to sailors, marine scientists, people who fish, and coastal residents.

 **Reading Checkpoint** **What two types of information help scientists predict the times of tides?**

Energy From Tides

Look at Figure 12. Can you almost hear the roar of the rushing water? **The movement of huge amounts of water between high and low tide is a source of potential energy—energy that is stored and can be used.** Engineers have designed tidal power plants that capture some of this energy as the tide moves in and out.

The first large-scale tidal power plant was built in 1967 on the Rance River in northwestern France. As high tide swirls up the river, the plant's gates open so that the water flows into a basin. As the tide retreats, the gates shut to trap the water. Gravity pulls the water back to sea through tunnels. The energy of the water moving through the tunnels powers generators that produce electricity, just as in a hydroelectric dam on a river.

Although tidal energy is a clean, renewable source of energy, it has several limitations. Harnessing tidal power is practical only where there is a large difference between high and low tides—at least 4 or 5 meters. There are very few places in the world where such a large difference occurs. Daily tides also may not occur at the time when there is a demand for electricity. However, tidal power can be a useful part of an overall plan to generate electricity that also includes other power sources between tides.

FIGURE 12
Tidal Power
Pulled by the tide, water rushes through this tidal power plant in France.
Making Generalizations
Why are so few locations suitable for tidal power plants?

✓ **Reading Checkpoint** Under what conditions is it practical to harness tidal power?

Section ② Assessment

🎯 **Target Reading Skill** Previewing Visuals
Refer to your questions and answers about Figure 11 to help you answer Question 2 below.

Reviewing Key Concepts

1. a. **Defining** What is a tide? What causes tides?
   b. **Explaining** Explain why the moon causes a tidal bulge to form on the side of Earth closest to it.
   c. **Inferring** The sun is much bigger than the moon. Why doesn't the sun affect tides more than the moon does?

2. a. **Reviewing** Why do the heights of tides change during the course of a month?
   b. **Describing** Describe the positions of the sun, moon, and Earth during a spring tide and during a neap tide.
   c. **Applying Concepts** Imagine that you are the captain of a fishing boat. Why would it be helpful to consult a monthly tide table?

3. a. **Reviewing** How can tides be used to generate electricity?
   b. **Predicting** Do you think that tidal power will ever be a major source of energy worldwide? Why or why not?

Writing in Science

Firsthand Account Imagine that you are fishing on a pier on the Bay of Fundy in Canada. It was high tide when you began fishing. Now it is low tide. Write a firsthand account describing the changes that you observed as the tide went out. Use clear, descriptive language in your writing.

Reading Preview

Key Concepts
- How salty is ocean water?
- How do the temperature and gas content of ocean water vary?
- How do conditions in the ocean change with depth?

Key Terms
- salinity • submersible

Target Reading Skill

Asking Questions Before you read, preview the red headings. In a graphic organizer like the one below, ask a *how* or *what* question for each heading. As you read, answer your questions.

Ocean Water Chemistry

Question	Answer
How salty is the ocean?	One kilogram of ocean water has . . .

If you've ever swallowed some water while you were swimming in the ocean, you know that the ocean is salty. Why? According to an old Swedish legend, it's all because of a magic mill. This mill could grind out anything its owner wanted, such as herring, porridge, or even gold. A greedy sea captain once stole the mill and took it away on his ship, but without finding out how to use it. He asked the mill to grind some salt but then could not stop it. The mill ground more and more salt, until the captain's ship sank from its weight. According to the tale, the mill is still at the bottom of the sea, grinding out salt!

Salt storage area ▼

The Salty Ocean

Probably no one ever took this legend seriously, even when it was first told. The scientific explanation for the ocean's saltiness begins with the early stages of Earth's history, when the ocean covered much of the surface of the planet. Undersea volcanoes erupted, spewing chemicals into the water. Gradually, the lava from these volcanic eruptions built up areas of land. Rain fell on the bare land, washing more chemicals from the rocks into the ocean. Over time, these dissolved substances built up to the levels present in the ocean today.

Salinity Just how salty is the ocean? If you boiled a kilogram of ocean water in a pot until all the water was gone, there would be about 35 grams of salts left in the pot. **On average, one kilogram of ocean water contains about 35 grams of salts—that is, 35 parts per thousand.** The total amount of dissolved salts in a sample of water is the **salinity** of that sample.

The substance you know as table salt—sodium chloride—is the salt present in the greatest amount in ocean water. When sodium chloride dissolves in water, it separates into sodium and chloride particles called ions. Other salts, such as magnesium chloride, form ions in water in the same way. Together, chloride and sodium make up almost 86 percent of the ions dissolved in ocean water. Ocean water also contains smaller amounts of about a dozen other ions, including magnesium and calcium, and other substances that organisms need, such as nitrogen and phosphorus.

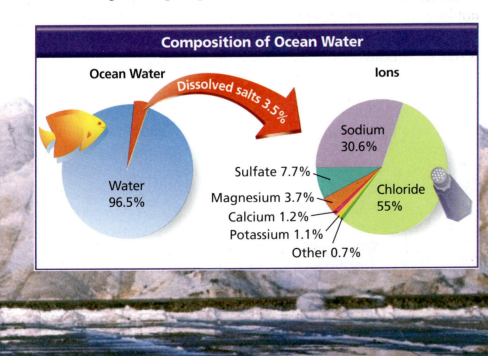

Composition of Ocean Water

Ocean Water

Dissolved salts 3.5%

Water 96.5%

Ions

Sodium 30.6%
Sulfate 7.7%
Magnesium 3.7%
Calcium 1.2%
Potassium 1.1%
Other 0.7%
Chloride 55%

FIGURE 13
Composition of Ocean Water
Ocean water contains many different dissolved salts. When salts dissolve, they separate into particles called ions.
Reading Graphs *Which ion is most common in ocean water?*

FIGURE 14
Salinity and Density
These people are relaxing with the paper while floating in the water! The Dead Sea between Israel and Jordan is so salty that people float easily on its surface.
Relating Cause and Effect
How is the area's hot, dry climate related to the Dead Sea's high salinity?

Math Skills

Calculating Density

To calculate the density of a substance, divide the mass of the substance by its volume.

$$\text{Density} = \frac{\text{Mass}}{\text{Volume}}$$

For example, 1 liter (L) of ocean water has a mass of 1.03 kilograms (kg). Therefore,

$$\text{Density} = \frac{1.03 \text{ kg}}{1.00 \text{ L}}$$

$$\text{Density} = 1.03 \text{ kg/L}$$

Practice Problems A 5-liter sample of one type of crude oil has a mass of 4.10 kg. What is its density? If this oil spilled on the ocean's surface, would it sink or float? Explain your answer in terms of density.

Variations in Salinity In most parts of the ocean, the salinity is between 34 and 37 parts per thousand. But near the ocean's surface, rain, snow, and melting ice add fresh water, lowering the salinity. Salinity is also lower near the mouths of large rivers such as the Amazon or Mississippi. These rivers empty great amounts of fresh water into the ocean. Evaporation, on the other hand, increases salinity, since the salt is left behind as the water evaporates. For example, in the Red Sea, where the climate is hot and dry, the salinity can be as high as 41 parts per thousand. Salinity can also be higher near the poles. As the surface water freezes into ice, the salt is left behind in the remaining water.

Effects of Salinity Salinity affects several properties of ocean water. For instance, ocean water does not freeze until the temperature drops to about −1.9°C. The salt acts as a kind of antifreeze by interfering with the formation of ice crystals. Salt water also has a higher density than fresh water. That means that the mass of one liter of salt water is greater than the mass of one liter of fresh water. Because its density is greater, seawater has greater buoyancy. It lifts, or buoys up, less dense objects floating in it. This is why an egg floats higher in salt water than in fresh water, and why the people in Figure 14 float so effortlessly in the Dead Sea.

Reading Checkpoint Why does salt water have greater buoyancy than fresh water?

◆ **H**

Other Ocean Properties

In New England, the news reports on New Year's Day often feature the shivering members of a "Polar Bear Club" taking a dip in the icy Atlantic Ocean. Yet on the same day, people enjoy the warm waters of a Puerto Rico beach. **Like temperatures on land, temperatures at the surface of the ocean vary with location and the seasons. Gases in ocean water vary as well.**

Temperature of Ocean Water Why do surface temperatures of the ocean vary from place to place? The broad surface of the ocean absorbs energy from the sun. Near the equator, surface ocean temperatures often reach 25°C, about room temperature. The temperature drops as you travel away from the equator.

Because warm water is less dense than cold water, warm water forms only a thin layer on the ocean surface. Generally, the deeper you descend into the ocean, the colder and denser the water becomes. When water temperature is lower, the water molecules stay closer together than at higher temperatures. So, a sample of cold water has more water molecules than a sample of warm water of the same volume. The sample of cold water is denser.

Gases in Ocean Water Just as land organisms use gases found in air, ocean organisms use gases found in ocean water. Two gases that ocean organisms use are carbon dioxide and oxygen.

Carbon dioxide is about 60 times as plentiful in the oceans as in the air. Algae need carbon dioxide for photosynthesis. Animals such as corals also use carbon dioxide, which provides the carbon to build their hard skeletons.

Unlike carbon dioxide, oxygen is scarcer in seawater than in air. Oxygen is most plentiful in seawater near the surface. Oxygen in seawater comes from the air and from algae in the ocean, as a product of photosynthesis. The amount of oxygen in seawater is affected by the water temperature. The cold waters in the polar regions contain more oxygen than warm, tropical waters. But there is still enough oxygen in tropical seas to support a variety of organisms.

 **Reading Checkpoint** What are two sources of oxygen in ocean water?

FIGURE 15
Organisms and Ocean Temperatures
From the warmest tropical waters to the coldest Antarctic sea, you can find organisms that are adapted to extreme ocean temperatures.

▲ This longfin anthias fish swimming near Hawaii lives in one of the warmest parts of the Pacific Ocean.

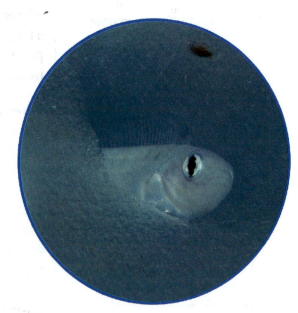

▲ This rockcod is swimming through a hole in an iceberg in near-freezing ocean water.

FIGURE 16

The Water Column

Conditions change as you descend to the ocean floor. **Interpreting Diagrams** *What two factors affect the density of ocean water?*

A scuba diver can descend to about 40 meters.

Surface Zone
Extends from the surface to about 200 meters. Average temperature worldwide is 17.5°C.

Transition Zone
Extends from bottom of the surface zone to about 1 kilometer. Temperature rapidly drops to 4°C.

The submersible *Alvin* can descend to about 4 kilometers.

Deep Zone
Extends from about 1 kilometer to ocean floor. Average temperature is 3.5°C.

In 1960, the submersible *Trieste* dived to a record depth of 11 kilometers.

Depth

PRESSURE INCREASES

Color and Light
Sunlight penetrates the surface of the ocean. It appears first yellowish, then blue-green, as the water absorbs the red light. No light reaches below about 200 meters.

Temperature
Near the surface, temperature is affected by the weather above. In the transition zone, the temperature drops rapidly. In the deep zone, the water is always extremely cold.

Salinity
Rainfall decreases salinity near the surface, while evaporation increases salinity in warm, dry areas. Below the surface zone, salinity remains fairly constant throughout the water column.

Density
The density of seawater depends on temperature and salinity. The ocean is generally least dense in the surface zone, where it is warmest. However, higher salinity also increases density. The most dense water is found in the cold deep zone.

Pressure
Pressure increases at the rate of 10 times the air pressure at sea level per 100 meters of depth.

0.5 km
1.0 km
1.5 km
2.0 km
2.5 km
3.0 km
3.5 km
4.0 km

3.8 km — Average ocean depth

Changes With Depth

If you could descend from the ocean's surface to the ocean floor, you would pass through a vertical section of the ocean referred to as the water column. Figure 16 on the previous page shows some of the dramatic changes you would observe.

Decreasing Temperature As you descend through the ocean, the water temperature decreases. There are three temperature zones in the water column. The surface zone is the warmest. It typically extends from the surface to between 100 and 500 meters. The transition zone extends from the bottom of the surface zone to about 1 kilometer. Temperatures drop very quickly as you descend through the transition zone, to about 4°C. Below the transition zone is the deep zone. Average temperatures there are 3.5°C in most of the ocean.

Increasing Pressure Water pressure is the force exerted by the weight of water. **Pressure increases continuously with depth in the ocean.** Because of the high pressure in the deep ocean, divers can descend safely only to about 40 meters. To observe the deep ocean, scientists must use a **submersible**, an underwater vehicle built of materials that resist pressure.

For: Links on ocean water chemistry
Visit: www.SciLinks.org
Web Code: scn-0833

 **Reading Checkpoint** What is a submersible?

Section 3 Assessment

🎯 **Target Reading Skill** Asking Questions Use the questions you wrote about the headings to help you answer the questions below.

Reviewing Key Concepts

1. a. Defining What is salinity? What is the average salinity of ocean water?
  b. Describing Describe one factor that increases the salinity of seawater and one factor that decreases its salinity.
  c. Inferring Would you expect the seawater just below the floating ice in the Arctic Ocean to be higher or lower in salinity than the water in the deepest part of the ocean? Explain.
2. a. Identifying Where would you find the warmest ocean temperatures on Earth?
  b. Comparing and Contrasting How do carbon dioxide and oxygen levels in the oceans compare to those in the air?

  c. Relating Cause and Effect How does the temperature of ocean water affect oxygen levels in the water?
3. a. Reviewing How do temperature and pressure change as you descend in the ocean?
  b. Predicting Where in the water column would you expect to find the following conditions: the highest pressure readings; the densest waters; the warmest temperatures?

Math Practice

4. Calculating Density Calculate the density of the following 1-L samples of ocean water. Sample A has a mass of 1.01 kg; Sample B has a mass of 1.06 kg. Which sample would likely have the higher salinity? Explain.

Investigating Changes in Density

Problem
Can you design and build an instrument that can detect differences in density?

Skills Focus
building a prototype, designing a solution, troubleshooting

Materials
- thumbtacks • 250-mL graduated cylinder
- unsharpened pencil with eraser • metric ruler
- fine-point permanent marker • thermometer
- ice • balance • water • spoon • salt
- additional materials provided by your teacher

Procedure

PART 1 Research and Investigate

1. One way to measure the density of a liquid is with a tool called a hydrometer. You can make a simple hydrometer using an unsharpened wooden pencil.

2. Starting at the unsharpened end of a pencil, use a permanent marker to make marks every 2 mm along the side of the pencil. Make longer marks for every whole centimeter. Continue until you have marked off 5 cm.

3. Label each of the long marks, starting at the unsharpened end of the pencil.

4. Insert 3 thumbtacks as weights into the eraser end of the pencil. **CAUTION:** *Be careful not to cut yourself on the sharp points of the thumbtacks.*

5. Fill the graduated cylinder with 250 mL of water at room temperature. Place the pencil in the water, eraser end down.

6. Add or remove thumbtacks and adjust their placement until the pencil floats upright, with about 2 cm sticking up above the surface of the water.

7. In your notebook, record the temperature of the water. Next to that number, record the reading on the pencil hydrometer at the surface of the water.

8. Fill the graduated cylinder with cold water. Place the pencil hydrometer into the water, eraser end down. Then repeat Step 7.

PART 2 Design and Build

9. Using what you learned in Part 1, design and build a hydrometer that can detect density differences among different samples of water. Your hydrometer should
   - be able to measure density differences between hot water and cold water
   - be able to measure density differences between salt water and fresh water
   - be constructed of materials approved by your teacher

10. Sketch your design in your notebook and make a list of the materials you will need. Write a plan for how you will construct your hydrometer. After you have received your teacher's approval for your design, build your hydrometer.

PART 3 Evaluate and Redesign

11. Test your hydrometer by using it to measure the density of water at different temperatures. Then test samples of water that have different salinities. Create a data table in which to record your results.

Data Table		
Temperature (°C)	Salinity $\left(\dfrac{g\ salt}{L\ water}\right)$	Hydrometer Reading

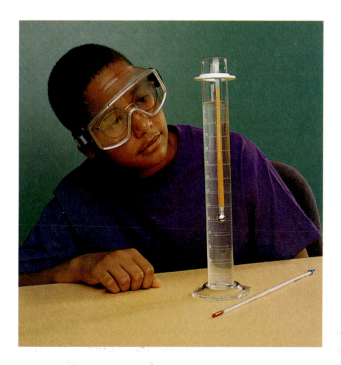

12. Based on your tests, decide how you could improve the design of your hydrometer. For example, how could you change your design so your hydrometer is able to detect smaller differences in density? Obtain your teacher's approval, then make the necessary changes, and test how your redesigned hydrometer functions.

Analyze and Conclude

1. **Inferring** Explain why cold water is more dense than hot water. Explain why salt water is more dense than fresh water.

2. **Building a Prototype** How well did the pencil hydrometer you built in Part 1 work? What problems did you encounter with the hydrometer?

3. **Designing a Solution** How did you incorporate what you learned in Part 1 into your hydrometer design in Part 2? For example, how did your hydrometer address the problems you encountered in Part 1?

4. **Troubleshooting** In Part 3, how well did your hydrometer perform when you measured water samples of different densities? How did you redesign your hydrometer to improve its function?

5. **Evaluating the Design** What limitations did factors such as buoyancy, materials, time, costs, or other factors place on the design and function of your hydrometer? Describe how you adapted your design to work within these limitations.

Communicate

Create an informative poster that describes how your hydrometer works. Include illustrations of your hydrometer and any important background information on density.

Currents and Climate

Reading Preview

Key Concepts
- What causes surface currents and how do they affect climate?
- What causes deep currents and what effects do they have?
- How does upwelling affect the distribution of nutrients in the ocean?

Key Terms
- current
- climate
- Coriolis effect
- El Niño
- upwelling

⟳ Target Reading Skill
Relating Cause and Effect As you read, identify the main factors that cause surface and deep currents in the oceans. Write the information in graphic organizers like the one below.

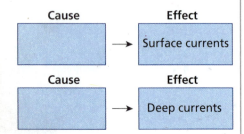

Cause		Effect
	→	Surface currents

Cause		Effect
	→	Deep currents

One spring day, people strolling along a beach in Washington State saw an amazing sight. Hundreds of sneakers of all colors and sizes were washing ashore from the Pacific Ocean! This "sneaker spill" was eventually traced to a cargo ship accident. Containers of sneakers had fallen overboard and now the sneakers were washing ashore.

But the most amazing part of the story is this—scientists could predict where the sneakers would wash up next. And just as the scientists had predicted, sneakers washed up in Oregon, and then thousands of kilometers away in Hawaii!

How did the scientists know that the sneakers would float all the way to Hawaii? The answer lies in a type of ocean movement known as a current. A **current** is a large stream of moving water that flows through the oceans. Unlike waves, currents carry water from one place to another. Some currents move water at the surface of the ocean, while other currents move water deep in the ocean.

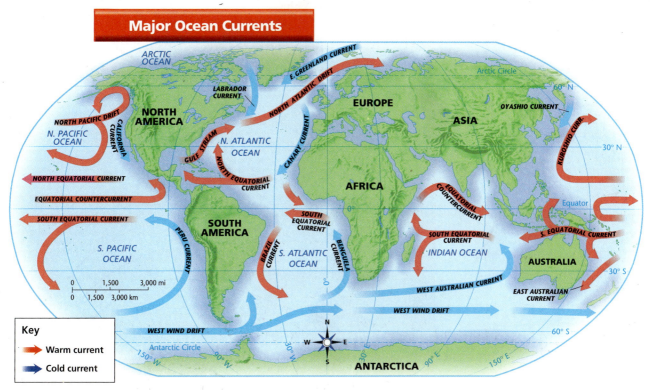

Major Ocean Currents

Key
→ Warm current
→ Cold current

Surface Currents

Figure 17 shows the major surface currents in Earth's oceans. **Surface currents, which affect water to a depth of several hundred meters, are driven mainly by winds.** Following Earth's major wind patterns, surface currents move in circular patterns in the five major oceans. Most of the currents flow east or west, and then double back to complete the circle.

Coriolis Effect Why do the currents move in these circular patterns? If Earth were standing still, winds and currents would flow in straight lines between the poles and the equator. But as Earth rotates, the paths of the winds and currents curve. This effect of Earth's rotation on the direction of winds and currents is called the **Coriolis effect** (kawr ee OH lis). In the Northern Hemisphere, the Coriolis effect causes the currents to curve to the right. In the Southern Hemisphere, the Coriolis effect causes the currents to curve to the left.

The largest and most powerful surface current in the North Atlantic Ocean, the Gulf Stream, is caused by strong winds from the west. It is more than 30 kilometers wide and 300 meters deep, and carries a volume of water 100 times greater than the Mississippi River. The Gulf Stream carries warm water from the Gulf of Mexico to the Caribbean Sea, then northward along the coast of the United States. Near Cape Hatteras, North Carolina, it curves eastward across the Atlantic, as a result of the Coriolis effect.

FIGURE 17
Large surface currents generally move in circular patterns in Earth's oceans. **Interpreting Maps** *Name four currents that flow along the coasts of North America. State whether each current is warm or cold.*

Go Online
SciLINKS NSTA

For: Links on ocean currents
Visit: www.SciLinks.org
Web Code: scn-0834

FIGURE 18

Surface Currents and Climate
This satellite image of the Atlantic Ocean has been enhanced with colors that show water temperature. Red and orange indicate warmer water, while green and blue indicate colder water.
Interpreting Maps *The Gulf Stream flows around Florida in the lower left of the map. Is the Gulf Stream a warm or cold current?*

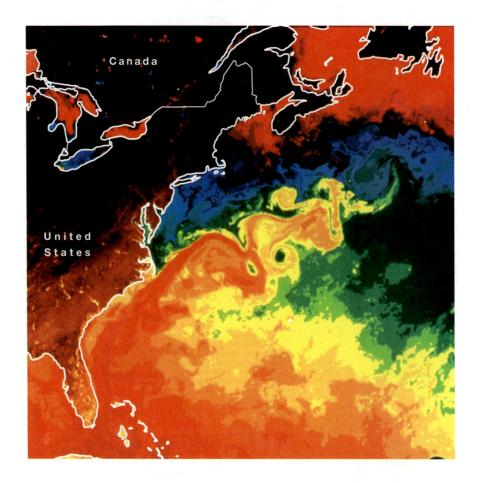

Canada

United States

Lab zone **Skills Activity**

Drawing Conclusions
Locate the Benguela Current in Figure 17 on the previous page. Near the southern tip of Africa, the winds blow from west to east. Using what you have learned about surface currents and climate, what can you conclude about the impact of this current on the climate of the south-western coast of Africa?

Effects on Climate The Gulf Stream and another warm current, the North Atlantic Drift, are very important to people in the city of Trondheim, Norway. Trondheim is located along Norway's western coast. Although it is very close to the Arctic Circle, winters there are fairly mild. Snow melts soon after it falls. And fortunately for the fishing boats, the local harbors are free of ice most of the winter. The two warm currents bring this area of Norway a mild climate. **Climate** is the pattern of temperature and precipitation typical of an area over a long period of time.

Currents affect climate by moving cold and warm water around the globe. In general, currents carry warm water from the tropics toward the poles and bring cold water back toward the equator. **A surface current warms or cools the air above it, influencing the climate of the land near the coast.**

Winds pick up moisture as they blow across warm-water currents. For example, the warm Kuroshio Current brings mild, rainy weather to the southern islands of Japan. In contrast, cold-water currents cool the air above them. Since cold air holds less moisture than warm air, these currents tend to bring cool, dry weather to the land areas in their path.

El Niño When changes in wind patterns and currents occur, they can have a major impact on the oceans and neighboring land. One example of such changes is **El Niño,** an abnormal climate event that occurs every two to seven years in the Pacific Ocean. El Niño begins when an unusual pattern of winds forms over the western Pacific. This causes a vast sheet of warm water to move eastward toward the South American coast. El Niño conditions can last for one to two years before the usual winds and currents return.

El Niño can have disastrous consequences. It causes shifts in weather patterns around the world, bringing unusual and often severe conditions to different areas. For example, a major El Niño occurred between 1997 and 1998 and caused an especially warm winter in the northeastern United States. However, it was also responsible for heavy rains, flooding, and mudslides in California, as well as a string of deadly tornadoes in Florida.

Although scientists do not fully understand the conditions that cause El Niño, they have been able to predict its occurrence using computer models of world climate. Knowing when El Niño will occur can reduce its impact. Scientists and public officials can plan emergency procedures and make changes to protect people and wildlife.

 **Reading Checkpoint** Why is it helpful to be able to predict when El Niño will occur?

FIGURE 19
El Niño's Impact
El Niño can cause severe weather all around the world.

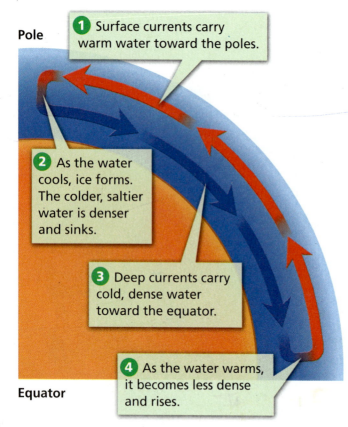

Pole

① Surface currents carry warm water toward the poles.

② As the water cools, ice forms. The colder, saltier water is denser and sinks.

③ Deep currents carry cold, dense water toward the equator.

④ As the water warms, it becomes less dense and rises.

Equator

FIGURE 20
Deep Currents
Deep currents are caused by differences in the density of ocean water.

Deep Currents

Deep below the ocean surface, another type of current causes chilly waters to creep slowly across the ocean floor. **These deep currents are caused by differences in the density of ocean water.**

As you read earlier, the density of water depends on its temperature and its salinity. When a warm surface current moves from the equator toward one of the poles, it gradually cools. As ice forms near the poles, the salinity of the water increases from the salt left behind during freezing. As its temperature decreases and its salinity increases, the water becomes denser and sinks. Then, the cold water flows back along the ocean floor as a deep current. Deep currents are affected by the Coriolis effect, which causes them to curve.

Deep currents move and mix water around the world. They carry cold water from the poles toward the equator. Deep currents flow slowly. They may take as long as 1,000 years to flow from the pole to the equator and back again!

Upwelling

In most parts of the ocean, surface waters do not usually mix with deep ocean waters. However, mixing sometimes occurs when winds cause upwelling. **Upwelling** is the movement of cold water upward from the deep ocean. As winds blow away the warm surface water, cold water rises to replace it.

Upwelling brings up tiny ocean organisms, minerals, and other nutrients from the deeper layers of the water. Without this motion, the surface waters of the open ocean would be very scarce in nutrients. Because nutrients are plentiful, zones of upwelling are usually home to huge schools of fish.

One major area of upwelling lies in the Pacific Ocean off the west coast of South America. Many people depend on this rich fishing area for food and jobs. The arrival of El Niño prevents upwelling from occurring. Without the nutrients brought by upwelling, fish die or go elsewhere to find food, reducing the fishing catch that season and hurting people's livelihoods.

 **Reading Checkpoint** What is upwelling?

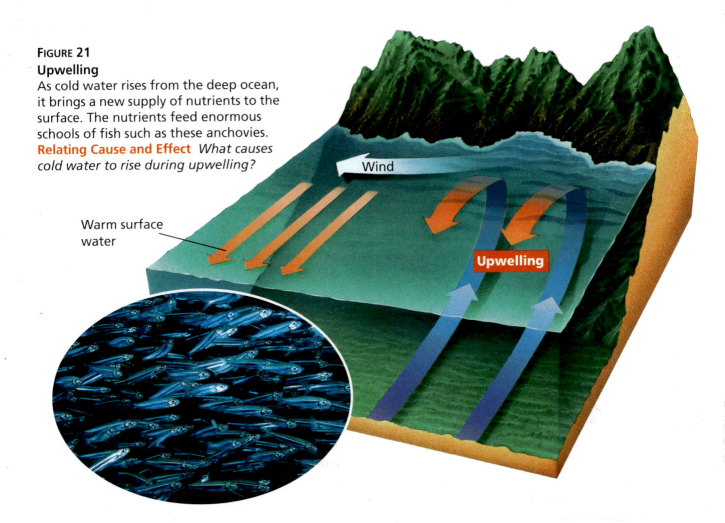

FIGURE 21
Upwelling
As cold water rises from the deep ocean, it brings a new supply of nutrients to the surface. The nutrients feed enormous schools of fish such as these anchovies.
Relating Cause and Effect *What causes cold water to rise during upwelling?*

Wind

Warm surface water

Upwelling

Section 4 Assessment

Target Reading Skill **Relating Cause and Effect** Refer to your graphic organizer about the causes of ocean currents to answer Questions 1 and 2 below.

Reviewing Key Concepts

1. a. **Defining** What is a current?
   b. **Describing** What causes surface currents to occur? How do surface currents affect the climate of coastal areas?
   c. **Predicting** What type of climate might a coastal area have if nearby currents are cold?

2. a. **Explaining** Explain how deep currents form and move in the ocean.
   b. **Comparing and Contrasting** Compare the causes and effects of deep currents and surface currents.

3. a. **Reviewing** What causes upwelling?

   b. **Explaining** Why are huge schools of fish usually found in zones of upwelling?
   c. **Applying Concepts** Why would the ability to predict the occurrence of El Niño be important for the fishing industry on the western coast of South America?

Lab zone **At-Home Activity**

Modeling the Coriolis Effect With the help of a family member, use chalk and a globe to model the Coriolis effect. Have your family member slowly rotate the globe in an easterly direction. As the globe rotates, draw a line from the North Pole to the equator. Use your knowledge of the Coriolis effect to explain why the line is curved.

Modeling Ocean Currents

Problem

How can you model the movement of ocean water caused by surface currents?

Skills Focus

making models, observing, inferring

Materials

- rectangular baking tray
- chalk
- modeling clay, 3 sticks
- ruler
- permanent marker
- hole puncher
- newspaper
- construction paper, blue and red
- jointed drinking straws, one per student
- light-reflecting rheoscopic fluid, 400 mL (or water and food coloring)

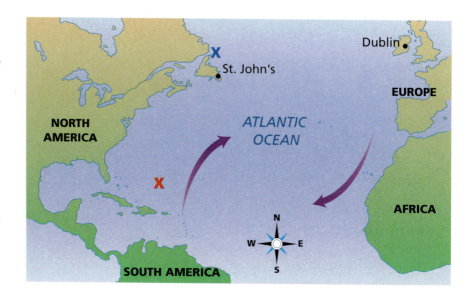

Procedure

1. Cover your work area with newspaper. Place the baking tray on top of the newspaper.

2. Using the map as a guide, draw a chalk outline of the eastern coast of North and South America on the left side of the tray. Draw the outline of the west coast of Europe and Africa on the right side of the tray.

3. Use modeling clay to create the continents, roughly following the chalk outlines you have drawn. Build the continents to a depth of about 3 cm. Press the clay tightly to the pan to form a watertight seal.

4. Fill the ocean area of your model with rheoscopic fluid (or water and food coloring) to a depth of 1 cm.

5. Place 10 blue paper punches in the ocean area marked with a blue X on the map. Place 10 red paper punches in the area marked with a red X.

6. Select a drinking straw and bend it at the joint. Write your initials on the short end of the straw with the marker.

7. With a partner, simulate the pattern of winds that blow in this region of the world. One partner should position his or her straw across the westernmost bulge of Africa and blow toward the west (see arrow on map). The other partner should position his or her straw across the northern end of South America and blow toward the northeast (see arrow on map). Make sure that the straws are bent and that the short ends are parallel to the ocean surface. Both partners should begin blowing gently through the straws at the same time. Try to blow as continuously as possible for one to two minutes.

8. Observe the motion of the fluid and paper punches over the surface of the ocean. Notice what happens when the fluid and punches flow around landmasses.

Analyze and Conclude

1. **Making Models** Draw a map that shows the pattern of ocean currents that was produced in your model. Use red arrows to show the flow of warm water moving north from the equator. Use blue arrows to show the flow of cold water away from the polar regions.

2. **Classifying** Use Figure 17 to add names to the currents you drew on your map. Which currents are warm-water currents? Which are cold-water currents?

3. **Observing** Based on what you observed with your model, describe the relationship between winds and surface currents in the ocean.

4. **Inferring** Dublin, Ireland, is located at the same latitude as St. John's in Newfoundland, Canada. However, when it's 8°C in Dublin in January, it's usually below 0°C in St. John's. Use your knowledge of ocean currents to explain why the climate in Dublin is different from the climate in St. John's.

5. **Communicating** Suppose you wanted to sail to Europe from the East Coast of the United States. Write a dialogue you might have with a crew member in which you discuss two natural factors that could help speed up the trip.

Design an Experiment

Design an investigation in which you simulate an upwelling off the coast of Africa. (*Hint:* You may use a model similar to the one used in this investigation.) *Obtain your teacher's permission before carrying out your investigation.*

1 Wave Action

Key Concepts

- Most waves form when winds blowing across the water's surface transmit their energy to the water.
- Near shore, wave height increases and wavelength decreases.
- As waves come ashore, water washes up the beach at an angle, carrying sand grains. The water and sand then run straight back down the beach. Waves shape a beach by eroding the shore in some places and building it up in others.

Key Terms

wave	tsunami
wavelength	longshore drift
frequency	rip current
wave height	groin

2 Tides

Key Concepts

- Tides are caused by the interaction of Earth, the moon, and the sun.
- Changes in the positions of Earth, the moon, and the sun affect the heights of the tides during a month.
- The movement of huge amounts of water between high and low tides is a source of potential energy.

Key Terms

tides	spring tide	neap tide

3 Ocean Water Chemistry

Key Concepts

- On average, one kilogram of ocean water contains about 35 grams of salts.
- Like temperatures on land, temperatures at the surface of the ocean vary with location and the seasons. Gases in ocean water vary as well.
- As you descend through the ocean, the water temperature decreases. Pressure increases continuously with depth in the ocean.

Key Terms

salinity	submersible

4 Currents and Climate

Key Concepts

- Surface currents, which affect water to a depth of several hundred meters, are driven mainly by winds. A surface current warms or cools the air above it, influencing the climate of the land near the coast.
- Deep currents are caused by differences in the density of ocean water. Deep currents move and mix water around the world. They carry cold water from the poles toward the equator.
- Upwelling brings up tiny ocean organisms, minerals, and other nutrients from the deeper layers of the water. Without this motion, the surface waters of the open ocean would be very scarce in nutrients.

Key Terms

current	El Niño
Coriolis effect	upwelling
climate	

Review and Assessment

For: Self-Assessment
Visit: PHSchool.com
Web Code: cfa-3030

Organizing Information

Sequencing Copy the flowchart about the movement of a wave onto a separate sheet of paper. Then complete it by putting the following three steps in the correct sequence: wave travels as low swell; wave breaks on shore; wavelength decreases and wave height increases. (For more on Sequencing, see the Skills Handbook.)

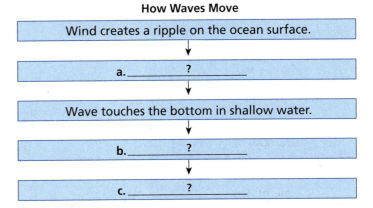

How Waves Move

Wind creates a ripple on the ocean surface.
↓
a. _____ ?
↓
Wave touches the bottom in shallow water.
↓
b. _____ ?
↓
c. _____ ?

Reviewing Key Terms

Choose the letter of the best answer.

1. Rolling waves with a large horizontal distance between crests have a long
   a. wave height.
   b. wavelength.
   c. frequency.
   d. trough.

2. Groins are built to reduce the effect of
   a. tsunamis.
   b. longshore drift.
   c. rip currents.
   d. deep currents.

3. At the full moon, the combined gravitational pulls of the sun and moon produce the biggest difference between low and high tide, called a
   a. surface current.
   b. neap tide.
   c. spring tide.
   d. rip current.

4. Ocean water is more dense than fresh water at the same temperature because of
   a. pressure.
   b. the Coriolis effect.
   c. upwelling.
   d. salinity.

5. Winds and currents move in curved paths because of
   a. the Coriolis effect.
   b. longshore drift.
   c. wave height.
   d. tides.

6. Cold and warm ocean water is carried around the world by
   a. spring tides.
   b. neap tides.
   c. currents.
   d. tsunamis.

Writing in Science

Essay Suppose you were planning to take part in an around-the-world sailing race. Write a short essay about the knowledge of currents that you will need to prepare for the race.

Ocean Motions

Video Preview
Video Field Trip
▶ Video Assessment

Review and Assessment

Checking Concepts

7. What factors influence the size of a wave?

8. Why does the height of a wave change as it approaches shore?

9. How does a rip current form?

10. Why are there two high tides a day in most places?

11. What is a spring tide? How does it differ from a neap tide?

12. Name two properties of ocean water affected by salinity. How does salinity affect each?

13. What is the Coriolis effect? How does it influence ocean currents?

14. How do warm-water currents influence climate?

15. What is El Niño? What are some of its effects?

16. Describe the cause and effects of upwelling.

Thinking Critically

17. **Predicting** How will the duck's location change as the wave moves? Explain your answer.

Direction of wave

18. **Applying Concepts** Would you expect the salinity of the ocean to be high or low in a rainy region near the mouth of a river? Why?

19. **Comparing and Contrasting** In what ways is the ocean at 1,000 meters deep different from the ocean at the surface in the same location?

20. **Relating Cause and Effect** How does the movement of ocean currents explain the fact that much of western Europe has a mild, wet climate?

21. **Classifying** Classify the following movements of ocean water by stating whether or not each is caused by winds: waves, tides, surface currents, deep currents, upwelling.

Math Practice

22. **Calculating Density** Two 1-liter samples of water were taken from the ocean. Both have the same salinity. Sample A has a mass of 1.02 kg. Sample B has a mass of 1.05 kg. Which sample was taken during the colder weather? Explain your answer.

Applying Skills

Use the data to answer Questions 23–25.

The temperature readings in the table were obtained in the Atlantic Ocean near Bermuda.

Ocean Temperatures

Depth (m)	Temp. (°C)	Depth (m)	Temp. (°C)
0	19	1,000	9
200	18	1,200	5
400	18	1,400	5
600	16	1,600	4
800	12	1,800	4

23. **Graphing** Construct a line graph using the data in the table. Plot depth readings on the horizontal axis and temperature readings on the vertical axis.

24. **Drawing Conclusions** Use your graph to identify the temperature range in the transition zone.

25. **Predicting** Predict how the ocean temperature at depths of 0 meters and at 1,400 meters would change with the seasons in this location. Explain your reasoning.

Lab zone Chapter **Project**

Performance Assessment Using your model, present your method of shoreline protection to the class. Show your classmates how the method you chose protects the lighthouse from ocean waves and the beach erosion that can result.

Standardized Test Prep

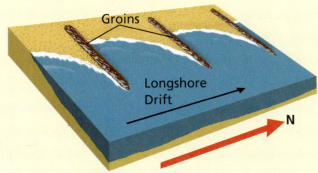
Choose the letter of the best answer.

1. A scientist plans to test the effect temperature has on the density of ocean water. What will the manipulated variable be in her experiment?
  A density   **B** salinity
  C temperature   **D** water depth

2. In which of the following areas would the salinity of the ocean water be the highest?
  F in a hot, dry area
  G near a rainy coastal area close to the equator
  H at the mouth of a large river
  J in cold, deep water, near the ocean bottom

3. A major warm ocean surface current flows along a coastal area. What type of climate would you most likely find in the area influenced by the current?
  A extremely hot and dry
  B cool and dry
  C extremely cool and wet
  D mild and wet

Use the wave diagram below and your knowledge of science to answer Questions 4–5.

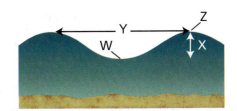

4. What is the wave feature labeled **W** in the diagram?
  F wave crest
  G wave trough
  H wavelength
  J wave height

5. What is the wave feature labeled **Y** in the diagram?
  A wave crest
  B wave trough
  C wavelength
  D wave height

Constructed Response

6. Some people refer to a tsunami as a tidal wave. Explain why this is incorrect. In your answer, describe what a tsunami is and how it forms.

Chapter

4

Ocean Zones

Interactive Textbook

Sea stars and green sea anemones color this tide pool. ▶

At Home in the Sea

Marine organisms are able to thrive in all ocean habitats, from sandy tropical beaches to the cold depths of the ocean floor. In this project, you will create a model of one ocean habitat.

Your Goal To build a three-dimensional model of a marine habitat and include some of the organisms that live there

To complete the project successfully, you will need to

- include the significant physical features of the habitat
- create a life-size model of one organism that lives in the habitat
- write an explanation of how the organism is adapted to its habitat
- follow the safety guidelines in Appendix A

Plan It! Begin now by previewing the visuals in the chapter to identify different ocean habitats. With your group, discuss which habitat you would like to learn more about. Make a list of questions you have about the habitat. Choose the materials you will need to build your model, then sketch your design. After your teacher approves your plan, begin to build the model and plan your written report.

Exploring the Ocean

Reading Preview

Key Concepts
- For what reasons have people studied the ocean?
- What are the main sections of the ocean floor?
- What processes have shaped the ocean floor?

Key Terms
- sonar • continental shelf
- continental slope
- abyssal plain
- mid-ocean ridge • trench
- plate • seafloor spreading

🎯 Target Reading Skill

Building Vocabulary A definition states the meaning of a word or phrase by telling about its most important feature or function. After you read the section, reread the paragraphs that contain definitions of Key Terms. Use all the information you have learned to write a definition of each Key Term in your own words.

What Can You Learn Without Seeing?

1. Your teacher will provide your group with ten plastic drinking straws and a covered box containing a mystery object. The top of the box has several holes punched in it. Using the straws as probes, try to determine the size, shape, and location of the object inside the box.
2. Based on the information you gathered, describe your object. What can you say about its length, shape, and position? Write down your hypothesis about the identity of the object.
3. Remove the box top to reveal the object.

Think It Over

Inferring Explain how you used the method of indirect observation to learn about the object.

Imagine going on a voyage around the world that will last three and a half years. Your assignment: to investigate everything about the sea. Your vessel: a ship powered by sails and a steam engine. On board there are thermometers for measuring the temperature of ocean water and cable for lowering dredges beneath the surface. With the dredges, you scrape sand, muck, and rock from the ocean floor. You drag nets behind the ship to collect ocean organisms.

The crew of a British ship, HMS *Challenger*, began such a voyage in 1872. By the end of the journey, scientists on the ship had gathered enough data to fill 50 volumes and had collected more than 4,000 new organisms! The scientists learned about ocean-water chemistry, currents, ocean life, and the shape of the ocean floor. The voyage of the *Challenger* was so successful that it became the model for many later ocean expeditions.

◀ HMS *Challenger*

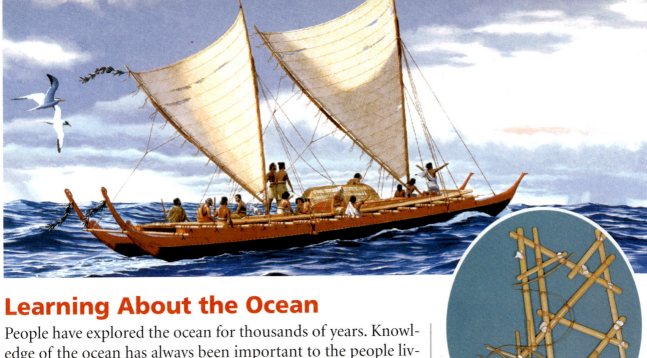

Learning About the Ocean

People have explored the ocean for thousands of years. Knowledge of the ocean has always been important to the people living along its coasts. **People have studied the ocean since ancient times, because the ocean provides food and serves as a route for trade and travel. Modern scientists have studied the characteristics of the ocean's waters and the ocean floor.**

Trading Routes The Phoenicians, who lived along the Mediterranean Sea, were one of the earliest cultures to explore the oceans. By about 1200 B.C., they had established sea routes for trade with other nations around the Mediterranean. After the Phoenicians, people of many European, African, and Asian cultures sailed along the coasts to trade with distant lands.

In the Pacific Ocean around 2,000 years ago, the Polynesians left the safety of their islands and boldly sailed into the open ocean. Their knowledge of winds and currents enabled the Polynesians to settle the widely scattered islands of Hawaii, Tahiti, and New Zealand. To navigate the ocean, they used devices such as the one shown in Figure 1.

Scientific Discoveries As modern science developed and trade increased, ocean exploration changed. Nations needed accurate maps of the oceans and lands bordering them. Governments also wanted their countries to be known for new scientific discoveries. For example, in the late 1700s, the British government hired Captain James Cook to lead three voyages of exploration. Cook's crew included scientists who studied the stars and those who collected new species of plants and animals.

Within a century of Cook's voyages, almost all of Earth's coastlines had been mapped. Scientists then turned to the study of the ocean's waters. The *Challenger* expedition marked the beginning of the modern science of oceanography.

FIGURE 1
Polynesian Explorers
Around 2,000 years ago, Polynesians explored the Pacific Ocean in boats such as the one above. They used stick charts (above right) to navigate.
Inferring *Why is careful navigation important to explorers?*

Exploring the Ocean Floor Until recently, the ocean floor was unexplored. Why did it take so long to reach the ocean floor? Studying the ocean floor is difficult because the ocean is so deep—3.8 kilometers deep on average, more than twice as deep as the Grand Canyon. At such depths, conditions are very harsh. First, because sunlight does not penetrate far below the surface, the deep ocean is in total darkness. Second, the water is very cold. Finally, deep ocean water exerts tremendous pressure due to the mass of water pushing down from above.

Humans cannot survive the darkness, cold temperatures, and extreme pressure of the deep ocean. So scientists have had to develop technology to study the ocean floor. Many of the inventions have involved indirect methods of gathering information.

• Tech & Design in History •

Ocean Exploration
The timeline includes several inventions that have helped scientists overcome the challenges of studying the oceans.

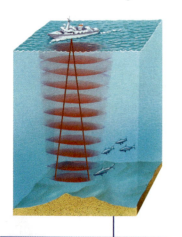

1943 SCUBA
Jacques Cousteau and Emile Gagnan invented SCUBA, which stands for "**s**elf **c**ontained **u**nderwater **b**reathing **a**pparatus." A tank containing compressed air is strapped to the diver's back and connected by a tube to a mouthpiece. SCUBA enables divers to explore to a depth of 40 meters.

1960 Submersibles
Explorers traveled to the bottom of Challenger Deep, 11 kilometers below the ocean surface, protected by the thick metal hull of the submersible *Trieste*.

1925 Sonar
Scientists aboard the German ship *Meteor* used sonar to map the ocean floor. They used a device called an echo sounder to produce pulses of sound. The ship's crew then timed the return of the echoes.

| 1920 | 1940 | 1960 |

One of the simplest methods, used by the *Challenger*'s crew, was to lower a weight on a long line into the water until the weight touched the bottom. The length of line that got wet was approximately equal to the water's depth. However, this method was slow and often inaccurate.

A major advance in ocean-floor mapping was **sonar,** which stands for **so**und **na**vigation and **r**anging. Sonar is a system that uses sound waves to calculate the distance to an object. The sonar equipment on a ship sends out pulses of sound that bounce off the ocean floor. The equipment then measures how quickly the sound waves return to the ship. Sound waves return quickly if the ocean floor is close. Sound waves take longer to return if the ocean floor is farther away.

✓ **Reading Checkpoint** What conditions exist in the depths of the ocean?

Writing in Science

Research and Write Each of the inventions shown in this timeline helped solve a challenge of ocean exploration. Find out more about one of these inventions. Write a short newspaper article telling the story of its development. Include details about the people who invented it and how it added to people's knowledge of the oceans.

1978 Satellites

Seasat A was the first satellite in Earth's orbit to study the oceans. Since satellites make millions of observations a day, they can provide data on rapidly changing ocean conditions. Such data include temperatures, algae growth patterns, and even the movement of large schools of fish.

1986 Remote Underwater Manipulator

The Remote Underwater Manipulator, or RUM III, is about the size of a small car. It is controlled by a computer aboard a ship at the surface. The RUM III can collect samples, take photographs, and map the ocean floor—all without a crew.

2003 Deep Flight Aviator

The Deep Flight Aviator, a new type of submersible, is launched in San Francisco Bay. Deep Flight Aviators maneuver faster and much more easily than other submersibles. Passengers can see much more, too.

| 1980 | 2000 | 2020 |

Features of the Ocean Floor

Once scientists were able to map the ocean floor, they discovered something surprising. The ocean floor was not a flat, sandy plain. The deep waters hid mountain ranges bigger than any on land, as well as deep canyons reaching into Earth's interior. If you could take a submarine voyage along the ocean floor, what would you see? **If you could travel along the ocean floor, you would see the continental shelf, the continental slope, the abyssal plain, and the mid-ocean ridge.** Trace your journey from the edge of one continent to the edge of another in Figure 2.

Shallow Water As you leave the harbor, your submarine first passes over the **continental shelf,** a gently sloping, shallow area of the ocean floor that extends outward from the edge of a continent. At a depth of about 130 meters, the slope of the ocean floor gets steeper. The steep edge of the continental shelf is called the **continental slope.** The continental slope marks the true edge of a continent, where the rock that makes up the continent stops and the rock of the ocean floor begins.

FIGURE 2
The Ocean Floor

The floor of the ocean has mountains, slopes, and other features. To show the major features of the ocean floor, thousands of kilometers have been "squeezed" into one illustration.
Interpreting Diagrams *Which is steeper, the continental slope or the continental shelf?*

Volcanic Island
When volcanoes on the ocean floor erupt, they can create mountains whose peaks break the surface of the ocean. As the lava cools, islands form.

Seamount
Mountains whose peaks do not break the surface of the ocean water above them are called seamounts.

Continental shelf

Continental slope

Abyssal Plain
Thick layers of sediment, formed by the sunken remains of dead organisms from the surface, cover these vast, flat plains.

Average depth of ocean: 3.8 km

Width of ocean: thousands of kilometers

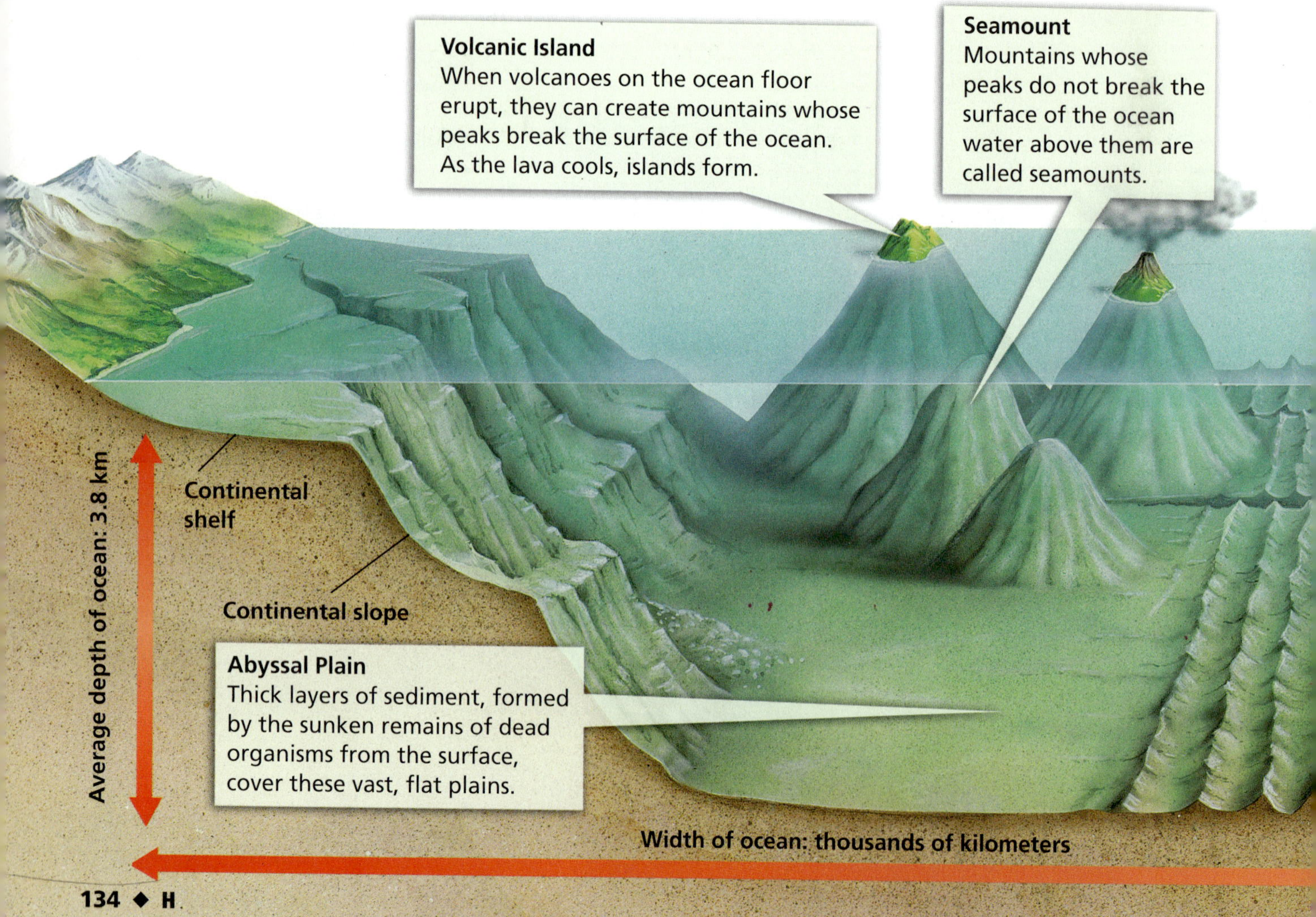

Open Ocean Your submarine descends more gradually now, following the ocean floor as it slopes toward the deep ocean. After some distance, you encounter a group of mountains. Some are tall enough to break the ocean's surface, forming islands. Others, called seamounts, are mountains that are completely underwater. Some seamounts have flat tops because their peaks have eroded away.

Next you cross a broad area covered with thick layers of mud and silt. This smooth, nearly flat region of the ocean floor is called the **abyssal plain** (uh BIHS ul). After gliding over the abyssal plain for many kilometers, you need to steer the submarine sharply upward to avoid a mountain range ahead. The **mid-ocean ridge** is a continuous range of mountains that winds around Earth, much as the line of stitches winds around a baseball. The mid-ocean ridge passes through all of Earth's oceans. Nearly 80,000 kilometers long, it is the longest mountain range on Earth.

Ocean Zones

Video Preview
▶ **Video Field Trip**
Video Assessment

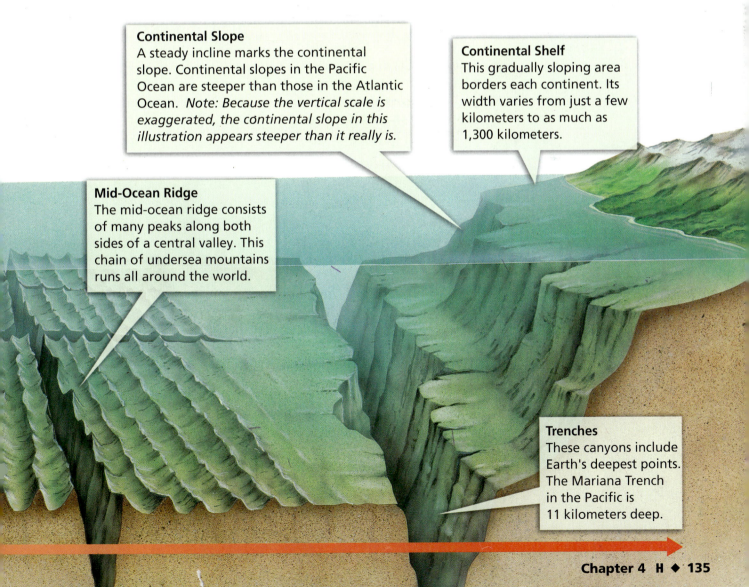

Continental Slope
A steady incline marks the continental slope. Continental slopes in the Pacific Ocean are steeper than those in the Atlantic Ocean. *Note: Because the vertical scale is exaggerated, the continental slope in this illustration appears steeper than it really is.*

Continental Shelf
This gradually sloping area borders each continent. Its width varies from just a few kilometers to as much as 1,300 kilometers.

Mid-Ocean Ridge
The mid-ocean ridge consists of many peaks along both sides of a central valley. This chain of undersea mountains runs all around the world.

Trenches
These canyons include Earth's deepest points. The Mariana Trench in the Pacific is 11 kilometers deep.

FIGURE 3

The Ocean Depths

On the dark ocean floor, huge masses of shrimp feed near a black smoker—a vent in the ocean floor that releases very hot, mineral-rich water.

Deepest Depths At the top of the mid-ocean ridge, your submarine is about two kilometers above the abyssal plain, but you are still at least one kilometer below the surface. From this vantage you can see that the mid-ocean ridge actually consists of two parallel chains of mountains separated by a central valley.

You cross the ocean floor from the mid-ocean ridge toward the abyssal plain. Soon your submarine's lights reveal a dark gash in the ocean floor ahead of you. As you pass over it, you look down into a canyon in the ocean floor called a **trench.** The trench is so deep you cannot see the bottom.

Your journey is nearly over as your submarine slowly climbs the continental slope. Finally you cross the continental shelf and maneuver the submarine into harbor.

Reading Checkpoint Which ocean-floor feature makes up the deepest parts of the ocean?

Movements of the Ocean Floor

As oceanographers mapped the ocean floor, their measurements told them about the features you saw on your imaginary journey between the continents. To gather more information about the floor of the deep ocean, scientists used a drilling ship named *Glomar Challenger*, in honor of the original *Challenger*.

The scientists collected samples of rock from the ocean floor. They drilled the rock samples from both sides of the mid-ocean ridge in the Atlantic Ocean. Tests on the samples showed that the rock closest to the ridge had formed much more recently than the rock farther away from the ridge. This information helped explain how the ocean floor formed. To understand how the ocean floor formed, you need to be familiar with Earth's structure.

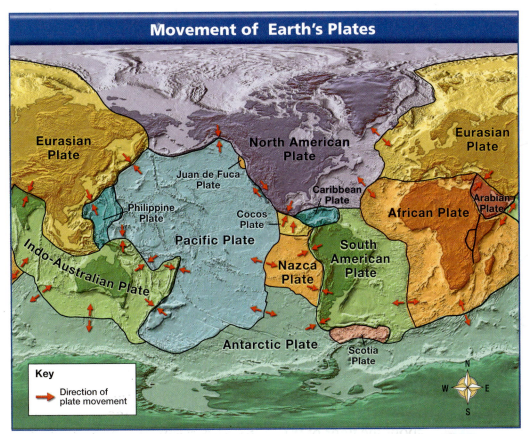

Movement of Earth's Plates

Eurasian Plate

North American Plate

Eurasian Plate

Juan de Fuca Plate

Caribbean Plate

African Plate

Arabian Plate

Philippine Plate

Cocos Plate

Pacific Plate

Indo-Australian Plate

Nazca Plate

South American Plate

Antarctic Plate

Scotia Plate

Key

→ Direction of plate movement

N W E S

Layers Inside Earth Earth consists of layers that cover the planet's center, or core. The thin, rocky, outer layer of Earth is called the crust. The thick layer between the crust and the core is the mantle. The high temperature inside Earth causes some of the material in the mantle to form a hot liquid called magma. Magma flows very slowly. It can escape upward through cracks in the crust and erupting volcanoes. Magma that reaches the surface is called lava. As lava cools, it forms new crust.

Earth's Plates Earth's crust is solid rock that is broken into irregularly shaped pieces like the shell of a cracked, hard-boiled egg. The pieces of Earth's crust, along with parts of the upper mantle, are called **plates.** Such plates move slowly on the underlying portion of the mantle.

About 14 major plates make up Earth's crust, as shown in Figure 4. They lie beneath the continents as well as the oceans. The plates move at an average speed of several centimeters per year—barely faster than your fingernails grow! Where two plates come together or spread apart, they create features such as mountains and trenches. **Plate movements have shaped many of the most dramatic features of Earth, both on land and under the ocean.** The sea floor, trenches, underwater volcanoes, and the mountain ranges of the mid-ocean ridges have all been formed by the interactions of Earth's plates.

FIGURE 4
Earth's Plates
Earth's crust and upper mantle are divided into 14 major plates.
Interpreting Maps
Name the plates that lie beneath parts of the continent of North America.

Go Online
SciLINKS ⟨NSTA⟩

For: Links on plate tectonics
Visit: www.SciLinks.org
Web Code: scn-0841

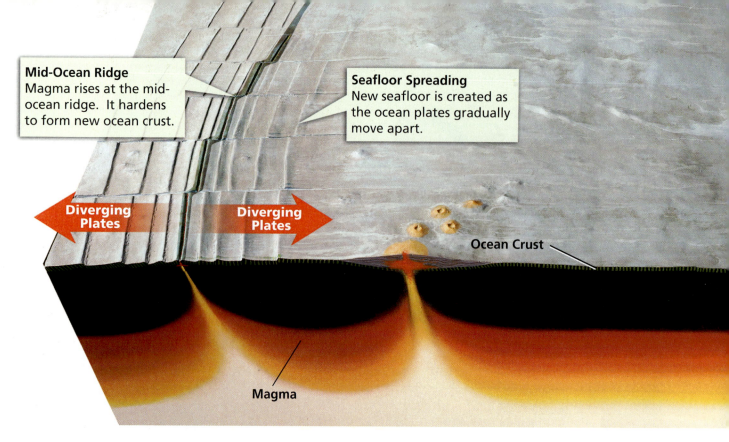

Mid-Ocean Ridge
Magma rises at the mid-ocean ridge. It hardens to form new ocean crust.

Seafloor Spreading
New seafloor is created as the ocean plates gradually move apart.

Diverging Plates

Diverging Plates

Ocean Crust

Magma

FIGURE 5

Moving Plates Beneath the Ocean

Where two plates diverge, magma from Earth's mantle rises up through the crack. Where two plates converge at a trench, one plate sinks under the other.
Interpreting Diagrams What happens when magma rises to the surface of the ocean floor?

Plates Moving Apart The mid-ocean ridge is located along the boundaries between plates that are moving apart, or diverging. Along the ridge, magma squeezes up through the cracks between the diverging plates. As the magma hardens along the ridge, it adds a new strip of rock to the ocean floor. Over millions of years, this process, called **seafloor spreading,** has produced the ocean floor.

The rock samples collected by the *Glomar Challenger* helped confirm the theory of seafloor spreading. Scientific analysis showed that the rocks closer to the ridge had been produced more recently than those farther away.

Plates Moving Together When the new ocean floor grows along the mid-ocean ridge, where does the old ocean floor farther away from the ridge go? Why doesn't Earth keep getting bigger? The answers to these questions lie in the deep ocean trenches you read about earlier. Where plates come together, or converge, one plate sinks under the other, as shown in Figure 5. As new rock is added along the mid-ocean ridge, old rock farther away from the mid-ocean ridge sinks into the trenches. The sinking rock is pushed back into Earth's interior. This process allows the ocean floor to spread while Earth itself remains the same size.

 **Reading Checkpoint** What happens to magma during seafloor spreading?

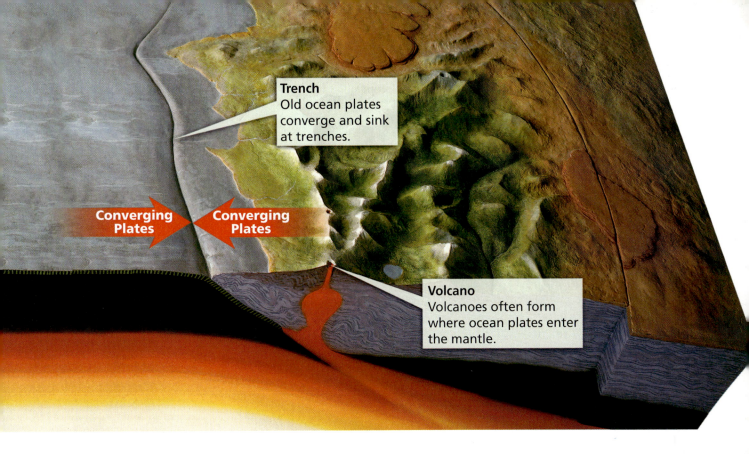

Trench
Old ocean plates converge and sink at trenches.

Converging Plates **Converging Plates**

Volcano
Volcanoes often form where ocean plates enter the mantle.

Section 1 Assessment

Target Reading Skill **Building Vocabulary** Use your definitions to help answer the questions below.

Reviewing Key Concepts

1. a. **Reviewing** What features of the ocean have modern scientists investigated?
   b. **Relating Cause and Effect** Why has this investigation been difficult?
   c. **Problem Solving** What is sonar? Explain how it has helped scientists solve problems associated with ocean investigation.

2. a. **Listing** List the four main sections of the ocean floor.
   b. **Interpreting Diagrams** Refer to Figure 2. Describe the characteristics of each of the four sections of the ocean floor that you listed above. Include specific features found in each section.

3. a. **Defining** What are Earth's plates?
   b. **Relating Cause and Effect** What is seafloor spreading? How does it relate to the behavior of Earth's plates?
   c. **Comparing and Contrasting** Compare the process of seafloor spreading to the process that occurs when plates converge.

Lab zone **At-Home Activity**

Mapping the Ocean With a family member, choose a room in your house and make a "room-floor" map based on depth readings. Imagine that the ceiling is the ocean surface and the floor is the bottom of the ocean. Follow a straight path across the middle of the room from one wall to another. At regular intervals, use a carpenter's measuring tape to take a depth reading from the ceiling to the floor or to the top of any furniture in that spot. Plot the depths on a graph. Then challenge another family member to identify the room by looking at the graph.

The Shape of the Ocean Floor

Nova Scotia, Canada

Soulac, France

Problem

Imagine you are an oceanographer traveling across the Atlantic along the 45° N latitude line marked on the map. You are gathering data on the depth of the ocean between Nova Scotia, Canada, and Soulac, France. How can you use data to determine the shape of the ocean floor?

Skills Focus

graphing, predicting, inferring

Materials

- pencil
- graph paper

Procedure

1. Draw the axes of a graph. Label the horizontal axis *Longitude*. Mark from 65° W to 0° from left to right. Label the vertical axis *Ocean Depth*. Mark 0 meters at the top of the vertical axis to represent sea level. Mark –5,000 meters at the bottom to represent the depth of 5,000 meters below sea level. Mark depths at equal intervals along the vertical axis.

2. Examine the data in the table. The numbers in the Longitude column give the ship's location at 19 points in the Atlantic Ocean. Location 1 is Nova Scotia, and Location 19 is Soulac. The numbers in the Ocean Depth column give the depth measurements recorded at each location. Plot each measurement on your graph. Remember that the depths are represented on your graph as numbers below 0, or sea level.

3. Connect the points you have plotted with a line to create a profile of the ocean floor.

Analyze and Conclude

1. **Graphing** On your graph, identify and label the continental shelf and continental slope.

2. **Predicting** Label the abyssal plain on your graph. How would you expect the ocean floor to look there?

3. **Graphing** Label the mid-ocean ridge on your graph. Describe the process that is occurring there.

4. **Inferring** What might the feature at 10° W be? Explain.

5. **Communicating** Imagine you are traveling along the ocean floor from Nova Scotia, Canada, to Soulac, France. Describe the features you would see along your journey.

More to Explore

Use the depth measurements in the table to calculate the average depth of the Atlantic Ocean between Nova Scotia and France.

Ocean Depth Sonar Data			
Longitude	Ocean Depth (m)	Longitude	Ocean Depth (m)
1. 64° W	0	11. 28° W	1,756
2. 60° W	91	12. 27° W	2,195
3. 55° W	132	13. 25° W	3,146
4. 50° W	73	14. 20° W	4,244
5. 48° W	3,512	15. 15° W	4,610
6. 45° W	4,024	16. 10° W	4,976
7. 40° W	3,805	17. 05° W	4,317
8. 35° W	4,171	18. 04° W	146
9. 33° W	3,439	19. 01° W	0
10. 30° W	3,073		

Ocean Habitats

Reading Preview

Key Concepts
- Into what zones do scientists divide the ocean?
- How are marine organisms classified?

Key Terms
- intertidal zone • neritic zone
- open-ocean zone • plankton
- nekton • benthos • food web

Target Reading Skill
Using Prior Knowledge Your prior knowledge is what you already know before you read about a topic. Before you read, write what you know about conditions that might determine where ocean organisms live. Use a graphic organizer like the one below. As you read, continue to write in what you learn.

What You Know
1. Many organisms need sunlight.
2.

What You Learned
1.
2.

Lab zone **Discover Activity**

How Complex Are Ocean Feeding Relationships?

1. Form a circle of five students. Each student will represent one of the following marine organisms: algae, shrimp, fish, sea otter, and whale. Each student should write the name of his or her organism on a card.
2. Discuss the possible feeding relationships among the five organisms. What might your organism eat? What might eat the organism you represent?
3. Use pieces of string to connect your card to the cards of all the organisms that may have feeding relationships with your organism.

Think It Over
Inferring Based on your results in Step 3, are the feeding relationships among ocean organisms simple or complex? Explain your answer.

At first glance, an ocean may seem lifeless. As you walk along the beach, your feet sink in the soft, wet sand. You may notice some dark, tangled seaweed that has washed up on the shore. A few sea gulls screech and swoop overhead. Otherwise, all is calm. You stop to gaze out at the horizon. The ocean stretches as far as the eye can see. Waves crash against the shore. But you see no sign of life in the water.

Look closer. Right beneath your feet you can see evidence of living things. Tiny, round holes are signs of burrowing clams. These clams dig down into the sand. This burrowing enables the clams to hide from predators and avoid being washed away by the tide. If you wade into the water, you may be able to spot a sand crab feeding in the surf. And far out to sea, a school of dolphins swims by. Their bodies form graceful arcs as they dive in and out of the water. An ocean may seem lifeless, but many different organisms inhabit this vast, watery environment.

A sea gull ▶

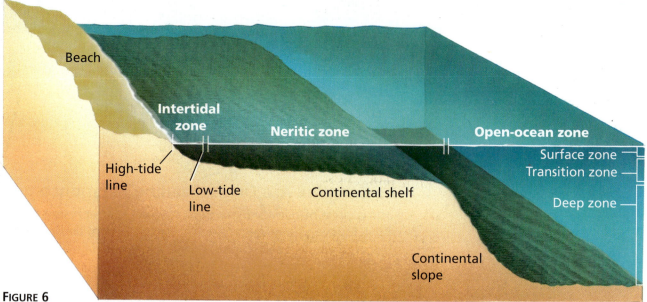

Beach

High-tide line

Intertidal zone

Low-tide line

Neritic zone

Open-ocean zone

Surface zone
Transition zone

Deep zone

Continental shelf

Continental slope

FIGURE 6
Ocean Zones
The three ocean zones are the intertidal zone, the neritic zone, and the open-ocean zone.
Classifying *Into what three zones is the open-ocean zone divided?*

Feeling the Pressure

1. ✂ Use a pen to poke two similar holes in an empty milk carton. One hole should be about one third of the way from the bottom. The other hole should be about two thirds of the way from the bottom.

2. Cover the holes with tape. Then fill the carton with water.

3. Hold the carton over a sink. Remove the tape. Note any differences in the flow of water from the two holes.

Making Models What physical condition in the ocean does this activity model? In which ocean zone is this condition most significant?

Ocean Zones and Conditions

You can think of the ocean as a huge community that includes living and nonliving things. In some ways, the ocean community resembles a human city or town. Typically, cities and towns are divided into several zones. Some zones consist mostly of houses and apartment buildings. Other zones have stores and shops or factories and office buildings.

Ocean Zones The ocean, too, can be divided into zones, as shown in Figure 6. Your walk on the sandy beach, for example, took place in the intertidal zone. **Ocean zones include the intertidal zone, the neritic zone, and the open-ocean zone.** At the highest high-tide line on land, the **intertidal zone** begins. From there, the zone stretches out to the point on the continental shelf exposed by the lowest low tide. The **neritic zone** extends from the low-tide line out to the edge of the continental shelf. Beyond the edge of the continental shelf lies the **open-ocean zone.** This zone includes the deepest, darkest part of the ocean. You will learn more about these ocean zones in Section 3 and Section 4.

Physical Conditions Each ocean zone has its characteristic physical conditions. These conditions help determine which organisms can live in that zone. For example, light does not penetrate very far beneath the ocean's surface. Organisms that need light for photosynthesis must live near the surface of the ocean. In contrast, in the deep ocean, pressure is high. Organisms that live deep in the ocean must be able to withstand this force.

 **Reading Checkpoint** **Which ocean zone is farthest from shore?**

Life in the Ocean

On land, most organisms live on or near the surface. The ocean, on the other hand, is inhabited by organisms at every depth. **Scientists classify marine organisms according to where they live and how they move.** Figure 7 shows the three categories of ocean organisms—plankton, nekton, and benthos.

Plankton Plankton are tiny algae and animals that float in the water and are carried by waves and currents. Algae plankton include geometrically shaped diatoms. Animal plankton include some tiny young fish and microscopic crustaceans, such as copepods.

Nekton Nekton are free-swimming animals that can move throughout the water column. Squid, most fishes, and marine mammals such as whales and seals are nekton.

Benthos Benthos are organisms that inhabit the ocean floor. Some benthos, like crabs, sea stars, octopus, and lobsters, move from place to place. Others, like sponges and sea anemones, stay in one location.

 **Reading Checkpoint** Are sharks plankton, nekton, or benthos? Why?

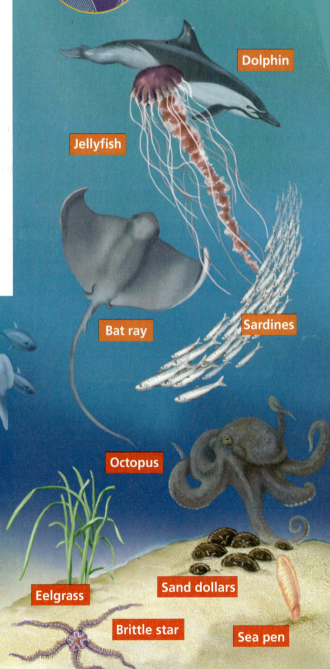

FIGURE 7
Marine Organisms
Marine organisms can be classified as plankton, nekton, or benthos.

Diatoms

Copepods

Dolphin

Jellyfish

Bat ray

Sardines

Key
- Plankton
- Nekton
- Benthos

Ocean sunfish

Octopus

Sturgeon

Eelgrass

Sand dollars

Crab

Brittle star

Sea pen

ne
tive art

n Food Web activity
.School.com
ode: cfp-3042

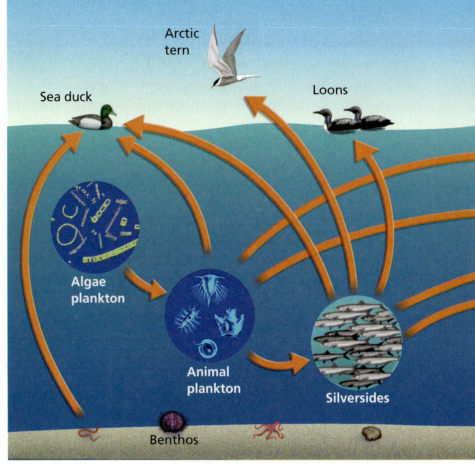

Arctic
tern

Sea duck

Loons

Algae
plankton

Animal
plankton

Silversides

Benthos

FIGURE 8

An Ocean Food Web

This ocean food web includes typical organisms found in the Arctic Ocean. The arrows indicate what each organism eats. **Interpreting Diagrams** *Which organisms feed directly on the Arctic cod? Which organisms depend indirectly on the cod?*

Relationships Among Organisms Plankton, nekton, and benthos are all found in most marine habitats. Many plankton and benthos are algae. Like plants, algae use sunlight to produce their own food through photosynthesis. Photosynthetic plankton are called producers. Other plankton and benthos, as well as all nekton, eat either algae or other organisms. They are called consumers. Finally, some organisms, including many benthos, break down wastes and the remains of other organisms. They are called decomposers.

Ocean Food Webs All of the feeding relationships that exist in a habitat make up a **food web.** A typical ocean food web is shown in Figure 8. Each organism in this Arctic food web depends either directly or indirectly on the algae plankton. Throughout the ocean, plankton are a source of food for other organisms of all sizes. If you think of sharks as sharp-toothed, meat-eating hunters, you might be surprised to learn that the biggest sharks of all feed directly on tiny plankton! Many whales, including Earth's largest animal—the blue whale—also feed only on plankton.

 **Reading Checkpoint** Which organisms in an ocean food web are the producers?

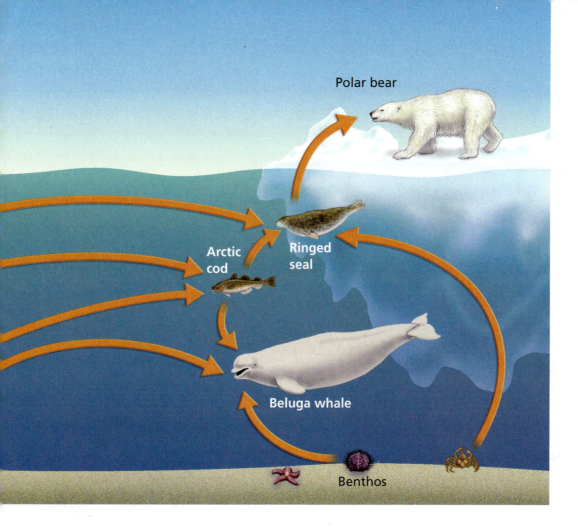

Polar bear

Arctic cod

Ringed seal

Beluga whale

Benthos

Section 2 Assessment

🎯 **Target Reading Skill** **Using Prior Knowledge**
Review your graphic organizer and revise it based on what you just learned in the section.

Reviewing Key Concepts

1. a. **Identifying** Identify the three ocean zones.
   b. **Sequencing** Put the ocean zones in order, beginning with the zone in which the water is least deep and ending with the zone that is deepest.
   c. **Inferring** Which zone probably has the greatest variety of living things? How is this variety related to the water's depth?

2. a. **Reviewing** What characteristics do scientists use to classify ocean organisms?
   b. **Describing** Identify the three categories of ocean organisms and describe their characteristics.

c. **Classifying** Sea cucumbers are small animals that crawl along the ocean floor. To which category of ocean organisms do they belong? Explain.

Writing in Science

Cause and Effect Paragraph Write a brief paragraph describing how the ocean food web in Figure 8 might be affected by a decrease in the Arctic cod population. Which populations might increase as a result and why? Which populations might decrease and why? To help plan your writing, you might use a cause-and-effect graphic organizer.

Intertidal Zone

Reading Preview

Key Concepts
- What conditions must organisms in the rocky intertidal zone tolerate?
- What are the major types of coastal wetlands?

Key Term
- estuary

🎯 Target Reading Skill
Outlining As you read, make an outline about the intertidal zone. Use the red headings for the main topics and the blue headings for the subtopics.

Intertidal Zone
I. Rocky shores
A. Along the rocks
B.
II. Where river meets ocean

Discover Activity

Can Your Animal Hold On?

1. Your teacher will give you a ping-pong ball, a rock, and some other materials. The ping-pong ball represents an ocean animal. Design a way for the animal to cling to the rock.
2. Attach the ping-pong ball to the rock.
3. Place the rock in a sink or deep pan. Run water over the rock. Observe how well your animal stays in place on the rock.

Think It Over

Inferring How might the ability to "hold on" be important to an animal that lives on the shore?

Imagine that your home has no walls or roof. Twice a day, a huge storm passes through, bringing a drenching downpour and winds so strong you can hardly keep your balance. At other times, the sun beats down, heating you and leaving you dry. This is what life is like for organisms that live on rocky shores, where the land meets the sea.

Rocky Shores

A rocky shore is one type of habitat found in the intertidal zone. You read about sandy shores, another type, in Section 2. **Organisms that live in the rocky intertidal zone must be able to tolerate the pounding of the waves and changes in both salinity and temperature. They must also withstand periods of being underwater and periods of being exposed to the air.** They must avoid drying out, hide from predators, and find food in this harsh setting. Luckily, they are well suited to these tasks.

Intertidal zone

Sea urchin

Abalone

Brittle star

Sea anemones

Sea lettuce

Along the Rocks Rocky shores are found along much of both coasts of the United States. Figure 9 shows some of the colorful organisms that typically live along the California coast.

The highest rocks, above the highest high-tide line, make up the spray zone. The spray zone is never completely covered with water, but it gets wet as the waves break against the rocks. A stripe of black algae indicates the highest high-tide line.

The rocks below this level are covered with barnacles. Barnacles can close up their hard shells. This action traps a drop of water inside to carry the barnacles through the dry period until the next high tide. The rocks are also home to flat animals called limpets. Limpets have a large, muscular foot that allows them to hold tightly to the rocks. They release drops of mucus around the edges of their shells. The mucus forms a tight seal.

In Tide Pools When the tide goes out, some water remains in depressions among the rocks called tide pools. As the water in a tide pool is warmed by the sun, the water begins to evaporate. The remaining water becomes saltier. If it rains, however, the salinity quickly decreases. Organisms in the tide pool must be able to withstand these changes in temperature and salinity. Tide-pool organisms must also withstand the force of the waves when the tide comes in again.

Sea stars cling to the rocks with rows of tiny suction cups. Spiny sea urchins crawl slowly along the bottom of the tide pool. If the bottom is sandy, a sea urchin can use its spines to dig a hole. The sea urchin buries itself in the hole during heavy surf.

Under shady rock ledges, sponges and sea anemones wait for the incoming tide to bring a fresh supply of plankton and other food particles. Most sea anemones look delicate. However, some sea anemones can survive out of water for more than two weeks. When out of the water, the anemone pulls its tentacles inside and folds up into a round blob.

 **Reading Checkpoint** How are sea stars able to cling to rocks?

FIGURE 9
A Rocky Shore
The constantly changing water level along a rocky shore in the intertidal zone creates different habitats.
Comparing and Contrasting How are conditions different for organisms near the top of the rocks compared to organisms at the bottom?

Rock lice

Blackline algae

Highest high tide

Barnacles

Periwinkle

Rockweed

Lowest high tide

Mussels

Chitons

Sea star

Highest low tide

Sea anemone

Hermit crab

Limpets

Lowest low tide

FIGURE 10
A Mangrove Forest
Arching prop roots anchor these mangrove trees firmly in the soft, sandy soil.
Relating Cause and Effect How do mangrove forests protect the coastline?

▲ **Roseate spoonbill**

▼ **American crocodile**

Where River Meets Ocean

Other important environments along the ocean's edge are estuaries. **Estuaries** are coastal inlets or bays where fresh water from rivers mixes with the salty ocean water. Water that is partly salty and partly fresh is brackish.

Coastal wetlands are found in and around estuaries. **Along the coasts of the United States, most wetlands are either mangrove forests or salt marshes.** Mangrove forests are found in southern Florida and along the coast of the Gulf of Mexico. Salt marshes are especially abundant along the east coast from Massachusetts to Florida.

Mangrove Forests Mangroves are short, gnarled trees that grow well in brackish water. These trees fringe the coastline of southern Florida. The mangroves' prop roots, shown in Figure 10, anchor the trees to the land. Mangroves can withstand all but the strongest hurricane winds. The mangroves break the action of winds and waves, protecting the coastline during storms. The prop roots also trap sediment from the land. They create a protected nursery, rich in nutrients, for many young animals.

Salt Marshes A salt marsh oozes with smelly mud. The mud is made up of sediments, animal and plant matter, and nutrients carried into the marsh by fresh water and tides.

Cordgrass is the most common plant in the marsh. Unlike most plants, cordgrass can survive in salt water. The plant releases salt through small openings in its long, narrow leaves. Some cordgrass is eaten by animals. The rest of the cordgrass is decomposed by bacteria and fungi in the water. The decomposed material supplies nutrients to marsh organisms.

Tidal channels run through the cordgrass. Waves break up as they enter the channels, so that organisms in the marsh are protected from the surf. Within the marsh, fish, crabs, shrimp, and oysters hatch and feed before entering the harsher ocean environment offshore. As the tide retreats, mud flats are exposed. Many crabs search for food in the rich mud. Herons, stilts, and egrets stalk across the mud to prey on the crabs and other benthos exposed by the low tide.

Protecting Estuaries The rivers that flow into estuaries can carry harmful substances. Pollutants such as pesticides, sewage, and industrial waste may end up in an estuary. Organisms that live in the estuary are affected by these pollutants.

For example, the Chesapeake Bay is a huge estuary located on the mid-Atlantic coast. It has been a rich source of oysters, clams, and blue crabs. However, pollutants from inland sources accumulated in the bay for years. Pollution, along with overfishing, greatly reduced the numbers of blue crabs in the Chesapeake Bay. When people realized the threat to the estuary, they took action. Laws were passed to regulate the water quality of rivers that empty into the Chesapeake Bay. Cleanup efforts have reduced much of the pollution in the bay. Today, pollution is less of a problem in the Chesapeake Bay than it once was.

FIGURE 11
Food From an Estuary
A crabber in the Chesapeake Bay pulls up the last trap of the day. As the health of the estuary improves, the blue crab population is increasing again.

Reading Checkpoint What has been done to help reduce pollution in the Chesapeake Bay?

Section 3 Assessment

Target Reading Skill **Outlining** Use the information in your outline about the intertidal zone to help you answer the questions below.

Reviewing Key Concepts

1. a. **Describing** What are conditions like in the rocky intertidal zone?
   b. **Explaining** Explain what a sea anemone does when it is not covered by water.
   c. **Applying Concepts** How does this behavior help the sea anemone survive in the intertidal zone?
2. a. **Identifying** Identify two types of coastal wetlands.
   b. **Comparing and Contrasting** List two ways that these environments are alike and two ways they are different.

c. **Making Judgments** A builder has proposed filling in a salt marsh to create a seaside resort. What positive and negative impacts might this action have on wildlife and local residents? Would you support the proposal? Explain.

Writing in Science

Fact Sheet Suppose you work for a national or state park that contains salt marshes. Your job is to take people on guided tours of a salt marsh. Before the tour, you distribute a fact sheet that points out the sights that visitors can expect to see. Write a fact sheet on salt marshes to distribute to park visitors. If you want, you can illustrate your fact sheet.

Neritic Zone and Open Ocean

Reading Preview

Key Concepts
- What are the conditions in the neritic zone?
- What environments support coral reefs and kelp forests?
- What are the conditions in the open ocean?

Key Terms
- atoll • bioluminescence
- hydrothermal vent

🎯 Target Reading Skill
Relating Cause and Effect As you read, identify the conditions that affect life in the neritic zone. Write the information in a graphic organizer like the one below.

Causes	Effect
☐ →	The neritic zone has a wide variety of organisms.
☐ →	

🔬Lab zone Discover **Activity**

How Deep Can You See?

1. With a permanent marker, divide a white plastic lid into four quarters. Shade in two quarters as shown.
2. ✂ Use a pair of scissors to carefully poke a small hole in the center of the lid.
3. Tie a piece of string to a paper clip. Place the clip underneath the lid and thread the string up through the hole.
4. Tape the string tightly to a meterstick so that the lid presses against the bottom of the meterstick.
5. Fill a large, deep bucket with tap water. While stirring the water, add one teaspoon of flour to represent the dissolved substances in seawater. The water should be slightly cloudy.
6. Lower the lid into the water so that it is 5 cm below the surface. Note whether the lid is still visible in the water.
7. Lower the lid 10 cm below the surface, then 15 cm, and so on until the lid is no longer visible.

Think It Over

Observing At what depth could you no longer see the lid? Based on your results, how do you think visibility changes with depth in the ocean?

▼ Sea otter in a kelp forest

Floating mats of algae on the ocean surface mark the location of a kelp forest. Bright-orange sheephead fish dart about. Young sea lions chase each other around the kelp stalks. A sea otter dives down to the rocky ocean bottom. When it rises, the otter is clutching a sea urchin between its paws. On the surface again, the otter rolls onto its back among the kelp. The otter skillfully uses its paws to scoop out the meat from the soft parts of the sea urchin.

FIGURE 12
Organisms in the Neritic Zone
Because it is so rich in nutrients, the neritic zone supports a huge variety of organisms. These include sea lions (left) and herring (below). **Inferring** *Why is the neritic zone so rich in nutrients?*

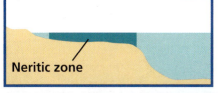

Neritic zone

Conditions in the Neritic Zone

A kelp forest is one type of habitat found in the neritic zone. Remember that the neritic zone extends from the low-tide line out to the edge of the continental shelf. A huge variety of organisms are found in the neritic zone, more than in any other ocean zone. Most of the world's major fishing grounds are found in this zone.

Why is the neritic zone home to so many living things? The answer has to do with its location over the continental shelf. **The shallow water over the continental shelf receives sunlight and a steady supply of nutrients washed from the land into the ocean. The light and nutrients enable large plantlike algae to grow.** These algae serve as a food source and shelter for other organisms.

In many parts of the neritic zone, upwelling currents bring additional nutrients from the bottom to the surface. These nutrients support large numbers of plankton, which form the base of ocean food webs. Schools of fish such as sardines and herrings feed on the plankton. Major fisheries in upwelling areas include Monterey Canyon off the California coast, Newfoundland's Grand Banks, and Georges Bank off the New England coast.

 **Reading Checkpoint** What are two ways that nutrients may be supplied to the neritic zone?

FIGURE 13
How an Atoll Forms

An atoll develops in stages, beginning with a fringing reef that surrounds a volcanic island. **Relating Cause and Effect** *For an atoll to form, what must happen to the volcanic island?*

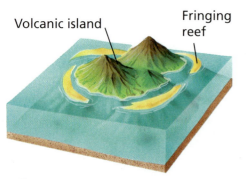

① A fringing reef closely surrounds an island.

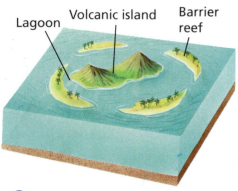

② As the island sinks, a lagoon forms inside the barrier reef.

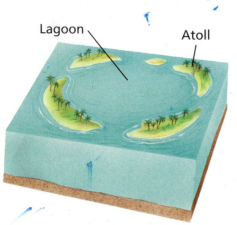

③ Finally, the island sinks, leaving a ring–shaped atoll.

Coral Reefs

A coral reef is another type of diverse habitat found in the neritic zone. Although a coral reef may look as if it is made of rock, it is actually made of living things. Coral reefs are created by colonies of tiny coral animals, each of which is not much larger than a pencil eraser. Each coral animal produces a hard structure that surrounds its soft body. After the coral dies, the empty structure remains. New coral animals attach and grow on top of it. Over many years, a reef is built.

Environment of Coral Reefs Microscopic algae live in the bodies of the coral animals and provide food for the corals. The algae need warm temperatures and sunlight. **Therefore, coral reefs can form only in shallow, tropical ocean waters.** The reefs grow above continental shelves or around volcanic islands, where the water is shallow.

Ring-Shaped Reefs In areas where the seafloor is sinking, a reef may develop over time into an atoll. An **atoll** is a ring-shaped reef surrounding a shallow lagoon. Figure 13 shows the development of an atoll. It begins as a fringing reef that closely surrounds the edges of the island. As the sea floor sinks, the island sinks with it, and the reef continues to grow upward. Water separates the top of the barrier reef from the island. The island continues to sink until it is entirely underwater, forming the atoll.

Life Around a Reef Coral can form a variety of shapes. These shapes are suggested by the names of coral species—elkhorn, brain, plate, star. Many animals live in and around a coral reef. Coral-reef animals include octopuses, spiny lobsters, shrimp, and fishes in all colors and sizes. Parrotfish scrape coral off the reef to eat. The parrotfish grind up the broken coral inside their bodies, producing the fine, soft sand commonly found around the reef.

▼ Clown fish

FIGURE 16
An Open-Ocean Organism
Orcas, or killer whales, are fierce predators of the surface zone.

Open-ocean zone

Conditions in the Open Ocean

The open ocean begins where the neritic zone ends, at the edge of the continental shelf. **The open ocean differs from the neritic zone in two important ways. First, only a small part of the open ocean receives sunlight. Second, the water has fewer nutrients.** As a result, the open ocean supports fewer organisms.

Diving into the open ocean is like walking down a long staircase that has a light only at the top. Sunlight penetrates only a short distance into the water. If the water is cloudy, sunlight does not reach as far. In clear tropical waters, however, sunlight may reach as deep as a few hundred meters.

Recall that the neritic zone receives a constant supply of nutrients from shore. In contrast, dissolved nutrients are less abundant in the open ocean.

The Surface Zone You have read that the water column in the open ocean can be divided into three zones. The surface zone extends as far as sunlight reaches below the surface. The surface zone is the only part of the open ocean that receives enough sunlight to support the growth of algae. These microscopic algae are the base of open-ocean food webs. Animal plankton that feed on the algae include shrimplike krill, as well as the young of crabs, mollusks, and fishes.

The Transition Zone The transition zone extends from the bottom of the surface zone to a depth of about 1 kilometer. The water here is darker and colder than in the surface zone.

Lab zone Skills Activity

Inferring
To keep from sinking, many plankton rely on the friction between their bodies and the surrounding water. More friction is needed to stay afloat in warm water than in denser cold water. One of the copepods below is found in tropical ocean waters, while the other is found near the poles. Which do you think is which? Explain your reasoning. (*Hint:* More streamlined shapes create less friction with their surroundings.)

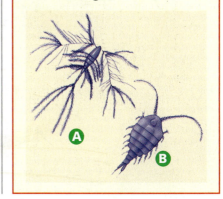

The Deep Zone In the deep zone, the water is even darker and colder than in the transition zone. Because of its harsh conditions, the deep ocean is often compared to a desert. Few organisms live in the deep zone, compared to other ocean and land environments. But unlike a desert, which bakes under the bright sun, the deep ocean is cold, dark, and wet.

Finding food in the darkness is a challenge. Many deep-sea fishes produce their own light. The production of light by living things is called **bioluminescence.** Chemical reactions in the cells of organisms produce bioluminescence.

In some cases, light is produced by bioluminescent bacteria that live on the bodies of fishes. In other cases, the chemical reactions take place in the bodies of the fishes, as they do in fireflies on land. For example, tiny light-producing structures are scattered over the surfaces of some fishes. Other fishes, such as the anglerfish, have light-producing organs. The anglerfish has a light organ on its head. The anglerfish lurks in the shadows below the pool of light created by its light organ. Shrimp and fishes that are attracted to the light become prey of the anglerfish.

The food supply in most of the deep ocean is much more limited than in shallower water. Therefore, animals in this zone must be good hunters to survive. The gaping mouths of many deep-sea fishes are filled with fanglike teeth. Rows of sharp teeth stick out at angles, ensuring that any animal it bites cannot escape.

FIGURE 17
Organisms of the Deep Zone
The anglerfish (above) and the deep sea octopus (right) are animals that flourish in the cold and dark of the deep zone.

Hydrothermal Vents In the deep zone, food is very scarce. As a result, organisms there tend to be small and slow-moving. However, there is one kind of deep-zone environment—a hydrothermal vent—that supports organisms of an unusual number, variety, and size. At a **hydrothermal vent,** hot water rises out of cracks in the ocean floor. This rising water has been heated by hot rock magma beneath the ocean floor. These vents are located along ocean ridges, where the plates are moving apart and new ocean floor is forming.

A hydrothermal vent is far from sunlight. What could organisms around a hydrothermal vent find to eat? The heated water coming from a vent carries gases and minerals from Earth's interior. Bacteria feed directly on these chemical nutrients. Like the algae in the surface zone that use sunlight to produce food, these bacteria use chemical nutrients to produce food.

These bacteria form the base of the food web at a hydrothermal vent. Other organisms, such as giant clams, feed on the bacteria. The giant red-tipped tube worms are supplied with food by bacteria living within their tissues. Meanwhile, the crabs feed on the remains of the other inhabitants of their unusual habitat.

FIGURE 18
A Hydrothermal Vent
Giant tube worms and crabs cluster around a hydrothermal vent on the ocean floor.

 **Reading Checkpoint** What is a hydrothermal vent?

Section 4 Assessment

Target Reading Skill **Relating Cause and Effect** Refer to your graphic organizer about conditions in the neritic zone to help you answer Question 1 below.

Reviewing Key Concepts

1. a. **Describing** Describe the physical conditions in the neritic zone.
   b. **Relating Cause and Effect** Explain how neritic-zone conditions support the growth of plankton.
   c. **Making Generalizations** Why are food webs in the neritic zone especially complex? (*Hint:* What is the role of plankton in food webs?)
2. a. **Describing** Describe life near a coral reef and life in a kelp forest.
   b. **Comparing and Contrasting** Compare and contrast the physical conditions that support coral reefs and kelp forests.

3. a. **Reviewing** How do conditions in the open ocean and the neritic zone differ?
   b. **Summarizing** Summarize the conditions that exist around hydrothermal vents.
   c. **Applying Concepts** Are the organisms around a hydrothermal vent typical of deep-zone organisms? Explain.

Writing in Science

Editorial You are a scientist studying a coral reef located near a tropical island. A forest on the island has been cut down. As a result, soil erosion is increasing. Write an editorial for the local newspaper explaining how this could affect the coral reef.

Resources From the Ocean

Reading Preview

Key Concepts
- How do people use living resources from the ocean?
- What are some nonliving ocean resources?
- What are the sources of ocean pollution?

Key Terms
- aquaculture • nodule

Target Reading Skill
Identifying Main Ideas As you read the Nonliving Resources section, write the main idea—the biggest or most important idea—in a graphic organizer like the one below. Then write three supporting details that give examples of the main idea.

Main Idea

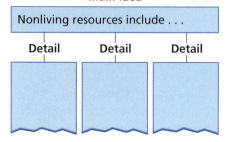

Nonliving resources include . . .		
Detail	Detail	Detail

Lab zone **Discover Activity**

Is It From the Ocean?

1. Your teacher will give you some labels from common household products. Read the ingredient information on each label.
2. Divide the products into two piles—those you think include substances that come from the ocean and those that do not.

Think It Over

Classifying For each product you classified as coming from the ocean, name the ocean resource that is used to produce it. In which ocean zone is it found?

When European explorers began sailing to North America, they were astounded by the huge number of codfish off its eastern coast. Sailors reported that this area was so "swarming with fish that they could be taken not only with a net but in baskets let down and weighted with a stone." Others reported sailing through schools of cod so thick they slowed the boats down!

This cod fishery stretched from Newfoundland to a hook of land appropriately named Cape Cod. For more than 400 years, the seemingly endless supply of "King Cod" supported a thriving fishing industry. But starting in the early 1900s, it became clear that the cod population was decreasing. With the price of cod rising, there was more competition to catch fewer fish. In 1992, the Canadian government closed the fishery.

A cod catch ▶

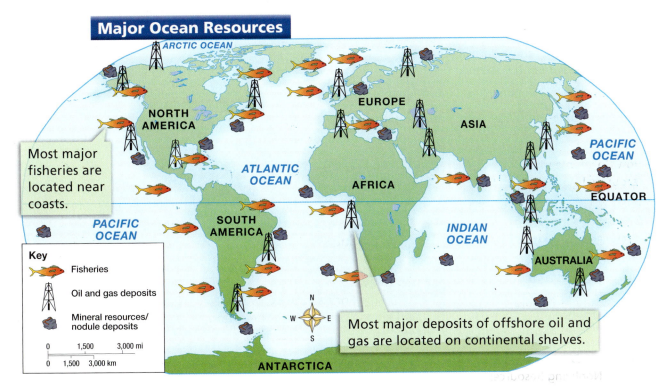

Major Ocean Resources

Most major fisheries are located near coasts.

Most major deposits of offshore oil and gas are located on continental shelves.

Key

🐟 Fisheries

⛏ Oil and gas deposits

🪨 Mineral resources/
nodule deposits

| 0 | 1,500 | 3,000 mi |
| 0 | 1,500 | 3,000 km |

Living Resources

Cod are just one example of a living resource from the ocean. How many other kinds of seafood have you tasted: tuna, shrimp, flounder, lobster, clams, squid, oysters, seaweed, or mussels? **People depend heavily on fishes and other ocean organisms for food. Ocean organisms also provide materials that are used in products such as detergents and paints.**

Harvesting Fish Many kinds of fishes are caught to be eaten. Anchovies, pollock, mackerel, herring, and tuna make up most of the worldwide catch. Locate the world's major fisheries in Figure 19. You can see that they are all located close to coasts. Nearly all fishes caught are harvested from coastal waters or areas of upwelling. These waters contain nutrients and plankton on which the fish feed.

If used wisely, fisheries naturally renew themselves each year. New fish are born, replacing those that are caught, but only as long as the fishery is not overfished. Overfishing causes the supply of fish to decrease.

Better technology has enabled people to catch large numbers of fish very quickly. Sometimes the fish can be caught faster than they can reproduce. When fish reproduction decreases, there are fewer and fewer fish each season. Eventually, the fish in the fishery may become very scarce. This is what happened in the cod fishery you read about earlier.

FIGURE 19
Resources From the Ocean
All over the world, the oceans are an important source of food, oil and gas, and minerals.
Interpreting Maps *Where are Africa's major fisheries located?*

Go Online
SciLINKS NSTA

For: Links on ocean resources
Visit: www.SciLinks.org
Web Code: scn-0845

FIGURE 20
Aquaculture
These "farmers" are raising catfish in fenced-in areas near the mouth of the Mississippi River.

Aquaculture As fish stocks decrease, **aquaculture,** the farming of saltwater and freshwater organisms, is likely to become more common. Aquaculture has been practiced in some Asian countries for centuries.

Aquaculture involves creating an environment for the organisms. To help the organisms thrive, nutrient levels, water temperature, light, and other factors must be controlled. Oysters, abalone, and shrimp have successfully been farmed in artificial saltwater ponds and protected bays. Even landlocked regions can produce seafood using aquaculture. For example, salmon are now being raised in Nebraska fields that once were cattle ranches.

Other Ocean Products People harvest ocean organisms for many purposes besides food. Algae is an ingredient in many household products. Its gelatin-like texture makes it an ideal base for detergents, shampoos, cosmetics, paints, and even ice cream! Sediments containing the hard pieces of diatoms are used for abrasives and polishes. Many researchers believe that other marine organisms may be important sources of chemicals for medicines in the future.

Reading Checkpoint What is aquaculture?

Nonliving Resources

In addition to living organisms, the ocean contains valuable nonliving resources. **Some nonliving ocean resources include water, fuels, and minerals.**

Water You have read how fresh water can be extracted from ocean water using desalination. Desalination provides fresh water for many dry areas and islands.

Fuels The remains of dead marine organisms are the source of another nonliving resource. The remains sink to the bottom of the ocean, where they are buried by sediments. As more sediments accumulate, the buried remains decompose. Over hundreds of thousands of years, the heat and pressure from the overlying layers gradually transform the organisms' remains into oil and natural gas.

As you know, many organisms live in the part of the ocean above the continental shelf. The thick sediments on the continental shelves bury the remains of living things. As a result, the richest deposits of oil and gas are often located on the continental shelves.

Oil rigs like the one in Figure 21 drill the rocky ocean floor as much as 300 meters below the surface. Imagine trying to dig a hole in the concrete bottom of a swimming pool, while standing on a raft floating on the surface of the water. You can see why drilling the ocean floor is very difficult! Ocean drilling is made even harder by strong currents, winds, and violent storms.

FIGURE 21
An Oil Rig
Lit up like a city at night, this Norwegian oil-drilling platform rises above the icy waters of the North Sea. Hundreds of people may live and work on an oil rig.
Relating Cause and Effect *How did oil deposits form beneath the ocean?*

Minerals Minerals are solid substances that are obtained from the ground and the water. When fresh water is removed from ocean water, the salts that are left behind are a valuable mineral resource. More than half of the world's supply of magnesium, a strong, light metal, is obtained from seawater in this way.

The ocean floor is another source of mineral resources. From the sediments covering the continental shelves, gravel and sand are mined for use in building construction. In some areas of the world, diamonds and gold are mined from sand deposits. Metals such as manganese also accumulate on the ocean floor. The metals concentrate around pieces of shell, forming black lumps called **nodules** (NAHJ oolz). Nodules sometimes occur in waters as deep as 5,000 meters. Therefore, recovering the nodules is a difficult process. The technology to gather them is still being developed.

 **Reading Checkpoint** **What minerals are obtained from the oceans?**

Ocean Pollution

The ocean is a self-cleaning system that can absorb some wastes without permanent damage. But dumping large amounts of wastes into the ocean threatens many marine organisms. Most ocean pollution comes from the land. **Although some ocean pollution is the result of natural occurrences, most pollution is related to human activities.**

Math Analyzing Data

Ocean Oil Pollution

The bar graph shows the main sources of oil pollution in the ocean. The source *Natural Seeps* refers to the natural process by which oil leaks out of oil deposits in the oceans. Study the graph, and then answer the following questions.

1. **Reading Graphs** How many sources of ocean oil pollution are shown on the graph?

2. **Interpreting Data** Which source causes the most oil pollution? The least?

3. **Classifying** Classify each source of oil pollution as either a natural cause or one that is caused by human actions.

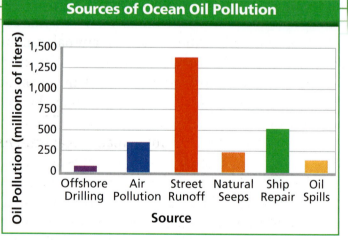

4. **Problem Solving** Which source or sources of ocean oil pollution could you personally reduce? What actions could you take to reduce the sources?

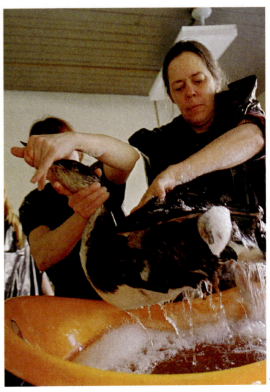

Natural Occurrences Some pollution is the result of weather. For example, heavy rains wash fresh water into estuaries and out into the water offshore. This surge of fresh water pollutes the ocean by lowering its salinity. A sudden change in salinity may kill ocean animals that are unable to adjust to it.

Human Activities Sewage, chemicals, and trash dumped into coastal waters all come from human sources. Substances that run off fields and roads often end up in the ocean. These substances can harm ocean organisms directly. The pollutants can also build up in the organisms' bodies and poison other animals, including people, that feed on them. Trash can cause serious problems, too. Air-breathing marine mammals can drown if they get tangled in fishing lines or nets. Other animals are harmed when they swallow plastic bags that block their stomachs.

Another major threat to ocean life is oil pollution. When an oil tanker or drilling platform is damaged, oil leaks into the surrounding ocean. Oil is harmful to many organisms. As Figure 22 shows, oil from a spill can coat the bodies of animals that live near the spill. This destroys their natural insulation and affects their ability to float. Oil is also harmful to animals that swallow it.

There is a natural cleaning process that slowly takes place after oil spills. Certain bacteria that live in the ocean feed on the oil and multiply. It takes many years, but these bacteria can eventually clean an oil-covered beach. Of course, oil can cause much damage to an area in that time, so people often help to clean up large spills.

FIGURE 22
Cleaning Up Oil
This cleanup worker is using absorbent mops to remove oil from the sand (left). On the right, two workers try to clean oil from a bird's beak and feathers.
Inferring *What might have caused this oil pollution?*

FIGURE 23
A Marine Refuge
This scientist is tagging an elephant seal in a marine refuge in California. Scientists will then be able to monitor the seal's travels.

Protecting Earth's Oceans Who owns the ocean and its resources? Who has the responsibility of protecting them? These are questions that nations have been struggling to answer for hundreds of years. Because the world ocean is a continuous body of water that has no boundaries, it is difficult to determine who, if anyone, should control portions of it. Nations must cooperate to manage and protect the oceans.

The United Nations has established different boundaries in the oceans. According to one treaty, a nation now controls the first 22 kilometers out from its coasts. The nation also controls the resources in the waters or on the continental shelf within 370 kilometers of shore. This treaty leaves approximately half of the ocean's surface waters as "high seas," owned by no nation. Ownership of the ocean floor beneath the high seas is still under debate.

Other international efforts have resulted in cooperation aimed at reducing ocean pollution. Examples include the establishment of marine refuges and regulations for building safer oil tankers.

 **Reading Checkpoint** Why is it difficult to determine who controls ocean resources?

Section 5 Assessment

Target Reading Skill Identifying Main Ideas Use your graphic organizer about Nonliving Resources to help you answer Question 2 below.

Reviewing Key Concepts

1. a. **Reviewing** What are two ways in which people use ocean organisms?
   b. **Summarizing** What is aquaculture? What problem does it help address?

2. a. **Listing** List three nonliving ocean resources.
   b. **Describing** How is oil obtained from the ocean floor?
   c. **Inferring** Oil deposits are found beneath dry land as well the ocean. From which location— ocean or dry land—is it more difficult to obtain oil? Explain your answer.

3. a. **Reviewing** Identify one natural occurrence and three human activities that can pollute the oceans.
   b. **Explaining** Explain why one nation by itself cannot control ocean pollution.

   c. **Making Judgments** Should mineral resources on the ocean floor belong to whomever finds them, or to the closest nation? Consider each position and write a short paragraph stating your opinion.

Lab zone **At-Home Activity**

Modeling Ocean Pollution Have a family member hook one end of a rubber band around his or her wrist. Stretch the rubber band across the back of the hand and hook the free end over three fingers as shown. Now ask the person to try to remove the rubber band without using the other hand. Explain that this shows how difficult it is for seals or dolphins to free themselves from a plastic beverage ring or piece of net. Can you propose any ways to reduce this threat to marine mammals?

Cleaning Up an Oil Spill

Problem

How can an oil spill be cleaned up?

Skills Focus

making models, observing

Materials

- water
- feather
- marking pen
- shallow pan
- paper towels
- paper cup
- cotton balls
- vegetable oil
- plastic dropper
- wooden sticks
- graduated cylinder, 100-mL

Procedure

1. Place a pan on a table or desk covered with newspaper. Label one end of the pan "Beach" and the other end "Open Ocean."

2. Pour water into the pan to a depth of 2 cm.

3. Gently pour 20 mL of vegetable oil into the center of the pan. Record your observations.

4. Dip a feather and your finger into the oil. Observe how each is affected by the oil.

5. Try to wipe oil off the feather and your finger using cotton balls or paper towels. Record whether any oil is left on the feather or your skin.

6. Now try to clean up the spill. First, using the wooden sticks, try to keep the oil from reaching the "beach." Next, gently blow across the surface of the water from the "open ocean" side to simulate wind and waves. Then use the cotton balls, paper towels, and dropper to recover as much of the oil as possible. Record your observations with each step.

7. When you are finished, dispose of the oil and used items in the paper cup. Wash your hands.

Analyze and Conclude

1. **Observing** How successful were you in cleaning up the oil? Did the water end up as clean as it was at the start?

2. **Making Models** How well were you able to keep the oil from reaching the beach? How does this activity model the problems that actual cleanup workers encounter?

3. **Inferring** Describe what happened when you cleaned the feather and your finger. What might happen to fish, birds, and other animals if they were coated with oil as a result of an oil spill?

4. **Predicting** Predict how storms with strong winds and waves would affect the cleanup of an oil spill.

5. **Communicating** Look at the used cleanup materials in the paper cup. What additional problems does this suggest for cleanup crews? Write instructions for procedures that cleanup crews might follow to deal with these problems.

More to Explore

One way to reduce the threat of oil spills is to transport less oil across the oceans. To make that possible, people would need to use less oil in their daily lives. Use reference materials or the Internet to find tips on oil conservation. Then list at least three ways to reduce the amount of oil you and your family use.

Shrimp Farms—At What Cost?

About one quarter of the world's shrimp are raised on shrimp farms. Many shrimp farms are created by clearing trees from mangrove forests and digging shallow, fenced-in ponds. Farmers then fill the ponds with ocean water and shrimp larvae. After about six months, when the shrimp are big enough to sell, the farmers drain the pond water back into the ocean.

To grow healthy shrimp, farmers often add fertilizers, medicines, and pesticides to the ponds. When the pond water is drained, these chemicals can harm other animals in the ocean. The United Nations has estimated that shrimp farming has destroyed 25 percent of the world's mangrove forests.

Shrimp Farming
This shrimper in Honduras is one of many who believe that local shrimp farming is reducing their catches and hurting their livelihood.

The Issues

How Important Is Shrimp Farming?

For many people in the world, shrimp is more than luxury food: It is a staple of their diet and their main source of animal protein. The current demand for shrimp is greater than the natural supply in the oceans. To meet the demand, many countries, including the United States, have turned to shrimp farming. Some people believe that the food and jobs that shrimp farms provide are worth a certain amount of damage to the environment.

Can the Pollution be Reduced?

Shrimp farmers are exploring ways to reduce the impact of their farms on the coastal environment. Better pond construction can help stop chemicals from leaking into the surrounding waters. Some governments have passed laws regulating where shrimp farms may be built. Farmers must investigate the impact their ponds will have on nearby mangrove forests and get approval before choosing a location. These methods of reducing environmental damage, however, are expensive and time-consuming for shrimp farmers.

Should Farmers Use Alternative Methods?

In some parts of Asia, a less destructive method of shrimp farming has been practiced for centuries. Shrimp are raised in ditches dug around clusters of mangroves. This provides the young shrimp with a natural nutrient supply that includes debris from the trees. A gate keeps the shrimp from escaping and allows the motion of the tides to replenish the water in the ditches. The disadvantage of this method is that it is much less profitable than the constructed shrimp ponds. Many shrimp farmers could not afford to switch to this method. If they did, the price of shrimp worldwide would rise.

You Decide

1. Identify the Problem

In your own words, summarize the problem facing shrimp farmers.

2. Analyze the Options

Make a list of the solutions mentioned. List the advantages and drawbacks of each. Who would benefit from each plan? Who might suffer?

3. Find a Solution

Write a brochure or pamphlet for shrimp farmers that states your proposed solution to their problem. After you have written the text, illustrate your brochure.

Go Online PHSchool.com

For: More on shrimp farms
Visit: PHSchool.com
Web Code: cfh-3040

① Exploring the Ocean

Key Concepts

- People have studied the ocean since ancient times, because the ocean provides food and serves as a route for trade and travel. Modern scientists have studied the characteristics of the ocean's waters and the ocean floor.

- If you could travel along the ocean floor, you would see the continental shelf, the continental slope, the abyssal plain, and the mid-ocean ridge.

- Plate movements have shaped many of the most dramatic features of Earth, both on land and under the ocean.

Key Terms

sonar	mid-ocean ridge
continental shelf	trench
continental slope	plate
abyssal plain	seafloor spreading

② Ocean Habitats

Key Concepts

- Ocean zones include the intertidal zone, the neritic zone, and the open-ocean zone.

- Scientists classify marine organisms according to where they live and how they move.

Key Terms

intertidal zone	nekton
neritic zone	benthos
open-ocean zone	food web
plankton	

③ Intertidal Zone

Key Concepts

- Organisms that live in the rocky intertidal zone must be able to tolerate the pounding of the waves and changes in both salinity and temperature. They must also withstand periods of being underwater and periods of being exposed to the air.

- Along the coasts of the United States, most wetlands are mangrove forests or salt marshes.

Key Term

estuary

④ Neritic Zone and Open Ocean

Key Concepts

- The shallow water over the continental shelf receives sunlight and a steady supply of nutrients washed from the land into the ocean. The light and nutrients enable large plantlike algae to grow.

- Coral reefs can form only in shallow, tropical ocean waters. Kelp forests grow in cold neritic waters where the ocean has a rocky floor.

- The open ocean differs from the neritic zone in two important ways. First, only a small part of the open ocean receives sunlight. Second, the water has fewer nutrients.

Key Terms

atoll
bioluminescence
hydrothermal vent

⑤ Resources From the Ocean

Key Concepts

- People depend heavily on fishes and other ocean organisms for food. Ocean organisms also provide materials that are used in products such as detergents and paints.

- Some nonliving ocean resources include water, fuels, and minerals.

- Although some ocean pollution is the result of natural occurrences, most pollution is related to human activities.

Key Terms

aquaculture
nodule

Review and Assessment

Organizing Information

Comparing and Contrasting Copy the table about ocean habitats onto a separate sheet of paper. Then complete it and add a title. (For more on Comparing and Contrasting, see the Skills Handbook.)

Habitat	Zone	Conditions	Organisms
Tide pool	Intertidal	a. ___?___	b. ___?___
Coral reef	c. ___?___	d. ___?___	Coral, fishes, shrimp, eels
Surface zone	Open ocean	e. ___?___	f. ___?___
Hydrothermal vent	g. ___?___	High pressure, dark, warm	h. ___?___

Reviewing Key Terms

Choose the letter of the best answer.

1. A smooth, nearly flat region of the ocean floor is called a(n)
   a. trench.
   b. mid-ocean ridge.
   c. abyssal plain.
   d. seamount.

2. Free-swimming animals that can move throughout the water column are called
   a. plankton.
   b. benthos.
   c. coral.
   d. nekton.

3. An area where rivers flow into the ocean and fresh water and salt water mix is a(n)
   a. tide pool.
   b. hydrothermal vent.
   c. estuary.
   d. kelp forest.

4. Hydrothermal vents are located
   a. in coral reefs.
   b. in the intertidal zone.
   c. in kelp forests.
   d. along ocean ridges.

5. Nodules consist of
   a. metals.
   b. algae.
   c. sediments.
   d. chemical nutrients.

If the statement is true, write *true*. If it is false, change the underlined word or words to make the statement true.

6. The mid-ocean ridge is formed where two plates <u>converge</u>.

7. The area between the high- and low-tide lines is the <u>neritic zone</u>.

8. An <u>estuary</u> is a coastal inlet or bay where fresh water mixes with salt water.

9. Many deep-sea fishes use their <u>bioluminescence</u> to attract prey.

10. <u>Aquaculture</u> is the farming of saltwater and freshwater organisms.

Writing in Science

Firsthand Account Suppose you were going to travel to the deepest part of the ocean floor in a submersible. Write about your journey, describing each feature of the ocean floor that you see along the way.

Discovery CHANNEL SCHOOL™

Ocean Zones
Video Preview
Video Field Trip
▶ Video Assessment

Review and Assessment

Checking Concepts

11. Why do scientists use indirect methods to study the ocean floor?

12. What is seafloor spreading, and what causes it?

13. Describe a typical marine food web.

14. Describe three physical factors that organisms in the rocky intertidal zone must overcome.

15. Explain why estuaries are especially vulnerable to pollution.

16. What is an atoll? How is it formed?

17. Explain why scientists were surprised to discover the variety of organisms living around hydrothermal vents.

Thinking Critically

18. Drawing Conclusions Mauna Kea projects about 4,200 meters above sea level. Its base is on the floor of the Pacific Ocean, about 6,000 meters below sea level. Mt. Everest rises 8,850 meters from base to summit. Its base is located on land. Which mountain is taller: Mauna Kea or Mt. Everest?

19. Classifying Classify the organisms in each photo below as plankton, nekton, or benthos.

20. Making Generalizations Explain why many of the world's fisheries are located in the neritic zone.

21. Relating Cause and Effect How might fertilizers used on farmland result in ocean pollution near shore?

Applying Skills

Use the diagram of a portion of the ocean floor to answer Questions 22–25.

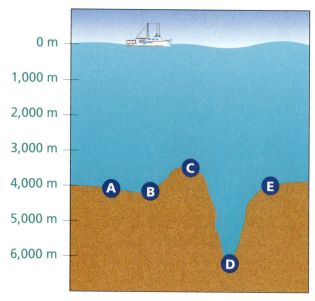

22. Interpreting Diagrams What is the approximate depth of the ocean floor at point A? At point C?

23. Inferring What might the feature between locations A and B be? The feature at point D?

24. Describing What would you expect the physical conditions at point D to be like?

25. Posing Questions What other information would help you determine which point—A or E—is closer to the mid-ocean ridge? Explain.

Lab zone Chapter Project

Performance Assessment Prepare a guided tour of your marine environment. First, rehearse the tour with your group. As you rehearse, check to see that your marine environment is complete. Make any final changes now. Then take your classmates through your tour.

Standardized Test Prep

Choose the letter of the best answer.

1. In which category of ocean organisms do sharks, tuna, killer whales, and squid belong?
   A plankton
   B nekton
   C benthos
   D none of the above

2. Use your knowledge of ocean zones to infer which adaptation would be most important for organisms in the intertidal zone.
   F the ability to use bioluminescence
   G the ability to withstand high pressures
   H the ability to use chemical nutrients in the water
   J the ability to withstand periods underwater and periods exposed to the air

Use the diagram below and your knowledge of science to answer Questions 3–4.

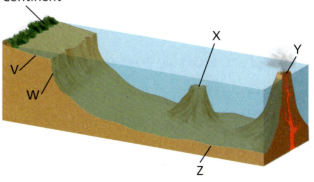

Continent

3. What is the feature labeled **X** on the diagram above?
   A seamount   **B** abyssal plain
   C mid-ocean ridge   **D** continental slope

4. In which part of the diagram would the greatest variety of organisms be found?
   F part V
   G part W
   H part X
   J part Z

5. If you were constructing a model of an estuary, which of the following elements would be the most important?
   A the depth of water to which sunlight can penetrate
   B the water temperature
   C the mix of fresh water and salt water
   D the presence of hydrothermal vents

Constructed Response

6. The coral reef ecosystem has a higher diversity of organisms than any other ecosystem. Explain the conditions necessary for coral reefs to form. Include in your explanation the relationship between coral and algae. Predict whether a coral reef would be likely to form near the mouth of a major river. Explain why or why not.

The Mississippi

What would you name a river that—

- carries about 420 million metric tons of cargo a year,
- drains 31 states and 2 Canadian provinces,
- flows at about 18,100 cubic meters of water per second?

Native Americans called the river *misi sipi*, an Algonquin name meaning "big water," or "father of waters."

You might have traveled on a river or lake that feeds into the mighty Mississippi but never realized it. The map below shows the watershed of this great river. From the west, the Missouri River—the "Big Muddy"— carries soft silt eroded from the Great Plains. The Missouri joins the Mississippi near St. Louis, turning the river's clear water to muddy brown. From the east, the Ohio River flows in from the rocky Appalachian plateau, nearly doubling the volume of water in the river. In all, the huge Mississippi watershed drains about 40 percent of the United States.

The Mississippi River
The Mississippi starts at Lake Itasca and flows through 10 states to the Gulf of Mexico. The river is a drainage point for hundreds of tributaries in the Mississippi watershed.

A National Trade Route

Since Native Americans settled in villages along the Mississippi around 1,200 years ago, the river has served as a water highway for trade and travel.

In the late 1600s, French explorers, fur traders, and soldiers arrived in the Mississippi Valley. They chose strategic sites for forts and fur-trading posts —Prairie du Chien, St. Louis, and St. Genevieve. At first, traders used canoes, rafts, and flatboats to carry goods downstream. But traveling up the river was difficult. Crews had to use long poles to push narrow keelboats upstream against the current.

In 1811, the arrival of *The New Orleans,* the first steamboat on the Mississippi River, changed the river forever. Within 40 years, there were hundreds more steamboats and many new river towns. On the upper Mississippi, the city of Minneapolis grew up around flour mills near St. Anthony Falls. Farther downstream, Memphis became a center for transporting cotton. Later, it was a stopping point for showboats and musicians. New Orleans quickly became a world port. It received cotton, tobacco, and sugar cane from southern plantations and exported corn, wheat, and indigo to Europe. Imported luxury items, such as soap, coffee, shoes, and textiles, traveled upstream from the port of New Orleans. Up and down the river townspeople eagerly waited for the cry, "Steamboat comin'!"

Flatboats
Flatboat crews rode the river currents, steering with long oars.

New Orleans
The city has been a major trading port since its founding in 1718.

The Mississippi River in Minnesota

Social Studies Activity

Research a city on the Mississippi River. Imagine that you are an early settler there. Write a letter to convince relatives to move to your city. Before writing, research the city's history by finding the answers to these questions:

- Who founded the city? When was it founded? Why did settlers move there? Where did they come from?

- What part did the Mississippi River play in the city's founding?

- What other physical features were important to the city?

- Where did the city's name come from?

- What products were grown, bought, or sold there?

Taming the River

Navigating the sandbars, shallow water, and rocky rapids on the upper Mississippi River was treacherous in the 1800s. To make traveling easier, engineers in the early 1900s built a "water staircase," a series of 29 locks and dams between Minneapolis, Minnesota, and Alton, Illinois, above St. Louis.

A lock is an enclosed basin, with gates at each end. Locks allow engineers to raise or lower the water level in a certain area of the river. Between the locks on the upper Mississippi, the river forms wide pools of quiet water, maintaining a channel deep enough for large boats. Use the diagrams to trace how a boat "locks through" as it travels upstream.

❶ The lock gate opens.
Your boat moves in and you tie up to the wall.

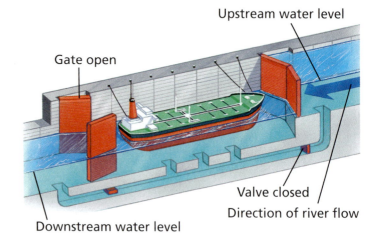

Upstream water level

Gate open

Valve closed

Direction of river flow

Downstream water level

❷ The gate closes, and water pours in.
As water fills the lock—like a bathtub filling—it lifts the boat a meter or more. When the water in the lock is even with the water level upstream, the gates at the upstream end open. You untie your boat and move out into the river.

If you were going downstream, you would "lock through" in reverse. The water would empty out of the lock, lowering the water level to match the level downstream.

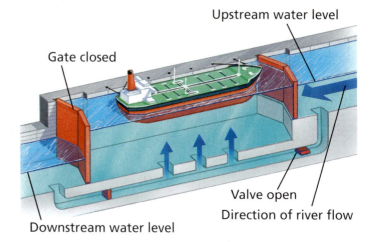

Upstream water level

Gate closed

Valve open

Direction of river flow

Downstream water level

Science Activity

Use a cardboard milk container to build a working model of a lock. Set up your lock following the illustration. Then demonstrate how your lock works, using a cork or pen cap as your ship and sailing it through the lock.

Modeling wax

Duct tape

Cut-out side view

All Aboard

The whistle blows. The gleaming white steamboat pulls away from the dock just below Fort Snelling, Minnesota. You head downstream toward New Orleans. As you watch the paddlewheel splashing in the water, you think of the old-time steamboats that traveled the Mississippi River in the 1800s.

Today you are cruising at a speed of 11.3 kilometers per hour. You want to stay awake until you enter Lock 3 at Red Wing, Minnesota. It's 4:30 P.M. on Monday now. You know that it's about 78.8 kilometers to Red Wing. It should take about 7 hours to reach the lock. So you'll be there at 11:30 P.M. and through the lock by midnight.

As your boat travels along the river, it will follow the schedule you see below. You will arrive in Mark Twain's hometown of Hannibal, Missouri, on Friday.

Look at the Upper Mississippi River schedule to answer the questions below. Distances are given from Fort Snelling.

- What is your average speed between Dubuque and Hannibal? Use the following equation:

$$\text{Speed} = \frac{\text{Distance}}{\text{Time}}$$

Round to the nearest tenth.

- How long will you spend in Prairie du Chien?
- About how long does it take to travel from Prairie du Chien to Dubuque?

Upper Mississippi Riverboat Schedule May–Sept.			
Port	**Arrival Time**	**Departure Time**	**Distance From Fort Snelling**
Fort Snelling, MN		4:30 P.M. Mon.	0 km
Lock 3, Red Wing, MN	11:30 P.M. Mon.	12:00 midnight	78.8 km
Prairie du Chien, WI	11:00 P.M. Tues.	10:30 A.M. Wed.	337.8 km
Dubuque, IA	6:30 P.M. Wed.	7:00 P.M. Wed.	426.3 km
Hannibal, MO	1:00 A.M. Fri.	_____	863.9 km

Math Activity

Now complete the riverboat schedule for the Lower Mississippi. Your boat will leave Hannibal at 6 P.M. Friday and will travel at a speed of 14.7 kilometers per hour for the rest of the journey.

- When will you arrive at Lock 26?
- You spend 34 minutes in the lock. When will you depart from Lock 26? Your boat travels on. When will it arrive in St. Louis?
- The boat will spend 4 hours in St. Louis and head to Cape Girardeau, arriving at 6:30 A.M. Sunday. How far is it from St. Louis to Cape Girardeau?

Lower Mississippi Riverboat Schedule May–Sept.			
Port	**Arrival Time**	**Departure Time**	**Distance From Fort Snelling**
Hannibal, MO		6 P.M. Fri.	863.9 km
Lock 26, Alton, IL	a. _?_	b. _?_	1,033.0 km
St. Louis, MO	c. _?_	d. _?_	1,070.7 km
Cape Girardeau, MO	6:30 A.M. Sun.	_____	e. _?_

Mark Three!
Mark Twain!

To steer a boat on the Mississippi, early riverboat pilots had to memorize landmarks at every bend and curve of the river, going both upstream and down. They had to know where the channel was deep enough for the boat, where the current was strong, and where there were sandbars or sunken logs.

When Samuel Clemens was growing up in the small river town of Hannibal, Missouri, his ambition was to become a Mississippi River steamboat pilot. He was a pilot for a while. Later he became one of America's most famous writers, using the pen name Mark Twain. In the passage at right from his book *Life on the Mississippi*, Twain describes a lesson he learned from an experienced pilot, Mr. Bixby.

"My boy," [Bixby said] "you've got to know the shape of the river perfectly. It is all there is left to steer by on a very dark night. Everything else is blotted out and gone. But mind you, it hasn't the same shape in the night that it has in the daytime."

"How on earth am I ever going to learn it, then?"

"How do you follow a hall at home in the dark? Because you know the shape of it. You can't see it."

"Do you mean to say that I've got to know all the million trifling variations of shape in the banks of this interminable [endless] river as well as I know the shape of the front hall at home?"

"On my honor, you've got to know them better than any man ever did know the shapes of the halls in his own house."

"I wish I was dead!"

"Now I don't want to discourage you, but— . . . . You see, this has got to be learned; there isn't any getting around it. . . ."

What's in a Name?
Mark Twain's name comes from a term that steamboat crews used to measure the depth of river water. *Twain* means "two." Dropping a weighted line, they would call out the depth:
"Mark twain!"—2 fathoms deep;
"Mark three!"—3 fathoms deep.
(Note: One fathom equals 1.8 meters.)

Sunrise over the Mississippi River in Iowa

"The river is a very different shape on a pitch-dark night from what it is on a starlight night. All shores seem to be straight lines, then, and mighty dim ones, too; and you'd run them for straight lines, only you know better. Then there's your gray mist. You take a night when there's one of these grisly, drizzly gray mists, and then there isn't any particular shape to a shore. A gray mist would tangle the head of the oldest man that ever lived. Well, then, different kinds of moonlight change the shape of the river in different ways. You see—"

"Oh, don't say any more, please! Have I got to learn the shape of the river according to all these five hundred thousand different ways? If I tried to carry all that cargo in my head, it would make me stoop-shouldered."

"No! You only learn the shape of the river; and you learn it with such absolute certainty that you can always steer by the shape that's in your head, and never mind the one that's before your eyes."

Language Arts Activity

Read the excerpt, focusing on what the dialogue tells you about the characters of Mark Twain and Mr. Bixby.

- What lesson does Mark Twain learn?
- How does Mr. Bixby feel about the Mississippi River?

How can you tell?

Now, use dialogue to write an ending to this riverboat excerpt. Before you begin writing, think carefully about the characters, setting, and your conclusion.

Tie It Together

Celebrate the River

Plan a class fair featuring cities on the Mississippi River today, such as St. Louis (above). Set up a booth for each city and create a travel brochure to persuade people to visit.

Choose a city to represent. Then, research the city to find information on

- interesting attractions and events— zoos, museums, parks, sports events, and music festivals.
- influences of different groups on food, customs, music, and architecture.
- physical features around the city.
- famous people—writers, political figures, entertainers—who lived there.
- historic places to visit—monuments, houses, battlefields, and statues.
- illustrations and pictures of special attractions.
- maps of walking tours and historic areas.
- native plants and animals in the area.

Before starting your brochure, decide which attractions to highlight. Then set up your booth, display your brochure, and celebrate life on the Mississippi today.

Think Like a Scientist

Scientists have a particular way of looking at the world, or scientific habits of mind. Whenever you ask a question and explore possible answers, you use many of the same skills that scientists do. Some of these skills are described on this page.

Observing

When you use one or more of your five senses to gather information about the world, you are **observing.** Hearing a dog bark, counting twelve green seeds, and smelling smoke are all observations. To increase the power of their senses, scientists sometimes use microscopes, telescopes, or other instruments that help them make more detailed observations.

An observation must be an accurate report of what your senses detect. It is important to keep careful records of your observations in science class by writing or drawing in a notebook. The information collected through observations is called evidence, or data.

Inferring

When you interpret an observation, you are **inferring,** or making an inference. For example, if you hear your dog barking, you may infer that someone is at your front door. To make this inference, you combine the evidence— the barking dog—and your experience or knowledge—you know that your dog barks when strangers approach—to reach a logical conclusion.

Notice that an inference is not a fact; it is only one of many possible interpretations for an observation. For example, your dog may be barking because it wants to go for a walk. An inference may turn out to be incorrect even if it is based on accurate observations and logical reasoning. The only way to find out if an inference is correct is to investigate further.

Predicting

When you listen to the weather forecast, you hear many predictions about the next day's weather—what the temperature will be, whether it will rain, and how windy it will be. Weather forecasters use observations and knowledge of weather patterns to predict the weather. The skill of **predicting** involves making an inference about a future event based on current evidence or past experience.

Because a prediction is an inference, it may prove to be false. In science class, you can test some of your predictions by doing experiments. For example, suppose you predict that larger paper airplanes can fly farther than smaller airplanes. How could you test your prediction?

Activity

Use the photograph to answer the questions below.

Observing Look closely at the photograph. List at least three observations.

Inferring Use your observations to make an inference about what has happened. What experience or knowledge did you use to make the inference?

Predicting Predict what will happen next. On what evidence or experience do you base your prediction?

Classifying

Could you imagine searching for a book in the library if the books were shelved in no particular order? Your trip to the library would be an all-day event! Luckily, librarians group together books on similar topics or by the same author. Grouping together items that are alike in some way is called **classifying.** You can classify items in many ways: by size, by shape, by use, and by other important characteristics.

Like librarians, scientists use the skill of classifying to organize information and objects. When things are sorted into groups, the relationships among them become easier to understand.

Activity

Classify the objects in the photograph into two groups based on any characteristic you choose. Then use another characteristic to classify the objects into three groups.

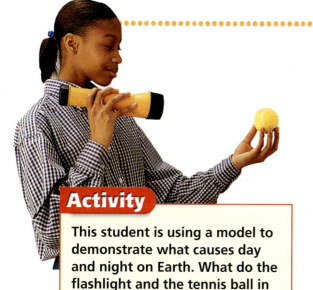

Activity

This student is using a model to demonstrate what causes day and night on Earth. What do the flashlight and the tennis ball in the model represent?

Making Models

Have you ever drawn a picture to help someone understand what you were saying? Such a drawing is one type of model. A model is a picture, diagram, computer image, or other representation of a complex object or process. **Making models** helps people understand things that they cannot observe directly.

Scientists often use models to represent things that are either very large or very small, such as the planets in the solar system, or the parts of a cell. Such models are physical models—drawings or three-dimensional structures that look like the real thing. Other models are mental models—mathematical equations or words that describe how something works.

Communicating

Whenever you talk on the phone, write a report, or listen to your teacher at school, you are communicating. **Communicating** is the process of sharing ideas and information with other people. Communicating effectively requires many skills, including writing, reading, speaking, listening, and making models.

Scientists communicate to share results, information, and opinions. Scientists often communicate about their work in journals, over the telephone, in letters, and on the Internet.

They also attend scientific meetings where they share their ideas with one another in person.

Activity

On a sheet of paper, write out clear, detailed directions for tying your shoe. Then exchange directions with a partner. Follow your partner's directions exactly. How successful were you at tying your shoe? How could your partner have communicated more clearly?

Making Measurements

By measuring, scientists can express their observations more precisely and communicate more information about what they observe.

Measuring in SI

The standard system of measurement used by scientists around the world is known as the International System of Units, which is abbreviated as SI (**Système International d'Unités,** in French). SI units are easy to use because they are based on multiples of 10. Each unit is ten times larger than the next smallest unit and one tenth the size of the next largest unit. The table lists the prefixes used to name the most common SI units.

Common SI Prefixes		
Prefix	**Symbol**	**Meaning**
kilo-	k	1,000
hecto-	h	100
deka-	da	10
deci-	d	0.1 (one tenth)
centi-	c	0.01 (one hundredth)
milli-	m	0.001 (one thousandth)

Length To measure length, or the distance between two points, the unit of measure is the **meter (m).** The distance from the floor to a doorknob is approximately one meter. Long distances, such as the distance between two cities, are measured in kilometers (km). Small lengths are measured in centimeters (cm) or millimeters (mm). Scientists use metric rulers and meter sticks to measure length.

Common Conversions		
1 km	=	1,000 m
1 m	=	100 cm
1 m	=	1,000 mm
1 cm	=	10 mm

Activity

The larger lines on the metric ruler in the picture show centimeter divisions, while the smaller, unnumbered lines show millimeter divisions. How many centimeters long is the shell? How many millimeters long is it?

Liquid Volume To measure the volume of a liquid, or the amount of space it takes up, you will use a unit of measure known as the **liter (L).** One liter is the approximate volume of a medium-size carton of milk. Smaller volumes are measured in milliliters (mL). Scientists use graduated cylinders to measure liquid volume.

Activity

The graduated cylinder in the picture is marked in milliliter divisions. Notice that the water in the cylinder has a curved surface. This curved surface is called the *meniscus*. To measure the volume, you must read the level at the lowest point of the meniscus. What is the volume of water in this graduated cylinder?

Common Conversion
1 L = 1,000 mL

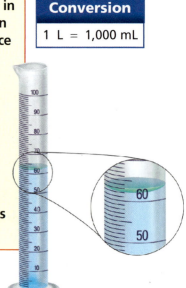

Mass To measure mass, or the amount of matter in an object, you will use a unit of measure known as the **gram (g).** One gram is approximately the mass of a paper clip. Larger masses are measured in kilograms (kg). Scientists use a balance to find the mass of an object.

Common Conversion

1 kg = 1,000 g

Activity

The mass of the potato in the picture is measured in kilograms. What is the mass of the potato? Suppose a recipe for potato salad called for one kilogram of potatoes. About how many potatoes would you need?

0.25 KG

Temperature To measure the temperature of a substance, you will use the **Celsius scale.** Temperature is measured in degrees Celsius (°C) using a Celsius thermometer. Water freezes at 0°C and boils at 100°C.

Time The unit scientists use to measure time is the **second (s).**

Activity

What is the temperature of the liquid in degrees Celsius?

Converting SI Units

To use the SI system, you must know how to convert between units. Converting from one unit to another involves the skill of **calculating,** or using mathematical operations. Converting between SI units is similar to converting between dollars and dimes because both systems are based on multiples of ten.

Suppose you want to convert a length of 80 centimeters to meters. Follow these steps to convert between units.

1. Begin by writing down the measurement you want to convert—in this example, 80 centimeters.

2. Write a conversion factor that represents the relationship between the two units you are converting. In this example, the relationship is 1 meter = 100 centimeters. Write this conversion factor as a fraction, making sure to place the units you are converting from (centimeters, in this example) in the denominator.

3. Multiply the measurement you want to convert by the fraction. When you do this, the units in the first measurement will cancel out with the units in the denominator. Your answer will be in the units you are converting to (meters, in this example).

Example

80 centimeters = ■ meters

$$80 \text{ centimeters} \times \frac{1 \text{ meter}}{100 \text{ centimeters}} = \frac{80 \text{ meters}}{100}$$

$$= 0.8 \text{ meters}$$

Activity

Convert between the following units.

1. 600 millimeters = ■ meters
2. 0.35 liters = ■ milliliters
3. 1,050 grams = ■ kilograms

Conducting a Scientific Investigation

In some ways, scientists are like detectives, piecing together clues to learn about a process or event. One way that scientists gather clues is by carrying out experiments. An experiment tests an idea in a careful, orderly manner. Although experiments do not all follow the same steps in the same order, many follow a pattern similar to the one described here.

Posing Questions

Experiments begin by asking a scientific question. A scientific question is one that can be answered by gathering evidence. For example, the question "Which freezes faster—fresh water or salt water?" is a scientific question because you can carry out an investigation and gather information to answer the question.

Developing a Hypothesis

The next step is to form a hypothesis. A **hypothesis** is a possible explanation for a set of observations or answer to a scientific question. In science, a hypothesis must be something that can be tested. A hypothesis can be worded as an *If . . . then . . .* statement. For example, a hypothesis might be *"If I add salt to fresh water, then the water will take longer to freeze."* A hypothesis worded this way serves as a rough outline of the experiment you should perform.

Designing an Experiment

Next you need to plan a way to test your hypothesis. Your plan should be written out as a step-by-step procedure and should describe the observations or measurements you will make.

Two important steps involved in designing an experiment are controlling variables and forming operational definitions.

Controlling Variables In a well-designed experiment, you need to keep all variables the same except for one. A **variable** is any factor that can change in an experiment. The factor that you change is called the **manipulated variable**. In this experiment, the manipulated variable is the amount of salt added to the water. Other factors, such as the amount of water or the starting temperature, are kept constant.

The factor that changes as a result of the manipulated variable is called the **responding variable.** The responding variable is what you measure or observe to obtain your results. In this experiment, the responding variable is how long the water takes to freeze.

An experiment in which all factors except one are kept constant is called a **controlled experiment.** Most controlled experiments include a test called the control. In this experiment, Container 3 is the control. Because no salt is added to Container 3, you can compare the results from the other containers to it. Any difference in results must be due to the addition of salt alone.

Forming Operational Definitions Another important aspect of a well-designed experiment is having clear operational definitions. An **operational definition** is a statement that describes how a particular variable is to be measured or how a term is to be defined. For example, in this experiment, how will you determine if the water has frozen? You might decide to insert a stick in each container at the start of the experiment. Your operational definition of "frozen" would be the time at which the stick can no longer move.

Experimental Procedure

1. Fill 3 containers with 300 milliliters of cold tap water.

2. Add 10 grams of salt to Container 1; stir. Add 20 grams of salt to Container 2; stir. Add no salt to Container 3.

3. Place the 3 containers in a freezer.

4. Check the containers every 15 minutes. Record your observations.

Interpreting Data

The observations and measurements you make in an experiment are called **data.** At the end of an experiment, you need to analyze the data to look for any patterns or trends. Patterns often become clear if you organize your data in a data table or graph. Then think through what the data reveal. Do they support your hypothesis? Do they point out a flaw in your experiment? Do you need to collect more data?

Drawing Conclusions

A **conclusion** is a statement that sums up what you have learned from an experiment. When you draw a conclusion, you need to decide whether the data you collected support your hypothesis or not. You may need to repeat an experiment several times before you can draw any conclusions from it. Conclusions often lead you to pose new questions and plan new experiments to answer them.

Activity

Is a ball's bounce affected by the height from which it is dropped? Using the steps just described, plan a controlled experiment to investigate this problem.

Technology Design Skills

Engineers are people who use scientific and technological knowledge to solve practical problems. To design new products, engineers usually follow the process described here, even though they may not follow these steps in the exact order. As you read the steps, think about how you might apply them in technology labs.

Identify a Need

Before engineers begin designing a new product, they must first identify the need they are trying to meet. For example, suppose you are a member of a design team in a company that makes toys. Your team has identified a need: a toy boat that is inexpensive and easy to assemble.

Research the Problem

Engineers often begin by gathering information that will help them with their new design. This research may include finding articles in books, magazines, or on the Internet. It may also include talking to other engineers who have solved similar problems. Engineers often perform experiments related to the product they want to design.

For your toy boat, you could look at toys that are similar to the one you want to design. You might do research on the Internet. You could also test some materials to see whether they will work well in a toy boat.

Drawing for a boat design ▼

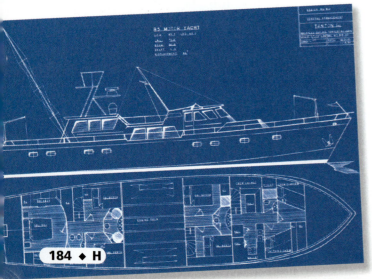

Design a Solution

Research gives engineers information that helps them design a product. When engineers design new products, they usually work in teams.

Generating Ideas Often design teams hold brainstorming meetings in which any team member can contribute ideas. **Brainstorming** is a creative process in which one team member's suggestions often spark ideas in other group members. Brainstorming can lead to new approaches to solving a design problem.

Evaluating Constraints During brainstorming, a design team will often come up with several possible designs. The team must then evaluate each one.

As part of their evaluation, engineers consider constraints. **Constraints** are factors that limit or restrict a product design. Physical characteristics, such as the properties of materials used to make your toy boat, are constraints. Money and time are also constraints. If the materials in a product cost a lot, or if the product takes a long time to make, the design may be impractical.

Making Trade-offs Design teams usually need to make trade-offs. In a **trade-off,** engineers give up one benefit of a proposed design in order to obtain another. In designing your toy boat, you will have to make trade-offs. For example, suppose one material is sturdy but not fully waterproof. Another material is more waterproof, but breakable. You may decide to give up the benefit of sturdiness in order to obtain the benefit of waterproofing.

Build and Evaluate a Prototype

Once the team has chosen a design plan, the engineers build a prototype of the product. A **prototype** is a working model used to test a design. Engineers evaluate the prototype to see whether it works well, is easy to operate, is safe to use, and holds up to repeated use.

Think of your toy boat. What would the prototype be like? Of what materials would it be made? How would you test it?

Troubleshoot and Redesign

Few prototypes work perfectly, which is why they need to be tested. Once a design team has tested a prototype, the members analyze the results and identify any problems. The team then tries to **troubleshoot,** or fix the design problems. For example, if your toy boat leaks or wobbles, the boat should be redesigned to eliminate those problems.

Communicate the Solution

A team needs to communicate the final design to the people who will manufacture and use the product. To do this, teams may use sketches, detailed drawings, computer simulations, and word descriptions.

Activity

You can use the technology design process to design and build a toy boat.

Research and Investigate

1. Visit the library or go online to research toy boats.

2. Investigate how a toy boat can be powered, including wind, rubber bands, or baking soda and vinegar.

3. Brainstorm materials, shapes, and steering for your boat.

Design and Build

4. Based on your research, design a toy boat that
   - is made of readily available materials
   - is no larger than 15 cm long and 10 cm wide
   - includes a power system, a rudder, and an area for cargo
   - travels 2 meters in a straight line carrying a load of 20 pennies

5. Sketch your design and write a step-by-step plan for building your boat. After your teacher approves your plan, build your boat.

Evaluate and Redesign

6. Test your boat, evaluate the results, and troubleshoot any problems.

7. Based on your evaluation, redesign your toy boat so it performs better.

Creating Data Tables and Graphs

How can you make sense of the data in a science experiment? The first step is to organize the data to help you understand them. Data tables and graphs are helpful tools for organizing data.

Data Tables

You have gathered your materials and set up your experiment. But before you start, you need to plan a way to record what happens during the experiment. By creating a data table, you can record your observations and measurements in an orderly way.

Suppose, for example, that a scientist conducted an experiment to find out how many Calories people of different body masses burn while doing various activities. The data table shows the results.

Notice in this data table that the manipulated variable (body mass) is the heading of one column. The responding variable (for

Calories Burned in 30 Minutes			
Body Mass	Experiment 1: Bicycling	Experiment 2: Playing Basketball	Experiment 3: Watching Television
30 kg	60 Calories	120 Calories	21 Calories
40 kg	77 Calories	164 Calories	27 Calories
50 kg	95 Calories	206 Calories	33 Calories
60 kg	114 Calories	248 Calories	38 Calories

Experiment 1, the number of Calories burned while bicycling) is the heading of the next column. Additional columns were added for related experiments.

Bar Graphs

To compare how many Calories a person burns doing various activities, you could create a bar graph. A bar graph is used to display data in a number of separate, or distinct, categories. In this example, bicycling, playing basketball, and watching television are the three categories.

To create a bar graph, follow these steps.

1. On graph paper, draw a horizontal, or *x*-, axis and a vertical, or *y*-, axis.

2. Write the names of the categories to be graphed along the horizontal axis. Include an overall label for the axis as well.

3. Label the vertical axis with the name of the responding variable. Include units of measurement. Then create a scale along the axis by marking off equally spaced numbers that cover the range of the data collected.

4. For each category, draw a solid bar using the scale on the vertical axis to determine the height. Make all the bars the same width.

5. Add a title that describes the graph.

Line Graphs

To see whether a relationship exists between body mass and the number of Calories burned while bicycling, you could create a line graph. A line graph is used to display data that show how one variable (the responding variable) changes in response to another variable (the manipulated variable). You can use a line graph when your manipulated variable is **continuous,** that is, when there are other points between the ones that you tested. In this example, body mass is a continuous variable because there are other body masses between 30 and 40 kilograms (for example, 31 kilograms). Time is another example of a continuous variable.

Line graphs are powerful tools because they allow you to estimate values for conditions that you did not test in the experiment. For example, you can use the line graph to estimate that a 35-kilogram person would burn 68 Calories while bicycling.

To create a line graph, follow these steps.

1. On graph paper, draw a horizontal, or *x*-, axis and a vertical, or *y*-, axis.

2. Label the horizontal axis with the name of the manipulated variable. Label the vertical axis with the name of the responding variable. Include units of measurement.

3. Create a scale on each axis by marking off equally spaced numbers that cover the range of the data collected.

4. Plot a point on the graph for each piece of data. In the line graph above, the dotted lines show how to plot the first data point (30 kilograms and 60 Calories). Follow an imaginary vertical line extending up from the horizontal axis at the 30-kilogram mark. Then follow an imaginary horizontal line extending across from the vertical axis at the 60-Calorie mark. Plot the point where the two lines intersect.

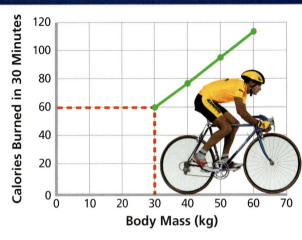

Effect of Body Mass on Calories Burned While Bicycling

5. Connect the plotted points with a solid line. (In some cases, it may be more appropriate to draw a line that shows the general trend of the plotted points. In those cases, some of the points may fall above or below the line. Also, not all graphs are linear. It may be more appropriate to draw a curve to connect the points.)

6. Add a title that identifies the variables or relationship in the graph.

Activity

Create line graphs to display the data from Experiment 2 and Experiment 3 in the data table.

Activity

You read in the newspaper that a total of 4 centimeters of rain fell in your area in June, 2.5 centimeters fell in July, and 1.5 centimeters fell in August. What type of graph would you use to display these data? Use graph paper to create the graph.

Circle Graphs

Like bar graphs, circle graphs can be used to display data in a number of separate categories. Unlike bar graphs, however, circle graphs can only be used when you have data for *all* the categories that make up a given topic. A circle graph is sometimes called a pie chart. The pie represents the entire topic, while the slices represent the individual categories. The size of a slice indicates what percentage of the whole a particular category makes up.

The data table below shows the results of a survey in which 24 teenagers were asked to identify their favorite sport. The data were then used to create the circle graph at the right.

Favorite Sports	
Sport	Students
Soccer	8
Basketball	6
Bicycling	6
Swimming	4

To create a circle graph, follow these steps.

1. Use a compass to draw a circle. Mark the center with a point. Then draw a line from the center point to the top of the circle.

2. Determine the size of each "slice" by setting up a proportion where *x* equals the number of degrees in a slice. (*Note:* A circle contains 360 degrees.) For example, to find the number of degrees in the "soccer" slice, set up the following proportion:

$$\frac{\text{Students who prefer soccer}}{\text{Total number of students}} = \frac{x}{\text{Total number of degrees in a circle}}$$

$$\frac{8}{24} = \frac{x}{360}$$

Cross-multiply and solve for x.

$$24x = 8 \times 360$$
$$x = 120$$

The "soccer" slice should contain 120 degrees.

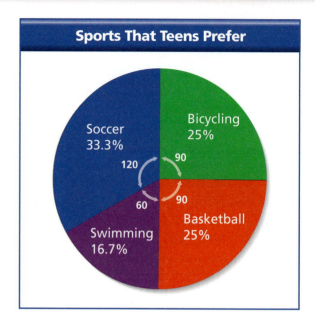

Sports That Teens Prefer

Soccer 33.3% — 120
Bicycling 25% — 90
Basketball 25% — 90
Swimming 16.7% — 60

3. Use a protractor to measure the angle of the first slice, using the line you drew to the top of the circle as the 0° line. Draw a line from the center of the circle to the edge for the angle you measured.

4. Continue around the circle by measuring the size of each slice with the protractor. Start measuring from the edge of the previous slice so the wedges do not overlap. When you are done, the entire circle should be filled in.

5. Determine the percentage of the whole circle that each slice represents. To do this, divide the number of degrees in a slice by the total number of degrees in a circle (360), and multiply by 100%. For the "soccer" slice, you can find the percentage as follows:

$$\frac{120}{360} \times 100\% = 33.3\%$$

6. Use a different color for each slice. Label each slice with the category and with the percentage of the whole it represents.

7. Add a title to the circle graph.

Activity

In a class of 28 students, 12 students take the bus to school, 10 students walk, and 6 students ride their bicycles. Create a circle graph to display these data.

Math Review

Scientists use math to organize, analyze, and present data. This appendix will help you review some basic math skills.

Mean, Median, and Mode

The **mean** is the average, or the sum of the data divided by the number of data items. The middle number in a set of ordered data is called the **median**. The **mode** is the number that appears most often in a set of data.

Example

A scientist counted the number of distinct songs sung by seven different male birds and collected the data shown below.

Male Bird Songs							
Bird	A	B	C	D	E	F	G
Number of Songs	36	29	40	35	28	36	27

To determine the mean number of songs, add the total number of songs and divide by the number of data items—in this case, the number of male birds.

Mean $= \frac{231}{7} = $ **33 songs**

To find the median number of songs, arrange the data in numerical order and find the number in the middle of the series.

27 28 29 35 36 36 40

The number in the middle is 35, so the median number of songs is 35.

The mode is the value that appears most frequently. In the data, 36 appears twice, while each other item appears only once. Therefore, 36 songs is the mode.

Practice

Find out how many minutes it takes each student in your class to get to school. Then find the mean, median, and mode for the data.

Probability

Probability is the chance that an event will occur. Probability can be expressed as a ratio, a fraction, or a percentage. For example, when you flip a coin, the probability that the coin will land heads up is 1 in 2, or $\frac{1}{2}$, or 50 percent.

The probability that an event will happen can be expressed in the following formula.

$P(\text{event}) = \dfrac{\text{Number of times the event can occur}}{\text{Total number of possible events}}$

Example

A paper bag contains 25 blue marbles, 5 green marbles, 5 orange marbles, and 15 yellow marbles. If you close your eyes and pick a marble from the bag, what is the probability that it will be yellow?

$P(\text{yellow marbles}) = \dfrac{\text{15 yellow marbles}}{\text{50 marbles total}}$

$P = \frac{15}{50}$, or $\frac{3}{10}$, or 30%

Practice

Each side of a cube has a letter on it. Two sides have *A*, three sides have *B*, and one side has *C*. If you roll the cube, what is the probability that *A* will land on top?

Area

The **area** of a surface is the number of square units that cover it. The front cover of your textbook has an area of about 600 cm².

Area of a Rectangle and a Square
To find the area of a rectangle, multiply its length times its width. The formula for the area of a rectangle is

$$A = \ell \times w, \text{ or } A = \ell w$$

Since all four sides of a square have the same length, the area of a square is the length of one side multiplied by itself, or squared.

$$A = s \times s, \text{ or } A = s^2$$

Example

A scientist is studying the plants in a field that measures 75 m × 45 m. What is the area of the field?

$$A = \ell \times w$$
$$A = 75 \text{ m} \times 45 \text{ m}$$
$$A = 3{,}375 \text{ m}^2$$

Area of a Circle
The formula for the area of a circle is

$$A = \pi \times r \times r, \text{ or } A = \pi r^2$$

The length of the radius is represented by r, and the value of π is approximately $\frac{22}{7}$.

Example

Find the area of a circle with a radius of 14 cm.

$$A = \pi r^2$$
$$A = 14 \times 14 \times \frac{22}{7}$$
$$A = 616 \text{ cm}^2$$

Practice

Find the area of a circle that has a radius of 21 m.

Circumference

The distance around a circle is called the circumference. The formula for finding the circumference of a circle is

$$C = 2 \times \pi \times r, \text{ or } C = 2\pi r$$

Example

The radius of a circle is 35 cm. What is its circumference?

$$C = 2\pi r$$
$$C = 2 \times 35 \times \frac{22}{7}$$
$$C = 220 \text{ cm}$$

Practice

What is the circumference of a circle with a radius of 28 m?

Volume

The volume of an object is the number of cubic units it contains. The volume of a wastebasket, for example, might be about 26,000 cm³.

Volume of a Rectangular Object
To find the volume of a rectangular object, multiply the object's length times its width times its height.

$$V = \ell \times w \times h, \text{ or } V = \ell w h$$

Example

Find the volume of a box with length 24 cm, width 12 cm, and height 9 cm.

$$V = \ell w h$$
$$V = 24 \text{ cm} \times 12 \text{ cm} \times 9 \text{ cm}$$
$$V = 2{,}592 \text{ cm}^3$$

Practice

What is the volume of a rectangular object with length 17 cm, width 11 cm, and height 6 cm?

Fractions

A **fraction** is a way to express a part of a whole. In the fraction $\frac{4}{7}$, 4 is the numerator and 7 is the denominator.

Adding and Subtracting Fractions

To add or subtract two or more fractions that have a common denominator, first add or subtract the numerators. Then write the sum or difference over the common denominator.

To find the sum or difference of fractions with different denominators, first find the least common multiple of the denominators. This is known as the least common denominator. Then convert each fraction to equivalent fractions with the least common denominator. Add or subtract the numerators. Then write the sum or difference over the common denominator.

Example

$$\frac{5}{6} - \frac{3}{4} = \frac{10}{12} - \frac{9}{12} = \frac{10 - 9}{12} = \frac{1}{12}$$

Multiplying Fractions

To multiply two fractions, first multiply the two numerators, then multiply the two denominators.

Example

$$\frac{5}{6} \times \frac{2}{3} = \frac{5 \times 2}{6 \times 3} = \frac{10}{18} = \frac{5}{9}$$

Dividing Fractions

Dividing by a fraction is the same as multiplying by its reciprocal. Reciprocals are numbers whose numerators and denominators have been switched. To divide one fraction by another, first invert the fraction you are dividing by—in other words, turn it upside down. Then multiply the two fractions.

Example

$$\frac{2}{5} \div \frac{7}{8} = \frac{2}{5} \times \frac{8}{7} = \frac{2 \times 8}{5 \times 7} = \frac{16}{35}$$

Practice

Solve the following: $\frac{3}{7} \div \frac{4}{5}$.

Decimals

Fractions whose denominators are 10, 100, or some other power of 10 are often expressed as decimals. For example, the fraction $\frac{9}{10}$ can be expressed as the decimal 0.9, and the fraction $\frac{7}{100}$ can be written as 0.07.

Adding and Subtracting With Decimals

To add or subtract decimals, line up the decimal points before you carry out the operation.

Example

$$\begin{array}{r} 27.4 \\ + \ 6.19 \\ \hline 33.59 \end{array} \qquad \begin{array}{r} 278.635 \\ - \ 191.4 \\ \hline 87.235 \end{array}$$

Multiplying With Decimals

When you multiply two numbers with decimals, the number of decimal places in the product is equal to the total number of decimal places in each number being multiplied.

Example

$$\begin{array}{r} 46.2 \ \text{(one decimal place)} \\ \times \ 2.37 \ \text{(two decimal places)} \\ \hline 109.494 \ \text{(three decimal places)} \end{array}$$

Dividing With Decimals

To divide a decimal by a whole number, put the decimal point in the quotient above the decimal point in the dividend.

Example

$$15.5 \div 5$$
$$\begin{array}{r} 3.1 \\ 5\overline{)15.5} \end{array}$$

To divide a decimal by a decimal, you need to rewrite the divisor as a whole number. Do this by multiplying both the divisor and dividend by the same multiple of 10.

Example

$$1.68 \div 4.2 = 16.8 \div 42$$
$$\begin{array}{r} 0.4 \\ 42\overline{)16.8} \end{array}$$

Practice

Multiply 6.21 by 8.5.

Ratio and Proportion

A **ratio** compares two numbers by division. For example, suppose a scientist counts 800 wolves and 1,200 moose on an island. The ratio of wolves to moose can be written as a fraction, $\frac{800}{1,200}$, which can be reduced to $\frac{2}{3}$. The same ratio can also be expressed as 2 to 3 or 2 : 3.

A **proportion** is a mathematical sentence saying that two ratios are equivalent. For example, a proportion could state that $\frac{800 \text{ wolves}}{1,200 \text{ moose}} = \frac{2 \text{ wolves}}{3 \text{ moose}}$. You can sometimes set up a proportion to determine or estimate an unknown quantity. For example, suppose a scientist counts 25 beetles in an area of 10 square meters. The scientist wants to estimate the number of beetles in 100 square meters.

> **Example**
>
> 1. Express the relationship between beetles and area as a ratio: $\frac{25}{10}$, simplified to $\frac{5}{2}$.
>
> 2. Set up a proportion, with x representing the number of beetles. The proportion can be stated as $\frac{5}{2} = \frac{x}{100}$.
>
> 3. Begin by cross-multiplying. In other words, multiply each fraction's numerator by the other fraction's denominator.
>
> $5 \times 100 = 2 \times x$, or $500 = 2x$
>
> 4. To find the value of x, divide both sides by 2. The result is 250, or 250 beetles in 100 square meters.

> **Practice**
>
> Find the value of x in the following proportion: $\frac{6}{7} = \frac{x}{49}$.

Percentage

A **percentage** is a ratio that compares a number to 100. For example, there are 37 granite rocks in a collection that consists of 100 rocks. The ratio $\frac{37}{100}$ can be written as 37%. Granite rocks make up 37% of the rock collection.

You can calculate percentages of numbers other than 100 by setting up a proportion.

> **Example**
>
> Rain falls on 9 days out of 30 in June. What percentage of the days in June were rainy?
>
> $$\frac{9 \text{ days}}{30 \text{ days}} = \frac{d\%}{100\%}$$
>
> To find the value of d, begin by cross-multiplying, as for any proportion:
>
> $9 \times 100 = 30 \times d$ $\quad d = \frac{900}{30}$ $\quad d = 30$

> **Practice**
>
> There are 300 marbles in a jar, and 42 of those marbles are blue. What percentage of the marbles are blue?

Significant Figures

The **precision** of a measurement depends on the instrument you use to take the measurement. For example, if the smallest unit on the ruler is millimeters, then the most precise measurement you can make will be in millimeters.

The sum or difference of measurements can only be as precise as the least precise measurement being added or subtracted. Round your answer so that it has the same number of digits after the decimal as the least precise measurement. Round up if the last digit is 5 or more, and round down if the last digit is 4 or less.

Example

Subtract a temperature of 5.2°C from the temperature 75.46°C.

75.46 − 5.2 = 70.26

5.2 has the fewest digits after the decimal, so it is the least precise measurement. Since the last digit of the answer is 6, round up to 3. The most precise difference between the measurements is 70.3°C.

Practice

Add 26.4 m to 8.37 m. Round your answer according to the precision of the measurements.

Significant figures are the number of nonzero digits in a measurement. Zeroes between nonzero digits are also significant. For example, the measurements 12,500 L, 0.125 cm, and 2.05 kg all have three significant figures. When you multiply and divide measurements, the one with the fewest significant figures determines the number of significant figures in your answer.

Example

Multiply 110 g by 5.75 g.

110 × 5.75 = 632.5

Because 110 has only two significant figures, round the answer to 630 g.

Scientific Notation

A **factor** is a number that divides into another number with no remainder. In the example, the number 3 is used as a factor four times.

An **exponent** tells how many times a number is used as a factor. For example, $3 \times 3 \times 3 \times 3$ can be written as 3^4. The exponent 4 indicates that the number 3 is used as a factor four times. Another way of expressing this is to say that 81 is equal to 3 to the fourth power.

Example

$$3^4 = 3 \times 3 \times 3 \times 3 = 81$$

Scientific notation uses exponents and powers of ten to write very large or very small numbers in shorter form. When you write a number in scientific notation, you write the number as two factors. The first factor is any number between 1 and 10. The second factor is a power of 10, such as 10^3 or 10^6.

Example

The average distance between the planet Mercury and the sun is 58,000,000 km. To write the first factor in scientific notation, insert a decimal point in the original number so that you have a number between 1 and 10. In the case of 58,000,000, the number is 5.8.

To determine the power of 10, count the number of places that the decimal point moved. In this case, it moved 7 places.

58,000,000 km = 5.8×10^7 km

Practice

Express 6,590,000 in scientific notation.

Reading Comprehension Skills

Each section in your textbook introduces a Target Reading Skill.
You will improve your reading comprehension by using the
Target Reading Skills described below.

Using Prior Knowledge

Your prior knowledge is what you already know before you begin to read about a topic. Building on what you already know gives you a head start on learning new information. Before you begin a new assignment, think about what you know. You might look at the headings and the visuals to spark your memory. You can list what you know. Then, as you read, consider questions like these.

• How does what you learn relate to what you know?

• How did something you already know help you learn something new?

• Did your original ideas agree with what you have just learned?

Asking Questions

Asking yourself questions is an excellent way to focus on and remember new information in your textbook. For example, you can turn the text headings into questions. Then your questions can guide you to identify the important information as you read. Look at these examples:

Heading: Using Seismographic Data

Question: How are seismographic data used?

Heading: Kinds of Faults

Question: What are the kinds of faults?

You do not have to limit your questions to text headings. Ask questions about anything that you need to clarify or that will help you understand the content. *What* and *how* are probably the most common question words, but you may also ask *why*, *who*, *when*, or *where* questions.

Previewing Visuals

Visuals are photographs, graphs, tables, diagrams, and illustrations. Visuals contain important information. Before you read, look at visuals and their labels and captions. This preview will help you prepare for what you will be reading.

Often you will be asked what you want to learn about a visual. For example, after you look at the normal fault diagram below, you might ask: What is the movement along a normal fault? Questions about visuals give you a purpose for reading—to answer your questions.

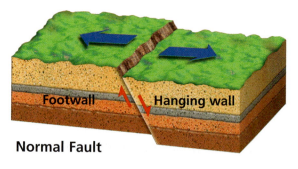

Footwall   Hanging wall

Normal Fault

Outlining

An outline shows the relationship between main ideas and supporting ideas. An outline has a formal structure. You write the main ideas, called topics, next to Roman numerals. The supporting ideas, called subtopics, are written under the main ideas and labeled A, B, C, and so on. An outline looks like this:

Technology and Society
I. Technology through history
II. The impact of technology on society
A.
B.

Identifying Main Ideas

When you are reading science material, it is important to try to understand the ideas and concepts that are in a passage. Each paragraph has a lot of information and detail. Good readers try to identify the most important—or biggest—idea in every paragraph or section. That's the main idea. The other information in the paragraph supports or further explains the main idea.

Sometimes main ideas are stated directly. In this book, some main ideas are identified for you as key concepts. These are printed in bold-face type. However, you must identify other main ideas yourself. In order to do this, you must identify all the ideas within a paragraph or section. Then ask yourself which idea is big enough to include all the other ideas.

Comparing and Contrasting

When you compare and contrast, you examine the similarities and differences between things. You can compare and contrast in a Venn diagram or in a table.

Venn Diagram A Venn diagram consists of two overlapping circles. In the space where the circles overlap, you write the characteristics that the two items have in common. In one of the circles outside the area of overlap, you write the differing features or characteristics of one of the items. In the other circle outside the area of overlap, you write the differing characteristics of the other item.

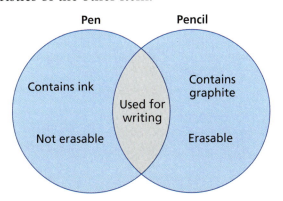

Pen — Pencil

Contains ink
Not erasable

Used for writing

Contains graphite
Erasable

Table In a compare/contrast table, you list the characteristics or features to be compared across the top of the table. Then list the items to be compared in the left column. Complete the table by filling in information about each characteristic or feature.

Blood Vessel	Function	Structure of Wall
Artery	Carries blood away from heart	
Capillary		
Vein		

Identifying Supporting Evidence

A hypothesis is a possible explanation for observations made by scientists or an answer to a scientific question. Scientists must carry out investigations and gather evidence that either supports or disproves the hypothesis.

Identifying the supporting evidence for a hypothesis or theory can help you understand the hypothesis or theory. Evidence consists of facts—information whose accuracy can be confirmed by testing or observation.

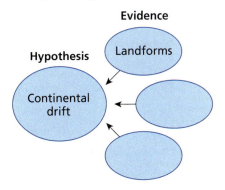

Evidence

Hypothesis — Landforms

Continental drift

Sequencing

A sequence is the order in which a series of events occurs. A flowchart or a cycle diagram can help you visualize a sequence.

Flowchart To make a flowchart, write a brief description of each step or event in a box. Place the boxes in order, with the first event at the top of the page. Then draw an arrow to connect each step or event to the next.

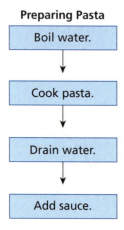

Preparing Pasta

Boil water.

↓

Cook pasta.

↓

Drain water.

↓

Add sauce.

Cycle Diagram A cycle diagram shows a sequence that is continuous, or cyclical. A continuous sequence does not have an end because when the final event is over, the first event begins again. To create a cycle diagram, write the starting event in a box placed at the top of a page in the center. Then, moving in a clockwise direction, write each event in a box in its proper sequence. Draw arrows that connect each event to the one that occurs next.

Seasons of the Year

Winter

Spring

Summer

Fall

Relating Cause and Effect

Science involves many cause-and-effect relationships. A cause makes something happen. An effect is what happens. When you recognize that one event causes another, you are relating cause and effect.

Words like *cause, because, effect, affect,* and *result* often signal a cause or an effect. Sometimes an effect can have more than one cause, or a cause can produce several effects.

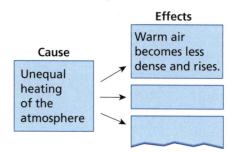

Cause

Unequal heating of the atmosphere

Effects

Warm air becomes less dense and rises.

Concept Mapping

Concept maps are useful tools for organizing information on any topic. A concept map begins with a main idea or core concept and shows how the idea can be subdivided into related subconcepts or smaller ideas.

You construct a concept map by placing concepts (usually nouns) in ovals and connecting them with linking words (usually verbs). The biggest concept or idea is placed in an oval at the top of the map. Related concepts are arranged in ovals below the big idea. The linking words connect the ovals.

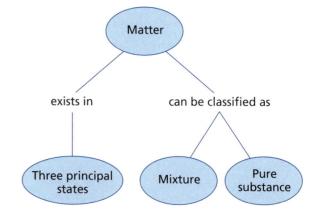

Matter

exists in

can be classified as

Three principal states

Mixture

Pure substance

Building Vocabulary

Knowing the meaning of these prefixes, suffixes, and roots will help you understand the meaning of words you do not recognize.

Word Origins Many science words come to English from other languages, such as Greek and Latin. By learning the meaning of a few common Greek and Latin roots, you can determine the meaning of unfamiliar science words.

Prefixes A prefix is a word part that is added at the beginning of a root or base word to change its meaning.

Suffixes A suffix is a word part that is added at the end of a root word to change the meaning.

Greek and Latin Roots

Greek Roots	Meaning	Example
ast-	star	astronaut
geo-	Earth	geology
metron-	measure	kilometer
opt-	eye	optician
photo-	light	photograph
scop-	see	microscope
therm-	heat	thermostat
Latin Roots	Meaning	Example
aqua-	water	aquarium
aud-	hear	auditorium
duc-, duct-	lead	conduct
flect-	bend	reflect
fract-, frag-	break	fracture
ject-	throw	reject
luc-	light	lucid
spec-	see	inspect

Prefixes and Suffixes

Prefix	Meaning	Example
com-, con-	with	communicate, concert
de-	from; down	decay
di-	two	divide
ex-, exo-	out	exhaust
in-, im-	in, into; not	inject, impossible
re-	again; back	reflect, recall
trans-	across	transfer
Suffix	**Meaning**	**Example**
-al	relating to	natural
-er, -or	one who	teacher, doctor
-ist	one who practices	scientist
-ity	state of	equality
-ology	study of	biology
-tion, -sion	state or quality of	reaction, tension

Safety Symbols

These symbols warn of possible dangers in the laboratory and remind you to work carefully.

 Safety Goggles Wear safety goggles to protect your eyes in any activity involving chemicals, flames or heating, or glassware.

 Lab Apron Wear a laboratory apron to protect your skin and clothing from damage.

 Breakage Handle breakable materials, such as glassware, with care. Do not touch broken glassware.

 Heat-Resistant Gloves Use an oven mitt or other hand protection when handling hot materials such as hot plates or hot glassware.

 Plastic Gloves Wear disposable plastic gloves when working with harmful chemicals and organisms. Keep your hands away from your face, and dispose of the gloves according to your teacher's instructions.

 Heating Use a clamp or tongs to pick up hot glassware. Do not touch hot objects with your bare hands.

 Flames Before you work with flames, tie back loose hair and clothing. Follow instructions from your teacher about lighting and extinguishing flames.

 No Flames When using flammable materials, make sure there are no flames, sparks, or other exposed heat sources present.

 Corrosive Chemical Avoid getting acid or other corrosive chemicals on your skin or clothing or in your eyes. Do not inhale the vapors. Wash your hands after the activity.

 Poison Do not let any poisonous chemical come into contact with your skin, and do not inhale its vapors. Wash your hands when you are finished with the activity.

 Fumes Work in a ventilated area when harmful vapors may be involved. Avoid inhaling vapors directly. Only test an odor when directed to do so by your teacher, and use a wafting motion to direct the vapor toward your nose.

 Sharp Object Scissors, scalpels, knives, needles, pins, and tacks can cut your skin. Always direct a sharp edge or point away from yourself and others.

 Animal Safety Treat live or preserved animals or animal parts with care to avoid harming the animals or yourself. Wash your hands when you are finished with the activity.

 Plant Safety Handle plants only as directed by your teacher. If you are allergic to certain plants, tell your teacher; do not do an activity involving those plants. Avoid touching harmful plants such as poison ivy. Wash your hands when you are finished with the activity.

 Electric Shock To avoid electric shock, never use electrical equipment around water, or when the equipment is wet or your hands are wet. Be sure cords are untangled and cannot trip anyone. Unplug equipment not in use.

 Physical Safety When an experiment involves physical activity, avoid injuring yourself or others. Alert your teacher if there is any reason you should not participate.

 Disposal Dispose of chemicals and other laboratory materials safely. Follow the instructions from your teacher.

 Hand Washing Wash your hands thoroughly when finished with the activity. Use antibacterial soap and warm water. Rinse well.

 General Safety Awareness When this symbol appears, follow the instructions provided. When you are asked to develop your own procedure in a lab, have your teacher approve your plan before you go further.

Science Safety Rules

General Precautions

Follow all instructions. Never perform activities without the approval and supervision of your teacher. Do not engage in horseplay. Never eat or drink in the laboratory. Keep work areas clean and uncluttered.

Dress Code

Wear safety goggles whenever you work with chemicals, glassware, heat sources such as burners, or any substance that might get into your eyes. If you wear contact lenses, notify your teacher.

Wear a lab apron or coat whenever you work with corrosive chemicals or substances that can stain. Wear disposable plastic gloves when working with organisms and harmful chemicals. Tie back long hair. Remove or tie back any article of clothing or jewelry that can hang down and touch chemicals, flames, or equipment. Roll up long sleeves. Never wear open shoes or sandals.

First Aid

Report all accidents, injuries, or fires to your teacher, no matter how minor. Be aware of the location of the first-aid kit, emergency equipment such as the fire extinguisher and fire blanket, and the nearest telephone. Know whom to contact in an emergency.

Heating and Fire Safety

Keep all combustible materials away from flames. When heating a substance in a test tube, make sure that the mouth of the tube is not pointed at you or anyone else. Never heat a liquid in a closed container. Use an oven mitt to pick up a container that has been heated.

Using Chemicals Safely

Never put your face near the mouth of a container that holds chemicals. Never touch, taste, or smell a chemical unless your teacher tells you to.

Use only those chemicals needed in the activity. Keep all containers closed when chemicals are not being used. Pour all chemicals over the sink or a container, not over your work surface. Dispose of excess chemicals as instructed by your teacher.

Be extra careful when working with acids or bases. When mixing an acid and water, always pour the water into the container first and then add the acid to the water. Never pour water into an acid. Wash chemical spills and splashes immediately with plenty of water.

Using Glassware Safely

If glassware is broken or chipped, notify your teacher immediately. Never handle broken or chipped glass with your bare hands.

Never force glass tubing or thermometers into a rubber stopper or rubber tubing. Have your teacher insert the glass tubing or thermometer if required for an activity.

Using Sharp Instruments

Handle sharp instruments with extreme care. Never cut material toward you; cut away from you.

Animal and Plant Safety

Never perform experiments that cause pain, discomfort, or harm to animals. Only handle animals if absolutely necessary. If you know that you are allergic to certain plants, molds, or animals, tell your teacher before doing an activity in which these are used. Wash your hands thoroughly after any activity involving animals, animal parts, plants, plant parts, or soil.

During field work, wear long pants, long sleeves, socks, and closed shoes. Avoid poisonous plants and fungi as well as plants with thorns.

End-of-Experiment Rules

Unplug all electrical equipment. Clean up your work area. Dispose of waste materials as instructed by your teacher. Wash your hands after every experiment.

The microscope is an essential tool in the study of life science. It allows you to see things that are too small to be seen with the unaided eye.

You will probably use a compound microscope like the one you see here. The compound microscope has more than one lens that magnifies the object you view.

Typically, a compound microscope has one lens in the eyepiece, the part you look through. The eyepiece lens usually magnifies 10 ×. Any object you view through this lens would appear 10 times larger than it is.

The compound microscope may contain one or two other lenses called objective lenses. If there are two objective lenses, they are called the low-power and high-power objective lenses. The low-power objective lens usually magnifies 10 ×. The high-power objective lens usually magnifies 40 ×.

To calculate the total magnification with which you are viewing an object, multiply the magnification of the eyepiece lens by the magnification of the objective lens you are using. For example, the eyepiece's magnification of 10 × multiplied by the low-power objective's magnification of 10 × equals a total magnification of 100 ×.

Use the photo of the compound microscope to become familiar with the parts of the microscope and their functions.

The Parts of a Compound Microscope

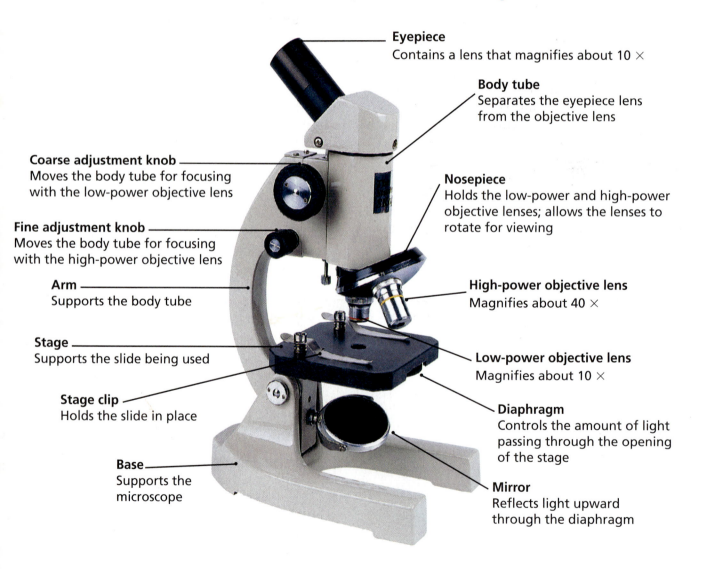

Eyepiece
Contains a lens that magnifies about 10 ×

Body tube
Separates the eyepiece lens from the objective lens

Coarse adjustment knob
Moves the body tube for focusing with the low-power objective lens

Nosepiece
Holds the low-power and high-power objective lenses; allows the lenses to rotate for viewing

Fine adjustment knob
Moves the body tube for focusing with the high-power objective lens

Arm
Supports the body tube

High-power objective lens
Magnifies about 40 ×

Stage
Supports the slide being used

Low-power objective lens
Magnifies about 10 ×

Stage clip
Holds the slide in place

Diaphragm
Controls the amount of light passing through the opening of the stage

Base
Supports the microscope

Mirror
Reflects light upward through the diaphragm

Using the Microscope

Use the following procedures when you are working with a microscope.

1. To carry the microscope, grasp the microscope's arm with one hand. Place your other hand under the base.
2. Place the microscope on a table with the arm toward you.
3. Turn the coarse adjustment knob to raise the body tube.
4. Revolve the nosepiece until the low-power objective lens clicks into place.
5. Adjust the diaphragm. While looking through the eyepiece, also adjust the mirror until you see a bright white circle of light. **CAUTION:** *Never use direct sunlight as a light source.*
6. Place a slide on the stage. Center the specimen over the opening on the stage. Use the stage clips to hold the slide in place. **CAUTION:** *Glass slides are fragile.*
7. Look at the stage from the side. Carefully turn the coarse adjustment knob to lower the body tube until the low-power objective almost touches the slide.
8. Looking through the eyepiece, very slowly turn the coarse adjustment knob until the specimen comes into focus.
9. To switch to the high-power objective lens, look at the microscope from the side. Carefully revolve the nosepiece until the high-power objective lens clicks into place. Make sure the lens does not hit the slide.
10. Looking through the eyepiece, turn the fine adjustment knob until the specimen comes into focus.

Making a Wet-Mount Slide

Use the following procedures to make a wet-mount slide of a specimen.

1. Obtain a clean microscope slide and a coverslip. **CAUTION:** *Glass slides and coverslips are fragile.*
2. Place the specimen on the slide. The specimen must be thin enough for light to pass through it.
3. Using a plastic dropper, place a drop of water on the specimen.
4. Gently place one edge of the coverslip against the slide so that it touches the edge of the water drop at a 45° angle. Slowly lower the coverslip over the specimen. If air bubbles are trapped beneath the coverslip, tap the coverslip gently with the eraser end of a pencil.
5. Remove any excess water at the edge of the coverslip with a paper towel.

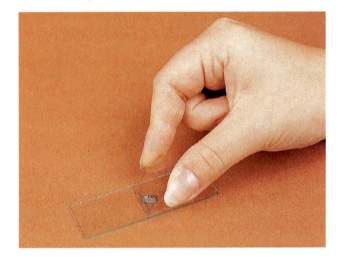

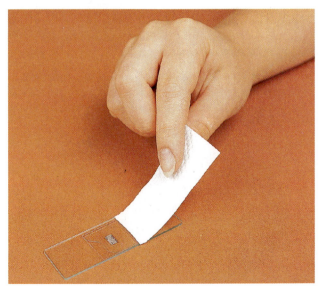

English and Spanish Glossary

A

abyssal plain A smooth, nearly flat region of the deep ocean floor. (p. 135)
llanura abisal Región llana, casi plana, de la cuenca oceánica profunda.

acid rain Rain or another form of precipitation that is more acidic than normal, caused by the release of molecules of sulfur dioxide and nitrogen oxide into the air. (p. 73)
lluvia ácida Lluvia u otra forma de precipitación que es más ácida de lo normal, debido a la contaminación del aire con moléculas de dióxido de azufre y óxido de nitrógeno.

aquaculture The farming of saltwater and freshwater organisms. (p. 160)
acuicultura Crianza de organismos de agua salada y dulce.

aquifer An underground layer of permeable rock or sediment that holds water. (p. 36)
acuífero Capa subterránea de roca o sedimento permeable que retiene agua.

artesian well A well in which water rises because of pressure within the aquifer. (p. 38)
pozo artesiano Pozo por el que el agua se eleva debido a la presión dentro del acuífero.

atoll A ring-shaped coral reef that surrounds a shallow lagoon. (p. 152)
atolón Arrecife de coral con forma de anillo que rodea a una laguna poco profunda.

B

benthos Organisms that live on the bottom of the ocean or other body of water. (p. 143)
bentos Organismos que viven en el fondo del océano u otro cuerpo de agua.

bioluminescence The production of light by living things. (p. 156)
bioluminiscencia Producción de luz por seres vivos.

C

capillary action The combined force of attraction among water molecules and with the molecules of surrounding materials. (p. 8)
acción capilar Fuerza de atracción combinada entre las moléculas de agua y entre esas moléculas y los materiales circundantes.

climate The pattern of temperature and precipitation typical of an area over a long period of time. (p. 118)
clima Patrón de temperatura y precipitación típico de un área a lo largo de mucho tiempo.

coagulation The process by which particles in a liquid clump together. (p. 60)
coagulación Proceso por el cual partículas presentes en un líquido forman cúmulos.

concentration The amount of one substance in a certain volume of another substance. (p. 58)
concentración Cantidad de una sustancia que hay en cierto volumen de otra sustancia.

condensation The process by which a gas changes to a liquid. (p. 11)
condensación Proceso por el cual un gas se convierte en líquido.

conservation The practice of using less of a resource so that it will not be used up. (p. 52)
conservación Práctica de usar menos de un recurso para que no se agote.

continental shelf A gently sloping, shallow area of the ocean floor that extends outward from the edge of a continent. (p. 134)
plataforma continental Área poco profunda con pendiente suave del suelo oceánico que se extiende desde los márgenes de un continente.

continental slope A steep incline of the ocean floor leading down from the edge of the continental shelf. (p. 134)
talud continental Región del suelo oceánico con pendiente empinada que baja del borde de la plataforma continental.

Coriolis effect The effect of Earth's rotation on the direction of winds and currents. (p. 117)
efecto de Coriolis Efecto de la rotación terrestre sobre la dirección de los vientos y las corrientes.

current A large stream of moving water that flows through the oceans. (p. 116)
corriente Un gran volumen de agua que fluye por los océanos.

desalination The process of obtaining fresh water from salt water by removing the salt. (p. 54)
desalinización Proceso mediante el cual se obtiene agua dulce a partir de agua salada eliminando la sal.

divide A ridge of land that separates one watershed from another. (p. 21)
divisoria de aguas Elevación de terreno que separa una cuenca hidrográfica de otra.

drought A long period of scarce rainfall. (p. 78)
sequía Período largo de escasas lluvias.

El Niño An abnormal climate event that occurs every two to seven years in the Pacific Ocean, causing changes in winds, currents, and weather patterns for one to two years. (p. 119)
El Niño Suceso climático anormal que se presenta cada dos a siete años en el océano Pacífico y que causa cambios en los vientos, corrientes y patrones meteorológicos que duran uno o dos años.

estuary A coastal inlet or bay where fresh water from rivers mixes with salty ocean water. (p. 148)
estuario Ensenada o bahía costera donde el agua dulce de los ríos se mezcla con el agua salada del mar.

eutrophication The process by which nutrients in a lake build up over time and cause an increase in the growth of algae. (p. 26)
eutrofización Proceso por el cual se van acumulando nutrientes en un lago y producen un aumento en el crecimiento de algas.

evaporation The process by which molecules at the surface of a liquid absorb enough energy to change to the gaseous state. (p. 10)
evaporación Proceso por el cual las moléculas en la superficie de un líquido absorben suficiente energía para pasar al estado gaseoso.

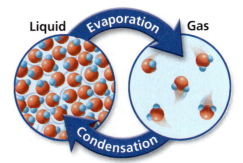

filtration The process of passing water through a series of screens that allow the water through, but not larger solid particles. (p. 60)
filtración Proceso en el que el agua pasa por una serie de mallas que impiden el paso de partículas sólidas grandes.

flash flood A sudden, violent flood that occurs within a few hours, or even minutes, of a storm. (p. 81)
crecida rápida Inundación repentina y violenta que ocurre en unas pocas horas, o incluso minutos, después de iniciada una tormenta.

food web The feeding relationships in a habitat. (p. 144)
red alimentaria Relaciones de alimentación en un hábitat.

frequency The number of waves that pass a specific point in a given amount of time. (p. 96)
frecuencia Número de ondas u olas que pasan por un punto dado en cierto tiempo.

English and Spanish Glossary

G

groin A wall made of rocks or concrete that is built outward from a beach to reduce erosion. (p. 101)
escollera Pared de piedra o concreto que se construye perpendicularmente a una playa para reducir la erosión.

groundwater Water that fills the cracks and spaces in underground soil and rock layers. (p. 15)
aguas freáticas Aguas que llenan las grietas y espacios de las capas subterráneas de suelo y roca.

H

habitat The place where an organism lives and where it obtains all the things it needs to survive. (p. 13)
hábitat Lugar donde vive un organismo y donde obtiene todo lo que necesita para sobrevivir.

hardness The level of the minerals calcium and magnesium in water. (p. 59)
dureza Cantidad de los minerales calcio y magnesio que contiene el agua.

hydroelectric power Electricity produced by the kinetic energy of water moving over a waterfall or dam. (p. 85)
energía hidroeléctrica Electricidad producida a partir de la energía cinética del agua que baja por una catarata o presa.

hydrothermal vent An area where ocean water sinks through cracks in the ocean floor, is heated by the underlying magma, and rises again through the cracks. (p. 157)
chimenea hidrotermal Área en la que aguas oceánicas se cuelan por grietas del suelo oceánico, son calentadas por el magma subyacente y ascienden otra vez por las grietas.

I

impermeable A characteristic of materials, such as clay and granite, through which water does not easily pass. (p. 35)
impermeable Característica de los materiales, como la arcilla y el granito, que no dejan pasar fácilmente el agua.

intertidal zone An area that stretches from the highest high-tide line on land out to the point on the continental shelf exposed by the lowest low tide. (p. 142)
zona intermareal Área que se extiende desde la línea más alta de pleamar en tierra hasta el punto de la plataforma continental expuesto por la bajamar más baja.

irrigation The process of supplying water to areas of land to make them suitable for growing crops. (p. 51)
irrigación Proceso mediante el cual se suministra agua a áreas de terreno para que pueda sembrarse en ellas.

K

kinetic energy The form of energy that an object has when it is moving. (p. 85)
energía cinética Forma de energía que tiene un objeto cuando está en movimiento.

L

levee A long ridge formed by deposits of sediments alongside a river channel. (p. 83)
dique Elevación larga formada por depósitos de sedimentos a lo largo del cauce de un río.

longshore drift The movement of sand along a beach. (p. 99)
deriva litoral Movimiento de arena a lo largo de una playa.

M

mid-ocean ridge A continuous range of mountains on the ocean floor that winds around Earth. (p. 135)
dorsal oceánica Cordillera continua en el suelo oceánico que serpentea por toda la Tierra.

N

neap tide A tide with the least difference between low and high tide that occurs when the sun and moon pull at right angles to each other at the first and third quarters of the moon. (p. 104)
marea muerta Marea con la mínima diferencia entre pleamar y bajamar; se presenta cuando el Sol y la Luna ejercen su atracción en direcciones que forman un ángulo recto, durante los cuartos creciente y menguante de la Luna.

nekton Free-swimming animals that can move throughout the water column. (p. 143)
necton Animales que nadan libremente y pueden desplazarse por la columna de agua.

neritic zone The area of the ocean that extends from the low-tide line out to the edge of the continental shelf. (p. 142)
zona nerítica Área del océano que se extiende desde la línea de bajamar hasta el borde de la plataforma continental.

nodule A lump on the ocean floor that forms when metals such as manganese build up around pieces of shell. (p. 162)
nódulo Protuberancia formada en el suelo oceánico cuando metales, como el manganeso, se depositan sobre pedazos de concha.

nonpoint source A widely spread source of pollution that is difficult to link to a specific point of origin. (p. 69)
fuente dispersa Fuente muy extendida de contaminación que es difícil vincular a un punto específico de origen.

nutrient A substance such as nitrogen or phosphorus that enables plants and algae to grow. (p. 26)
nutriente Sustancia, como el nitrógeno o el fósforo, que permite el crecimiento de plantas y algas.

O

open-ocean zone The deepest, darkest area of the ocean beyond the edge of the continental shelf. (p. 142)
zona de mar abierto Zona más profunda y oscura del océano, más allá de la plataforma continental.

P

permeable A characteristic of materials, such as sand and gravel, through which water easily passes. (p. 35)
permeable Característica de materiales, como la arena y la grava, por los que pasa fácilmente el agua.

pesticide A chemical intended to kill insects and other organisms that damage crops. (p. 74)
pesticida Sustancia química empleada para matar insectos y otros organismos que dañan los cultivos.

pH The measurement of how acidic or basic a substance is, on a scale of 0 (very acidic) to 14 (very basic). (p. 58)
pH Medida de qué tan ácida o básica es una sustancia, en una escala de 0 (muy ácida) a 14 (muy básica).

photosynthesis The process by which plants use water, along with carbon dioxide and energy from the sun, to make their own food. (p. 13)
fotosíntesis Proceso por el cual las plantas usan el agua, el dióxido de carbono y la energía del Sol para elaborar su propio alimento.

plankton Tiny algae and animals that float in water and are carried by waves and currents. (p. 143)
plancton Algas y animales diminutos que flotan en el agua a merced de las olas y las corrientes.

plate One of the major pieces of solid rock that make up Earth's upper layer. (p. 137)
placa Una de las grandes piezas de roca sólida que componen la capa superior de la Tierra.

point source A specific source of pollution that can be identified. (p. 69)
fuente localizada Fuente específica de contaminación que puede identificarse.

polar molecule A molecule that has electrically charged areas. (p. 7)
molécula polar Molécula que posee áreas con carga eléctrica.

pollutant A substance that causes pollution. (p. 69)
contaminante Sustancia que causa contaminación.

potential energy Energy that is stored and waiting to be used. (p. 85)
energía potencial Energía que está almacenada para usarse posteriormente.

precipitation Water that falls to Earth as rain, snow, hail, or sleet. (p. 17)
precipitación Agua que cae a la superficie terrestre en forma de lluvia, nieve, granizo o aguanieve.

R

reservoir A lake that stores water for human use. (p. 25)
embalse Lago en el que se almacena agua para uso humano.

rip current A rush of water that flows rapidly back to sea through a narrow opening in a sandbar. (p. 99)
corriente de resaca Torrente de agua que fluye con fuerza desde una playa hacia mar adentro por un canal estrecho en un banco de arena.

S

salinity The total amount of dissolved salts in a water sample. (p. 109)
salinidad Cantidad total de sales disueltas en una muestra de agua.

saturated zone The area of permeable rock or soil in which the cracks and pores are totally filled with water. (p. 35)
zona saturada Área de roca o suelo permeable cuyas grietas y poros están totalmente llenos de agua.

seafloor spreading A process by which new rock is added to the ocean floor along the boundary between diverging plates. (p. 138)
expansión del suelo oceánico Proceso por el cual se añade roca nueva al suelo oceánico a lo largo del borde de placas divergentes.

sewage Wastewater containing human wastes. (p. 62)
aguas residuales Aguas que contienen desechos humanos.

solution A mixture that forms when one substance dissolves another. (p. 8)
solución Mezcla que se forma cuando una sustancia disuelve a otra.

solvent A substance that dissolves another substance. (p. 8)
solvente Sustancia que disuelve otra sustancia.

sonar A system that uses sound waves to calculate the distance to an object, and that gets its name from *so*und *na*vigation and *r*anging. (p. 133)
sonar Sistema que utiliza ondas sonoras para calcular la distancia a la que está un objeto. Su nombre proviene de la frase en inglés "*so*und *na*vigation and *r*anging" (navegación y determinación de distancias por sonido).

specific heat The amount of heat needed to increase the temperature of a certain mass of a substance by 1°C. (p. 9)
calor específico Cantidad de calor necesaria para elevar en 1°C la temperatura de cierta masa de una sustancia.

spring tide A tide with the greatest difference between high and low tide that occurs when the sun and the moon are aligned with Earth at the new moon and the full moon. (p. 104)
marea viva Marea que presenta la mayor diferencia entre pleamar y bajamar; se presenta cuando el Sol y la Luna están alineados con la Tierra en la luna nueva y la luna llena.

submersible An underwater vehicle built of strong materials to resist pressure. (p. 113)
sumergible Vehículo submarino hecho de materiales fuertes para resistir la presión.

surface tension The tightness across the surface of water that is caused by the polar molecules pulling on one another. (p. 8)
tensión superficial Tirantez que hay en la superficie del agua debido a que sus moléculas polares tiran unas de otras.

T

tides The daily rise and fall of Earth's waters on its coastlines. (p. 103)
mareas Ascenso y descenso diario de las aguas de la Tierra en las costas.

transpiration The process by which plants give off water vapor through their leaves. (p. 16)
transpiración Proceso por el cual las plantas desprenden vapor de agua de sus hojas.

trench A deep, steep-sided canyon in the ocean floor.
fosa Cañón profundo, de lados empinados, en el suelo oceánico. (p. 136)

tributary A stream or smaller river that feeds into a main river. (p. 20)
afluente Arroyo o río más pequeño que desemboca en un río principal.

tsunami A giant wave usually caused by an earthquake beneath the ocean floor. (p. 98)
tsunami Ola gigantesca, casi siempre causada por un sismo bajo el suelo oceánico.

U

unsaturated zone The layer of rocks and soil above the water table in which the pores contain air as well as water. (p. 35)
zona insaturada Capa de rocas y suelo encima del nivel freático en la cual los poros contienen aire además de agua.

upwelling The movement of cold water upward from the deep ocean that is caused by wind. (p. 120)
atloramiento Movimiento ascendente de aguas frías desde las profundidades del mar, causado por los vientos.

W

water cycle The continuous process by which water moves from Earth's surface to the atmosphere and back. (p. 16)
ciclo del agua Proceso continuo por el cual el agua pasa de la superficie terrestre a la atmósfera y regresa.

water pollution The addition of any substance that has a negative effect on water or the living things that depend on the water. (p. 69)
contaminación del agua Adición de cualquier sustancia que tiene un efecto negativo al agua o los seres vivos que dependen de ella.

water quality The degree of purity of water, determined by measuring the substances in water besides water molecules. (p. 58)
calidad del agua Grado de pureza del agua, determinado por medición de las sustancias que el agua contiene además de sus propias moléculas.

watershed The land area that supplies water to a river system. (p. 21)
cuenca hidrográfica Área de terreno que suministra agua a un sistema fluvial.

water table The top of the saturated zone, or depth to the groundwater under Earth's surface. (p. 35)
nivel freático Límite superior de la zona saturada, o distancia hasta las aguas freáticas bajo la superficie terrestre.

wave The movement of energy through a body of water. (p. 95)
ola Movimiento de energía a través de un cuerpo de agua.

wave height The vertical distance from the crest of a wave to the trough. (p. 96)
altura de una ola Distancia vertical desde la cresta de una ola hasta el valle.

wavelength The horizontal distance between two wave crests. (p. 96)
longitud de una ola Distancia horizontal entre dos crestas de ola.

wetland A land area that is covered with a shallow layer of water during some or all of the year. (p. 28)
humedal Área de terreno cubierta por una capa superficial de agua durante una parte del año, o todo el tiempo.

Index

Page numbers for key terms are printed in **boldface** type.
Page numbers for illustrations, maps, and charts are printed in *italics*.

Index

Page numbers for key terms are printed in **boldface** type.
Page numbers for illustrations, maps, and charts are printed in *italics*.

Index

Page numbers for key terms are printed in **boldface** type.
Page numbers for illustrations, maps, and charts are printed in *italics*.

Acknowledgments

Staff Credits

Diane Alimena, Scott Andrews, Jennifer Angel, Michele Angelucci, Laura Baselice, Carolyn Belanger, Barbara A. Bertell, Suzanne Biron, Peggy Bliss, Stephanie Bradley, James Brady, Anne M. Bray, Sarah M. Carroll, Kerry Cashman, Jonathan Cheney, Joshua D. Clapper, Lisa J. Clark, Bob Craton, Patricia Cully, Patricia M. Dambry, Kathy Dempsey, Leanne Esterly, Emily Ellen, Thomas Ferreira, Jonathan Fisher, Patricia Fromkin, Paul Gagnon, Kathy Gavilanes, Holly Gordon, Robert Graham, Ellen Granter, Diane Grossman, Barbara Hollingdale, Linda Johnson, Anne Jones, John Judge, Kevin Keane, Kelly Kelliher, Toby Klang, Sue Langan, Russ Lappa, Carolyn Lock, Rebecca Loveys, Constance J. McCarty, Carolyn B. McGuire, Ranida Touranont McKneally, Anne McLaughlin, Eve Melnechuk, Natania Mlawer, Janet Morris, Karyl Murray, Francine Neumann, Baljit Nijjar, Marie Opera, Jill Ort, Kim Ortell, Joan Paley, Dorothy Preston, Maureen Raymond, Laura Ross, Rashid Ross, Siri Schwartzman, Melissa Shustyk, Laurel Smith, Emily Soltanoff, Jennifer A. Teece, Elizabeth Torjussen, Amanda M. Watters, Merce Wilczek, Amy Winchester, Char Lyn Yeakley. **Additional Credits:** Tara Alamilla, Louise Gachet, Allen Gold, Andrea Golden, Terence Hegarty, Etta Jacobs, Meg Montgomery, Stephanie Rogers, Kim Schmidt, Adam Teller, Joan Tobin.

Illustration

David Corrente: 127, 171; **John Edwards and Associates**: 64–65, 99, 143; **Kevin Jones and Associates**: 16, 76; **XNR Productions**: 49, 137. **All charts and graphs by Matt Mayerchak.**

Photography

Photo Research Paula Wehde

Cover Image top, Larry Ulrich; **bottom**, Stuart Westmoreland/Getty Images, Inc.

Page vi, Corbis; **vii**, Richard Haynes; **viii**, Richard Haynes; **x**, Norbert Wu; **1 both**, Norbert Wu; **2–3**, Dale Stokes/Norbert Wu; **3t**, Norbert Wu; **3b**, Dale Stokes/Norbert Wu.

Chapter 1

Pages 4–5, Larry Carver; **5 inset**, Richard Haynes; **6t**, Russ Lappa; **6–7b**, Randy Linchs/Sharpshooters; **8b**, Richard Haynes; **8m**, Visuals Unlimited; **8t**, Richard Haynes; **9**, Grafton Marshall-Smith/Corbis; **10l**, Karen Mancinelli; **10m**, Clive Streeter/Dorling Kindersley; **10r**, Japack/Leo de Wys; **12**, Rana Clamitans/Visuals Unlimited; **13**, AFP/Corbis; **17**, Norbert Schafer/Corbis; **18**, Richard Haynes; **19**, Dennis Welch/Imagestate; **24**, Dave G. Houser/Corbis; **25l**, Royalty Free/Corbis; **25r**, David Parker/Photo Researchers Inc.; **27**, AP/Wide World Photos; **28b**, Wolfgang Kaehler/Corbis; **28t**, Russ Lappa; **29l**, John Eastcott /Yva Momatiuk/Animals Animals/Earth Scenes; **29r**, Breck P. Kent/Animals Animals/Earth Scenes; **32**, Doug Perrine/Seapics; **33**, Salvatore Vasapolli/Earthscenes; **34**, Richard Haynes; **38**, John Paul Kay/Peter Arnold Inc.; **39**, Joseph Van Os/Getty Images, Inc.; **40**, Richard Haynes; **41**, Mark Thayer; **42**, Rana Clamitans/Visuals Unlimited.

Chapter 2

Pages 46–47, Julian Hirshowitz/Corbis; **47 inset**, Richard Haynes; **49b**, Jim Richardson; **49t**, Corbis; **50l**, Liba Taylor/Corbis; **50r**, O. Louis Mazzatenta/National Geographic Image Collection; **51l**, Tom Bean/Getty Images, Inc.; **51r**, Richard T. Nowitz/Corbis; **53**, L. Lefkowitz/Getty Images, Inc.; **55**, Ralph A. Clevenger/Corbis Westlight; **56**, Russ Lappa; **57**, Uniphoto; **58**, Richard Haynes; **59**, Jim Cummins/Getty Images, Inc.; **64–65 all**, Courtesy of Massachusetts Water Resources Authority, Boston, MA; **67**, Richard Haynes; **68t**, Russ Lappa; **68b**, Harrison Shull; **69**, Getty Images, Inc.; **71**, Bettmann/Corbis; **72 inset l**, Digital Vision/Getty Images, Inc.; **72 inset r**, Jouanne Thomas/Corbis; **72–73**, David Woodfall/Getty Images, Inc.; **73 inset l**, Getty Images, Inc.; **73 inset r**, Robert Goddyn/UPA; **74**, Tony Craddock/Photo Researchers, Inc.; **75**, Gabe Palmer/Corbis; **77**, Peter Essick/Aurora; **79**, AP/Wide World Photos; **79 inset**, Svenja-Foto/Masterfile; **80**, Comstock; **81**, Grant V. Faint/Getty Images, Inc.; **82**, AFP/Corbis; **84**, Julia Waterlow/Corbis; **85**, Hubert Stadler/Corbis; **87**, AP/Wide World Photos; **88**, Hubert Stadler/Corbis.

Chapter 3

Pages 92–93, Ron Sanford/Corbis; **93 inset**, Index Stock Imagery, Inc.; **94t**, Richard Haynes; **94–95b**, Aaron Chang/Corbis; **100l**, Robert Gill; Papilio/Corbis; **100r**, Jim Wark/Airphoto; **101**, Jim Wark/Airphoto; **102**, Gene Ahrens/Bruce Coleman, Inc.; **103**, Gene Ahrens/Bruce Coleman, Inc.; **104**, Fred Bruemmer/DRK Photo; **107**, Maher Attar/Corbis Sygma; **108–109**, Peter M. Fisher/Corbis; **110**, Alon Reininger/Corbis; **111b**, Norbert Wu; **111t**, Dave Fleetham/Seapics; **114**, Richard Haynes; **115**, Mark Thayer; **116**, Russ Lappa; **118**, Raven/Explorer/Photo Researchers, Inc.; **119**, Jeffrey Greenberg/Visuals Unlimited; **121**, Andrew J. Martinez; **123**, Richard Haynes; **124l**, Fred Bruemmer/DRK Photo; **124r**, Peter M. Fisher/Corbis.

Chapter 4

Pages 128–129, Darrell Gulin/Dembinsky Photo Associates; **129 inset**, Richard Haynes; **130b**, State Library of NSW; **130t**, Russ Lappa; **131**, Herb Kawainui/HawaiianEyes.com; **131 inset**, Photograph Courtesy Peabody Essex Museum; **132l**, Norbert Wu/Corbis; **132r**, Hulton Archive/Getty Images, Inc.; **133l**, Scott Camanzine/Photo Researchers, Inc.; **133r**, 2004 Jay Wade; **138–139t**, Dorling Kindersley; **139b**, Russ Lappa; **141**, Richard Dunoff/Corbis; **143l**, E.R. Degginger/Photo Researchers, Inc.; **143r**, Tim Heller/Mo Yung Productions; **148**, David R. Frazier; **148 inset l**, Corbis; **148 inset r**, George McCarthy/Nature Picture Library; **149b**, Andy Martinez/Photo Researchers, Inc.; **149t**, Lynda Richardson/Corbis; **150b**, Corbis; **150t**, Richard Haynes; **151l**, Doug Perrine/Seapics; **151r**, Andrew J. Martinez; **152**, Japack/Corbis; **153**, Australia Picture Library/Corbis; **153 inset l**, Seapics; **153 inset r**, Fred Bavendam; **154**, Corbis; **155**, Martin Ruegner/Image State/Picture Quest; **156**, Seapics; **156 inset**, Bruce Robinson/Corbis; **157**, WHOI; **158b**, Seapics; **158t**, Richard Haynes; **160b**, Russ Lappa; **160t**, Clyde H. Smith/Peter Arnold, Inc.; **161**, Arnulf Husmo/Getty Images, Inc.; **163l**, Bob Torrez/Getty Images, Inc.; **163r**, Bill Nation/Corbis Sygma; **164t**, Frans Lanting/Minden Pictures; **164b**, Richard Haynes; **165**, Richard Haynes; **166**, Corbis; **166–167 background**, Corbis; **168**, Russ Lappa; **170l**, Corbis; **170r**, Doug Perrine/Innerspace Visions.

Page 173b, Panoramic Images; **173m**, University Art Collection, Tulane; **173t**, North Wind Picture Archive; **175**, Richard Pasley/Liaison/Getty Images, Inc.; **176 inset**, Bettmann/Corbis; **176 journal page**, Russ Lappa; **176–177**, Clint Farlinger; **177 inset**, Richard Sisk/Panoramic Images; **178**, Tony Freeman/PhotoEdit; **179b**, Russ Lappa; **179m**, Richard Haynes; **179t**, Russ Lappa; **180**, Richard Haynes; **182**, Richard Haynes; **184**, Morton Beebe/Corbis; **185**, Richard Haynes; **187b**, Richard Haynes; **187t**, Dorling Kindersley; **189**, ImageStop/Phototake; **192**, Richard Haynes; **199**, Richard Haynes; **200**, Russ Lappa; **201 both**, Russ Lappa; **202**, Bruce Robinson/Corbis; **203**, AP/Wide World Photos; **204**, John Paul Kay/Peter Arnold Inc.; **205**, Doug Perrine/Seapics; **206**, Norbert Schafer/Corbis.